Some manuscripts of the book of Acts have a slightly longer version of the book that is familiar to us, a version called the Western text, which is made up of small amounts of additional material scattered throughout the work. Various theories have been proposed to account for the existence of the Western text, although no real consensus has emerged. In recent years this material, long thought to be inauthentic, has been re-examined by a number of scholars who have come to the conclusion that it may derive from Luke, the author of Acts. This study puts forward the ingenious thesis that Luke left Acts unfinished at his death, and that the work of his posthumous editors has led to the existence of the two versions of Acts which appear in our manuscripts.

SOCIETY FOR NEW TESTAMENT STUDIES

MONOGRAPH SERIES

General editor: G. N. Stanton

71

THE PROBLEM OF THE TEXT OF ACTS

The Problem of the Text of Acts

W. A. STRANGE

The right of the
University of Cambridge
to print and sell
all manner of books
was granted by
Henry VIII in 1534.
The University has printed
and published continuously
since 1584.

CAMBRIDGE UNIVERSITY PRESS

CAMBRIDGE
NEW YORK   PORT CHESTER
MELBOURNE   SYDNEY

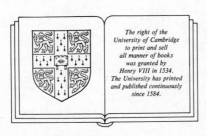

Published by the Press Syndicate of the University of Cambridge
The Pitt Building, Trumpington Street, Cambridge CB2 1RP
40 West 20th Street, New York, NY 10011-4211, USA
10 Stamford Road, Oakleigh, Victoria 3166, Australia

First published 1992

Printed in Great Britain at the University Press, Cambridge

*A cataloguing in publication record for this book is available
from the British Library*

Library of Congress cataloguing in publication data
Strange, W. A., 1953–
  The problem of the text of Acts / W. A. Strange.
      p.   cm.
  Includes bibliographical references and index.
  ISBN 0 521 41384 2
  1. Bible. N.T. Acts – Criticism, Textual.   I. Title.
BS2625.2.S776   1992
226.6′048–dc20   91–18372   CIP

ISBN 0 521 41384 2 hardback

CE

CONTENTS

PREFACE

The material in this book began its existence as an Oxford D.Phil. thesis, undertaken while the author was on the staff of Wycliffe Hall, Oxford, and a postgraduate student of The Queen's College, Oxford. In expressing my appreciation for the help I received from both institutions, I would like to thank in particular the then Principal of Wycliffe Hall, the Revd Geoffrey Shaw, for his support, and my colleagues there for their encouragement.

It was the late Professor G. D. Kilpatrick whose teaching first stimulated my interest in the discipline of textual criticism; for this I shall always remain grateful. As the work progressed the helpful and wise guidance of my supervisors, the late Professor G. B. Caird and Dr J. B. Muddiman (who acted as supervisor for the greater part of the time), put me enormously in their debt.

Comments and suggestions from Professor J. N. Birdsall, Dr J. K. Elliott, and Professor J. C. O'Neill have been of great help in the preparation of this work.

Finally, this book would not have seen the light of day had it not been for my wife's patient encouragement during the years in which Acts has become part of our lives.

It need scarcely be said that the imperfections of the work are wholly my own.

ABBREVIATIONS

Wherever possible, the abbreviations used here follow the conventions of S. Schwertner, *Internationales Abkürzungsverzeichnis für Theologie und Grenzgebiete* (Berlin and New York, 1974).

Periodicals

Ant.	*Antonianum*
AThR	*Anglican Theological Review*
AUSS	*Andrews University Seminary Studies*
BASP	*Bulletin of the American Society of Papyrologists*
BBezC	*Bulletin of the Bezan Club*
Bib	*Biblica*
CBQ	*Catholic Biblical Quarterly*
CQR	*Church Quarterly Review*
CR	*Classical Review*
ET	*Expository Times*
EtCl	*Etudes classiques*
EThL	*Ephemerides theologicae Lovanienses*
GGA	*Göttingische gelehrte Anzeigen*
GHÅ	*Göteborgas Högskolas Årsskrift*
Gn.	*Gnomon*
HThR	*Harvard Theological Review*
IrBibSt	*Irish Biblical Studies*
JBL	*Journal of Biblical Literature*
JHS	*Journal of Hellenic Studies*
JP	*Journal of Philology*
JR	*Journal of Religion*
JSNT	*Journal for the Study of the New Testament*
JThS	*Journal of Theological Studies*
LTP	*Laval théologique et philosophique*
Mn.	*Mnemosyne*

NT	*Novum Testamentum*
NTS	*New Testament Studies*
PBA	*Proceedings of the British Academy*
RB	*Revue biblique*
RBPH	*Revue belge de philologie et de l'histoire*
REAug	*Revue des études augustiniennes*
REG	*Revue des études grecques*
RHPhR	*Revue d'histoire et de philosophie religieuses*
RMP	*Rheinisches Museum für Philologie*
RSPhTh	*Revue des sciences philosophiques et théologiques*
RSR	*Recherches de science religieuse*
RThL	*Revue théologique de Louvain*
RThom	*Revue thomiste*
StTh	*Studia Theologica*
ThL	*Theologische Literaturzeitung*
ThR	*Theologische Rundschau*
ThSt	*Theological Studies*
ThStKr	*Theologische Studien und Kritiken*
ThZ	*Theologische Zeitschrift*
VigChr	*Vigiliae Christianae*
ZKG	*Zeitschrift für Kirchengeschichte*
ZNW	*Zeitschrift für die neutestamentliche Wissenschaft*
ZPE	*Zeitschrift für Papyrologie und Epigraphik*
ZThK	*Zeitschrift für Theologie und Kirche*

Other abbreviations

Actes	*Les Actes des Apôtres, traditions, rédactions, théologie,* ed. J. Kremer (EThL.B 48; Gembloux, 1979)
ANTT	Arbeiten zur neutestamentlichen Textforschung
AThANT	Abhandlungen zur Theologie der alten und neuen Testaments
Beg.	*The Beginnings of Christianity.* Part 1, *The Acts of the Apostles,* ed. F. J. Foakes Jackson and Kirsopp Lake, 5 vols. (London, 1920–33)
BEvTh	Beiträge zur evangelische Theologie
BHTh	Beiträge zur historischen Theologie
BZNW	Beihefte zur Zeitschrift für die neutestamentliche Wissenschaft
EThL.B	Ephemerides theologicae Lovanienses Bibliotheca

FRLANT   Forschungen zur Religion und Literatur der alten und neuen Testaments

HThS   Harvard Theological Studies

KPS   Klassisch-Philologische Studien

MSSNTS   Monograph Series. Society for New Testament Studies

N–A[26]   Nestle–Aland, *Novum Testamentum Graece*, 26th edn (1979)

NTTC   *New Testament Textual Criticism, Its Significance for New Testament Exegesis. Essays in Honour of Bruce M. Metzger*, ed. E. J. Epp and G. D. Fee (Oxford, 1981)

NTTS   New Testament Tools and Studies

NT.S   Supplements to Novum Testamentum

PG   J.-P. Migne, *Patrologia Graeca*

PL   J.-P. Migne, *Patrologia Latina*

PRE   *Pauly's Real Encyclopädie der classischen Altertumswissenschaft*

P.Oxy   B. P. Grenfell, A. S. Hunt, and others, *The Oxyrhynchus Papyri*, 53 vols. (London, 1898–1986: in progress)

PSI   *Pubblicazioni della Società italiana per la ricerca dei papiri greci e latini in Egitto* (Florence, 1912–   )

SAW   Studienhefte zur Altertumswissenschaft

SBL.DS   Society of Biblical Literature. Dissertation Series

SBL.MS   Society of Biblical Literature. Monograph Series

SLA   *Studies in Luke–Acts*, ed. L. E. Keck and J. L. Martyn (London, 1968)

SPT   W. M. Ramsay, *St.Paul the Traveller and the Roman Citizen* (London, 1895)

StUNT   Studien zur Umwelt der Neuen Testaments

TCGNT   B. M. Metzger, *A Textual Commentary on the Greek New Testament* (on behalf of and in cooperation with the Editorial Committee of the United Bible Societies' Greek New Testament) (London and New York, 2nd edn, 1975)

TDNT   G. Kittel and G. Friedrich (eds.), *A Theological Dictionary of the New Testament*, 10 vols. (Grand Rapids, 1963–76)

TeT   Temi e Testi

ThHNT   Theologisches Handkommentar zum Neuen Testament

ThWNT   G. Kittel and G. Friedrich (eds.), *Theologisches Wörter-buch zum Neuen Testament*, 10 vols. (Stuttgart, 1933–79)

TU   Texte und Untersuchungen

UBS[3]   United Bible Societies' *Greek New Testament*, 3rd edition (1975)

CONSTRUCTION OF APPARATUS

The apparatus is intended to assist in elucidating the Western variants under discussion. It does not, therefore, give details of every variant found in the texts cited.

When the term Maj (Majority) appears, it may be assumed that all witnesses detailed above are cited when they give readings at variance with that of the majority of witnesses and when their readings may be ascertained. Conversely, it may assumed that those which are not explicitly cited concur with the Majority.

1

THE STUDY OF THE TEXT OF ACTS

Introduction

Since the beginning of systematic study of the New Testament text, the textual peculiarities of Acts have been the subject of controversy. In the book of Acts, to a greater extent than anywhere else in the New Testament, the so-called Western text gives a large number of variant readings, which amount to virtually an alternative version of the book. The text-critical problem is thus forced upon the reader of Acts so that, to a degree unique in the New Testament, decisions about the text affect conclusions about the work in all its aspects. It is a matter of some consequence for the study of Luke's work to decide whether Acts acquired its textual peculiarities at its origin, or in the course of its transmission. It is also of consequence for the study of Christian literature in an obscure period, the early second century, to discover in what circumstances the book of Acts was transmitted, and how it happened that, as Patristic evidence suggests, Acts already existed in two forms by the last quarter of the second century.

The course of controversy over the text of Acts may be divided into three periods. The first was that before 1939. In this period the nature and scope of the problem became clear, and the main hypotheses were formulated which attempted to give comprehensive explanations of the textual peculiarities of Acts as a whole. None of these theories, however, succeeded in establishing an undisputed consensus, and from the time of the Second World War there may be detected a turning away from such comprehensive hypotheses, a movement occasioned by dissatisfaction with these hypotheses' results. This change of emphasis marks the second period in the study of the text of Acts, the three decades 1945–75, which may be described as the period of eclecticism, although it is to be noted that this eclecticism was often rather half-hearted. In this period, text-critical work on Acts appeared to be moving towards consensus after the radical disagreements of the pre-war period. The foundation of this consensus was a tacit acceptance that the Western text was the result of the activity of second-century 'improvement' of the text, and could therefore in practice be disregarded when Luke's own work was being considered. But this tacit and widespread assumption of the post-war decades lacked a coherent justification: it arose out of a decision to set aside the questions which had been debated before the war, rather than from a genuine resolution of these problems. Since the mid 1970s, text-critical study of Acts has entered its third period. In this period the unresolved problems of the text of Acts have been examined afresh. There has been a renaissance in the text-critical study of Acts, and as a result of much recent work, the possibility has re-emerged that substantial Lucan material may exist in the Western readings of Acts. If this should prove to be so, then eclecticism cannot be enough, because it fails to deal with the central problem: what sort of work can Acts be, to exist in two versions, both of which bear some relationship to the author? It is a question which has never received a satisfactory answer.

The purpose of this chapter will be to trace the characteristic features of the three periods in the study of the text of Acts, and to analyse the reasons for the transitions between them. This review will enable the current issues in the textual criticism of Acts to be seen in perspective. It will then be possible to see what problems need to be addressed today in the attempt to resolve the enigma of the text of Acts.

The period before 1939: the classic theories

Early criticism

The existence of the two great bilingual manuscripts Codex Bezae (D) and Codex Laudianus (E) drew scholars' attention from the sixteenth century onwards to the problem of what was later to be called the Western text, in the New Testament generally, and in Acts specifically. The readings of D first entered a printed text in Stephanus' third edition of his New Testament (1550), in which D is designated β' in the Preface, and cited as β in the text.[1] Laudianus, taken from Würzburg to Oxford in 1636, became widely known through its citation in Fell's edition of the New Testament (1675).

The problem of the text of Acts was therefore first posed when textual criticism of the New Testament was in its infancy. J. Leclerc suggested in 1686 that the textual peculiarities of Codex Bezae in Acts might indicate that Luke issued two editions of the work, one of which has given rise to the text of Bezae, and one to the usually accepted text. But having examined some Bezan variants, and noting that such readings occur elsewhere in Codex Bezae, Leclerc concluded that the Bezan text is more likely to be due to para-phrasing interpolations.[2] Leclerc's opinion was shared by his opponent, the astute critic Richard Simon.[3] In what was probably the first monograph to give extensive attention to Codex D, A. Arnaud argued that the peculiarities of D were due to the activities of a sixth-century falsifier.[4]

The seventeenth-century critics had seen the problems of Bezae and Laudianus as little more than the peculiarities of particular manuscripts. The organisation of witnesses into groups, which was the work of Bengel, Wettstein, and Semler in the eighteenth century, made it clear that there was a recognisable 'Western' group of witnesses, and that the textual problem of Acts was more than merely the idiosyncrasy of two manuscripts. Eighteenth-century criticism, valuable though it was in laying the foundations of ordering of witnesses, left critics with the unhappy choice of 'Western' as an adjective to describe the group of witnesses of which Codex D is the principal. This text is scarcely 'Western' in a geographical sense, as has been widely recognised for some time. The term 'Western text' will be used here though, because it is a familiar legacy from the eighteenth century, even if it is inaccurate.

Eighteenth-century criticism also led to a dismissal of the Western tradition from consideration. It was generally regarded as a late and degenerate form. So, although the text of D was published for the first time by Kipling in 1793, and the peculiarities of the Harclean Syriac became evident through White's edition of 1799, critics of the early nineteenth century took on the whole little notice either of D in particular, or of the Western text in general. A notable exception was F. A. Bornemann, who in 1848 proposed the theses that either the text of Acts had been interpolated from a travel narrative kept by Luke and preserved separately from the book of Acts, or the Western text was original, and the non-Western a later abbre-viation. Both theses were to reappear in later work on the text of Acts.[5] But the emerging German criticism showed little interest at this stage in the problems of the Western text.[6]

The classic theories

The refinement of textual criticism in the mid to late nineteenth century brought a renewed interest in the particular problems of the text of Acts, and the half-century before 1939 was the most fertile period in the study of Acts' text. Scrivener's edition of Codex Bezae (1864) had given critics a new tool for the study of D, more accessible, more accurate, and more critical than Kipling's edition.[7] At the same time, new studies of versional evidence were beginning to reveal the true extent of the Western textual tradition.

Interest in the text of Acts stemmed from two sources. On the one hand, it was widely recognised that the text itself required examination and explanation. From this perception of the problem, as one relating specifically to the book of Acts (and perhaps also to the Gospel of Luke), arose the work of Blass and A. C. Clark. For them, the problem was a Lucan one. On the other hand there were those critics who approached the text of Acts as a part of the more general problem of the Western text in the New Testament as a whole. For these critics, the text of Acts was one battlefield in the more general war provoked by the work of Westcott and Hort. Among those whose interest in Acts was of this sort, as well as Westcott and Hort themselves, were Rendel Harris and J. H. Ropes.

Westcott and Hort

Westcott and Hort ascribed the Western text of the New Testament as a whole to the free handling of the text by scribes in the process of copying.[8] They saw no reason to distinguish between the Western text in Acts and that elsewhere in the New Testament. In Acts, as elsewhere, the desire to smooth, to clarify, and to embellish the work has led scribes to alter passages, and even to insert new material. The differences between the Western text in Acts and that in other New Testament books could be accounted for, they suggested, by the continued circulation of stories about the apostolic era until well into the second century. From such sources as these, material was added to the text of Acts.[9] There was thus no unity in the Western text of Acts, since it was made up of a collection of readings which had accumulated over time, and as the result of the activity of various hands.

Blass

Blass approached the text of Acts as essentially a Lucan problem. Blass's thesis was first expressed in a study published in 1894[10] and was further developed in the following year by the publication of an edition of Acts according to the principles of his thesis.[11] Blass took issue with Westcott and Hort at two points: the 'Lucanism' of the Western variants, and the relative order in which the two texts were written. Blass proposed that such additional material as that found in 1.5, 14.2, or 21.16, could only have been added by someone with an intimate knowledge of the events themselves.[12] When it is also noted that the vocabulary of the Western variants remains faithful to that of Luke, then it is to be concluded, Blass maintained, that the material peculiar to the Western text was written by the author of Acts.[13]

Westcott and Hort had regarded the Western text as paraphrase and expansion. Blass, on the other hand, argued that the non-Western text was in fact secondary to the Western, since no one in possession of the polished and concise non-Western text would wish to rewrite it as the rough and verbose Western text.[14] Blass proposed that the two text-forms be regarded as a polished and an unpolished form of the work, both of which may be attributed to the author. His explanation for this phenomenon was that the Western text represents the author's first draft, and the non-Western the finished state of the work.[15] Blass cited the example of Catullus, who mentions the custom of writing first drafts on a palimpsest, and a fair copy on better materials.[16]

Blass's hypothesis remained a serious point of contention for some years. His case convinced a number of New Testament scholars, most notably T. Zahn and E. Nestle.[17] Blass's critics, however, were numerous. They questioned his assumptions about the relative priority of the texts. They argued that he had over-valued the literary tastes of second-century copyists, and that their reasons for producing the paraphrases of the Western text were quite clear. Critics also drew attention to passages in which there appeared to be a distance in point of view between the Western and non-Western texts: the Apostolic Decree (15.20,29,21.25) was a notable instance. They maintained that it was hard to see how the same author could be responsible for these alternative accounts. Several studies of the text of Acts appeared in the decade after the publication of Blass's edition which criticised his work in this manner.[18]

Ropes

The most effective answer to Blass, however, was the publication in 1926 of Ropes's study of the text of Acts.[19] Ropes's work was conceived as part of a thorough investigation of the book of Acts in all its aspects. It was so solidly done, that it has provided the basis for most subsequent work in the field.

Ropes reached two conclusions about the Western text of Acts: in the first place, it was the result of a specific revision, and not merely of accumulated additions, as Westcott and Hort had thought; and in the second, this revision was the work of a later reviser than the author of Acts. Ropes's first conclusion rested on two observations:

> In the first place it [the Western text] has an unmistakably homogeneous internal character. Secondly, its hundreds or thousands of variants are now known to have arisen in a brief period, scarcely, if at all, longer than the fifty years after the book first passed into circulation. In that period a pedigree of successive copies was short and to produce so many variants the mere natural licence of copyists would be insufficient. And since one rewriting would suffice, any theory that more than one took place in those years would seem to fall under the condemnation of Occam's razor.[20]

That the Western text of Acts was not written by the author of Acts himself is apparent, Ropes argued, from the nature of the Western readings themselves:

> The 'Western' fulness of words, the elaboration of religious expressions, such as the names for Christ and the *plus* of conventional religious phrases, the fact that the difference in language and mode of narration can often be explained as due to superficial difficulties in the other text, occasional misunderstanding, as would appear, or at least neglect, of the meaning of the other text (for instance Acts xx. 3–5), the relative colourlessness and a certain empty naiveté of the 'Western', all contrast unfavourably with the greater conciseness, sententiousness, and vigour, and occa-

sionally the obscurity, of the Old Uncial text. And even more decisive is the fact that in all the excess of matter which the 'Western' text shows, virtually nothing is to be found beyond what could be inferred from the Old Uncial text.[21]

The Western reviser had, according to Ropes, a few recognisable interests, for example, a concern with Gentiles, but taken as a whole, his was no tendentious revision.[22] What is more, in spite of the fact that the Western text is essentially a revised text, there are places at which the Western witnesses have preserved readings drawn from the ancient textual base on which they rest, and which have perished from the alternative text, the Old Uncial, as Ropes named it. Ropes notes three readings in this category: καὶ μείναντες ἐν Τρωγυλίᾳ (20.15), καὶ Μύρα (21.1), and δι᾽ ἡμερῶν δεκάπεντε (27.5). He noted that 'there may be others', and in fact there are several places at which his textual notes indicate a preference for the Western readings.[23] The omissions of the Western text are of particular importance, he argued, because of the reviser's tendency to expand. When there are Western 'omissions' in Acts, these deserve careful scrutiny, because they may well prove to be 'Western non-interpolations', and therefore genuine readings.[24] After examining other aspects of the text, Ropes drew his conclusion as to its origin:

> Our conclusion, then, is that the 'Western' text was made before, and perhaps long before, the year 150, by a Greek-speaking Christian who knew something of Hebrew, in the East, perhaps in Syria or Palestine. The introduction of 'we' in the 'Western' text of xi.27 possibly gives some colour to the guess that the place was Antioch.[25]

Ropes's work was taken further by G. Zuntz, in a study written in 1939 but published only in 1972, which for this reason did not attract the attention it deserved.[26] Zuntz accepted Ropes's case in all essentials, but added more precision in two respects. He took up the distinction within the Western text to which Ropes had alluded, between 'an ancient base, which would be of the greatest possible value if it could be recovered, and the paraphrastic rewriting of a second-century Christian'.[27] Zuntz detected two groups of Western readings, of quite contrary character: readings marked by 'brevity, harshness, omissions' on the one hand, and those marked by 'laxity, alleviations, additions' on the other.[28] These two tendencies point to the conclusion that two elements have given the Western text its present character, its sporadic faithfulness to the original text (shorter readings), and its habitual paraphrasing (longer readings). Both p[45] and Clement of Alexandria, Zuntz argued, are witnesses to the ancient, and shorter Western text.[29]

Zuntz was also more specific than Ropes had been about the place of origin of the Western text in its revised form. Ropes tentatively suggested Antioch (see n. 25 above). Zuntz believed that Edessa was more likely, because some Western readings showed evidence of adaptation for lectionary reading, according to the lections identified by Burkitt as in use at Edessa,[30] and because (reviving a thesis of F. H. Chase) some Western readings appear to have been translated into Greek from Syriac.[31]

Ropes was perhaps wise not to have been drawn to quite such precise conclusions as Zuntz. Zuntz, though, added some important observations to Ropes's thesis. One was to underline the distinction between the Western text's base and its later developments. This distinction was to play a major part, in a different form, in the work of Boismard and Lamouille (see pp. 30–2 below).

Another important observation was to supplement Ropes's denial of tendentious purpose behind the Western text by noting that while not reflecting the theological controversies of the second century,[32] the Western text manifests a concern to make the book of Acts relevant to its readers. Zuntz called one of the Western text's major techniques 'paradigmatical expansions' – that is, the transforming of narrative from historical scenes into models of church life at a particular point. The inclusion of a catechetical formula in the baptism of the Ethiopian eunuch is an example of this.[33] In this, Zuntz was anticipating the much later comments of C. K. Barrett (see p. 26 below).

Lake and Cadbury

The fourth volume of *The Beginnings of Christianity*, of which Ropes's *Text of Acts* was the third, was the *Commentary* by Kirsopp Lake and H. J. Cadbury.[34] Lake combined two sources of interest in the Western text of Acts: a concern with the text of the New Testament generally, and an interest in the book of Acts itself. In consequence, we are probably justified in regarding the bulk of the textual discussions in the book as being the work of Lake.[35] Lake's comments on the text are often an instructive supplement to the work of Ropes. Lake agreed with Ropes about the history of the text in general terms, but was in practice more willing to allow that the Western text has preserved readings from its ancient textual base, when the non-Western text may be corrupt.[36] This meant that in many instances Lake was willing to allow that the Western reading was original,[37] although he also thought that certainty was often unattainable.[38] Lake's discussions of variants therefore owed little to his professed convictions about the origin of the Western text as a whole, and proceeded instead in an eclectic manner, on the basis of the internal characteristics of the readings.

Clark

A more fundamental reappraisal of Ropes's conclusions was attempted seven years after the appearance of Ropes's study by A. C. Clark's *The Acts of the Apostles*.[39] In this book Clark extended observations which he had already made about the abbreviating habits of ancient copyists, and which had arisen from study of the manuscript tradition of classical authors as well as of biblical texts.[40] In his earlier work, Clark had argued that the Gospels were transmitted in manuscripts having very short lines, of only ten to twelve characters each, and that virtually all of our existing manuscripts have suffered from omission of single lines or numbers of lines.[41] In the case of Acts, though, the work had been written in sense-lines, much as Codex Bezae now is, and the shorter text, although it was produced by the accidental omission of lines, was more coherent than the shorter text of the Gospels because the omission of a line which was a self-contained unit did not leave such an evident gap as the omission of a line whose content was wholly arbitrary.[42]

Ropes noted this early work of Clark, and argued that it did not account for 'the facts ... which show a rational, not merely an accidental difference between the two types of text'.[43] In his major work on Acts, Clark was able to take account of Ropes's criticisms. In consequence he modified his thesis, and argued that in Acts the omissions in the non-Western text were deliberate. They represent the work of an Alexandrian abbreviator, who eliminated short passages throughout the work, inspired by various motives.[44] Clark's argument thus led to the conclusion that the Western text (which he designated Z) is original, while the non-Western (which he designated Γ = Graeci) is not, because it was the result of a deliberate process of abbreviation, for which there are parallels in other manuscript traditions.

The decline of the 'Western Problem'

In the years before the Second World War, Clark's view won some sympathisers, notable among them B. H. Streeter.[45] However, Ropes's analysis of the textual history of Acts prevailed, not only over Clark, but also over Blass, and to a certain extent, over that of Westcott and Hort also. Two reasons may be seen for this dominance of Ropes's thesis.

Those whose interest in the text of Acts arose from concern with the book of Acts itself could conclude that the monumental *Beginnings of Christianity* had in effect disposed of the textual problem, and that Acts-research could now proceed on a more secure base to more fruitful areas of enquiry. So, when Acts became in the post-war years 'one of the great storm-centres of New Testament scholarship',[46] the textual problem came to be regarded as a peripheral issue, in a way in which it had not been regarded by scholars of a previous generation.

The other reason for the dominance of Ropes's thesis was that interest in the Western text generally was waning in the inter-war years. During the 1920s and 1930s there existed, indeed, an international fraternity of scholars, the 'Bezan Club', concerned with the problems of the Western text, and publishing material in the form of an occasional *Bulletin*.[47] It was significant, though, that the driving force behind the group was the ageing Rendel Harris, one of the scholars who had kept open the issue of the Western text's value in the years after the publication of Westcott and Hort's edition.[48] The series of the *Bulletin of the Bezan Club* came to an end in 1937. From its pages, and from the editorial comments in particular, one may gather that its collapse was due chiefly to a lack of interest in the issues which it set itself to address. By the 1930s it was generally judged that textual criticism had established a secure working basis for New Testament scholarship. Minor difficulties might remain in places, but the majority of scholars were content to believe that in the fifty years since the appearance of Westcott and Hort's edition, the work of textual criticism had in large part been done. The Western text of Acts, like the Western text elsewhere in the New Testament, might prove to be of some antiquarian interest, but could scarcely claim the legitimate attention of New Testament scholarship.

Kenyon's careful statement, in an article published in 1938, of a position similar to that of Westcott and Hort may conveniently be taken to mark the end of an era in the study of the text of Acts.[49] The combined arguments of Westcott and Hort, Ropes and Kenyon appeared to close the matter. However they might differ on the issue of how the Western text arose, they were agreed against Blass and Clark that the Western text was secondary, and could in practice be ignored in the study of the book of Acts. This attitude, if not quite a consensus, was at least a majority opinion which strongly influenced the course of work on Acts after 1945.

The post-war period: eclecticism

The post-war approach

The three decades after 1945 were a period of curious indecision in the study of the text of Acts. On the one hand, there was a widespread ostensible recognition that none of the 'classic' theories about the origin of Acts' textual peculiarities carried full conviction. Henceforward, textual studies would not be devoted to the vindication of one text-form over another. Yet, on the other hand, this recognition was accompanied by a reluctance to follow the Western readings, even in places at which scholars such as Ropes and Lake, for all their doubts about the Western text, had been willing to do so. It was an attitude which G. D. Kilpatrick aptly characterised as acquiescence in Ropes's conclusions, but with a marked lack of conviction.[50] This post-war period was, then, one in which a theoretical espousal of eclecticism was accompanied by a practical rejection of the Western textual tradition.

The eclectic approach to Acts was encouraged by two studies published during the war years, both advocating the abandonment of the search for the authentic text-form of Acts, and calling for an acknowledgement of the faults and the merits of all existing text-forms. These two studies mark a turning point in the study of the text of Acts.

The eclectic method

Dibelius

The first of the war-time studies to appear was that of Dibelius: 'The Text of Acts: An Urgent Critical Task'.[51] His theme was the unsatisfactory nature of all the large-scale hypotheses which attempted to explain the existence of two textual traditions in Acts. Much work needed to be done, Dibelius argued, before we might safely commit ourselves to such comprehensive explanations. For the time being, the student of Acts should be content to acknowledge that both textual traditions are corrupt, and that neither Western nor non-Western witnesses invariably contain the true readings. Neither witness should be followed blindly, for both require critical attention.[52] Dibelius went further, though, and proposed a thesis of his own to account for the existence of textual divergence within Acts, suggesting that the circulation of Acts within the book trade had led to the text's being treated with greater freedom than in those exemplars which had been used by the church.[53] The thesis was novel, and deserves attention. We shall return to it at a later point (see pp. 15f. below).

Kilpatrick

The second war-time study to appear was that of Kilpatrick in 1943.[54] Kilpatrick had been greatly influenced by the work of C. H. Turner, and in particular by his insistence that author's usage was the surest canon of textual criticism.[55] To follow this canon meant as a corollary abandoning the notion that there is such a thing as 'the best manuscript' – in the New Testament tradition, at least. In the case of Acts, the application of this canon shows that the original text was not to be found exclusively in either the Western or the non-Western traditions. Both Western and non-Western texts were what later hands had made them, but equally the authentic text was to be sought in both.[56] Twenty years later, Kilpatrick returned to the theme in 'An Eclectic Study of the Text of Acts'.[57] Here, he maintained that the authentic text was on occasion to be found in the Western witnesses:

> Thus we do not concern ourselves with attempting to satisfy ourselves that the Egyptian text or the Western text as a whole is right, but we try to decide each variant by itself.[58]

Kilpatrick's work represents the most consistent attempt to apply an eclectic method to the textual criticism of the book of Acts.[59]

Black and Wilcox

An eclectic approach encouraged the search for Semitisms in the Western text of Acts, as well as the non-Western: if either tradition might preserve authentically Lucan material, then primitive linguistic elements (i.e. Semitisms) might be found in either. The seminal work on Semitisms and the textual tradition of the New Testament was done by A. J. Wensinck before the Second World War.[60] His suggestions were taken up and elaborated by M. Black, whose work *An Aramaic Approach to the Gospels and Acts* first appeared in 1946.[61] In the Western text of Acts, as well as in that of the Gospels, Black detected certain Semitic turns of phrase. He suggested that at these places the Western text stands nearer to the original than does the non-Western text in which these primitive, Semitic elements have been obliterated.[62]

Black's work was taken further, and the approach applied more thoroughly to Acts itself, by Wilcox in 1965.[63] After a careful study of the different types of Semitism to be found in Acts, Wilcox concluded that primitive Semitisms were sometimes to be found in the Western text of Acts, and that therefore:

> while we may not disregard the usual traditional methods of textual criticism, it seems that greater deference should be paid to the claims of individual readings of these [Western] and other manuscripts, in which primitive material may have survived unrevised (although we must remember that such Semitisms may be due to the Semitic-thinking scribes). The inquiry does not suggest, much less warrant, a double-edition theory of Acts, but it does tend to enhance the claims of the so-called 'eclectic' method of textual criticism.[64]

Criticism of the eclectic method

Overt criticism of the eclectic method and doubt about the presence of Semitic elements in the Western textual tradition were also expressed in the three decades after the Second World War.

One of the most thorough, and quite probably the most influential of scholars to work on Acts in this period, E. Haenchen, dissented clearly from Black in his estimate of Semitic elements in the Western text. Haenchen maintained that where such 'Semitisms' were to be found, they could better be explained as examples of scribal negligence, or in the case of those drawn from Codex D itself, as examples of the influence of the Latin translation on the Greek.[65] J. D. Yoder, as a result of his work on the language of the Greek variants of Codex D, concluded that D as a whole does not have a Semitising character. It is capable of eliminating Semitic constructions, as well as exhibiting them.[66] In spite of this criticism, though, it remains true that Wilcox's careful work has yet to be answered with equal care.[67] The case for detecting Semitic colour in some Western variants in Acts remains an open one.

The eclectic method itself also attracted criticism. A. F. J. Klijn at first welcomed the eclectic approach to the Western text,[68] but faced with the specific results of the method, particularly a study by L. Cerfaux of 1950 and Kilpatrick's study of 1963 (see n. 50 above), Klijn was less satisfied. An eclectic method, he concluded, can lead to arbitrary results, and indeed had done so in Cerfaux's and Kilpatrick's studies.[69] Klijn's reservations were shared by G. D. Fee, who also wrote of the dangers of subjective judgement inherent in the eclectic method.[70]

From the 1940s, however, the general attitude to the eclectic method as applied to Acts was not so much overtly critical as ambivalent. On the one hand, there was agreement that the quest to vindicate one text-form over another was no longer the appropriate way in which to conduct the textual criticism of the book. There was general agreement that the larger questions concerning the origins of the text-forms could be put to one side. There was a theoretical acceptance that any text may contain the authentic reading. In that sense most textual criticism of Acts in the period 1945–75 was eclectic in a sense in which Clark, for example, was not: it did not proceed from any clearly formulated theory about the origins of Acts' textual peculiarities. On the other hand, however, studies of the text of Acts published in this period showed a tacit acceptance of Ropes's account of the textual history of the book. Even though critics after the War consciously rejected the search for any comprehensive explanation of Acts' textual characteristics, such large-scale explanations frequently recurred as assumptions in their work. Critics in this period seldom embraced the thorough-going eclecticism of Kilpatrick, although by agreeing that none of the classic theories was fully convincing, they deprived themselves of any reason for not doing so.

The Western text as witness to the history of Acts

Attention in the period 1945–75 was in fact directed less at the establishment of the original text than at using the textual peculiarities of Acts in order to draw conclusions about the book's early history. In part, the text was used to throw light on the obscure 'tunnel period' of the book's transmission, that is, the early second century, and in part it was used to illustrate the practice of textual criticism as an exercise in hermeneutics.

Dibelius

Dibelius's essay of 1941 (see p. 12 above) made a significant attempt to find an appropriate *Sitz im Leben* for the transmission of the book of Acts. Dibelius addressed the problem, too often neglected, of why this book in particular should have undergone the processes which have produced its distinctive textual character. He suggested that the answer lay with the literary pretensions of the author. Acts, unlike any other New Testament work, was intended from the first to be read by a wider public than that of the Christian community alone. It was from the first intended to circulate in the book trade, and was actually accepted as an ecclesiastical reading-book at only a comparatively late stage – in the last third of the second century. In the course of its circulation outside ecclesiastical control, the text of Acts was subject to a multitude of minor 'improvements' which aimed to make the book more acceptable to its readers.[71]

A. D. Nock, in an otherwise warm review of Dibelius's *Aufsätze zur Apostelgeschichte*, took issue with Dibelius over this thesis. It rested, he argued, on a misconception of the notion of publication in antiquity, and made a quite unwarranted assumption that a text copied extra-ecclesially would be more likely to suffer corruption than one under the 'protection' of the church. What, after all, would 'ecclesiastical control' amount to in the early second century? It had not prevented the insertion of the *pericope de adultera* into John and Luke, nor had it protected the end of Mark. Indeed, professional copyists could have made a better job of copying than would Christians making copies for their own use.[72] Nock's criticisms were to the point, and he is generally judged to have dispensed with Dibelius' proposal. In fairness to Dibelius, though, it should be noted that the corruption of copies of books available through professional booksellers was a common complaint in antiquity.[73] A more telling criticism of Dibelius is that he assumed that Acts, in order to be a serious literary work, would have had to have been copied, bought, and sold through professional booksellers. But it will be argued at a later point in this study (pp. 171f.) that it was by no means necessary for a work to be disseminated through booksellers in order for it to be considered serious literature in the ancient world. The merit of Dibelius's study was to have made a possible proposal about the way in which two streams of textual transmission could have arisen during the 'tunnel period' of the book's existence, and to have related this proposal to the literary aspirations of the author himself. This line of enquiry was significant, even if Dibelius's specific suggestions have not withstood criticism.

Haenchen

E. Haenchen similarly drew attention to the 'tunnel period' of Acts' transmission as the key to its textual enigma. Successive editions of his Commentary since 1954 contained an introduction to the study of the text of Acts in which Haenchen attributed the existence of the Western text to the freedom to interpret the text enjoyed by scribes before Acts became regarded as sacred scripture.[74] Acts was accepted as scripture only in the late second century, a process to which Irenaeus is witness.[75] The Western readings, though, are not homogeneous. One can distinguish in Acts three classes of readings which have been called 'Western'. In the first class are those which are common to the Western text throughout the New Testament: 'a mass of small alterations intended to clarify and smooth'.[76] Secondly, there are certain readings which distinguish the Western text of Acts from that elsewhere in the New Testament. These readings are the result of work on the text by someone who has paid close attention to the book and its problems. The readings attempt to alleviate these problems, by obliterating 'seams' left in the narrative at the junction of pericopes, or by adding local details. These alterations Haenchen attributed to an assiduous reader of Acts at some early point in its history, a reader who was in effect 'Acts' earliest commentator'.[77] These are the readings which have tempted some critics to suppose that the author of Acts was responsible for the Western text, but in fact, Haenchen argued, it can be shown that they are the product of a later hand.[78] Finally, there are the readings which are in reality nothing more than the careless errors of the scribe of Codex D, although some of them have at times been treated as examples of Western readings. In this category are to be found many of the supposed Semitisms of the Western text. These are only apparent Semitisms which have arisen from careless transcription of the manuscript, or from the Latin column's influence upon the Greek.[79] Haenchen's conclusion is that virtually nothing can be learned from the Western readings about the original text of Acts – a more pessimistic view of the Western text than that of Dibelius – but that the first and second categories of readings are at least instructive of the way in which Acts was read and interpreted by some of its readers in the early second century.

By providing an explanation in outline of the origin of the Western text, Haenchen came closer than any other scholar in the period 1945–75 to formulating a theory which would account for the textual peculiarities of Acts. It is noteworthy, though, that Haenchen confined his remarks to general statements, illustrated with chosen examples. His thesis about the textual history of Acts, and his triple classification of readings, did not have to stand the test of being applied comprehensively to the text. None the less, his provision of a working hypothesis about the origin of the Western readings probably did as much as anything to hinder the free use of the eclectic method which so many critics ostensibly embraced.

Tendency criticism of the Western text of Acts

Haenchen's description of the Western reviser as 'Acts' earliest commentator' also indicates another approach to the text of Acts prominent in the three decades after the War: the use of the Western readings to throw light on the obscure period of Acts' transmission in the early second century. Indeed, since this is a period for which Christian source material in general is very scanty, the Western readings in Acts have been regarded by some as a valuable additional source for an obscure period of Christian history.

Tendency criticism of the Western readings in Acts had been

carried out sporadically in an earlier period. Rendel Harris, in his major study of Codex Bezae, had suggested that Montanist influences were responsible for some of the Western readings in Acts.[80] T. E. Page had pointed to the increase in the honorific titles of Jesus in D, as a sign that a trend towards veneration for the name of Jesus was already established at the time that these readings entered the text.[81] As noted earlier, though, Ropes detected no real tendency in the Western readings: 'Of any special point of view, theological or other, on the part of the "Western" reviser, it is difficult to find any trace.'[82]

Menoud

In this, as in other aspects of the study of the text, Ropes's view was highly influential, but the first sign of a reaction against it came in the publication in 1951 of an article by P. H. Menoud on 'The Western Text and the Theology of Acts'.[83] Starting by noting the recent interest in the eclectic method, and endorsing that method, Menoud went on to examine 'the peculiarities of the Western text which have, or may have, a theological significance'.[84] The passage to which he gave most attention was the 'Apostolic Decree' (Acts 15.20,29 and 21.25). In the textual history of the Decree, Menoud detected an intention:

> to emphasise the newness of the Christian faith as regards Judaism, and to do so both negatively and positively. Negatively, in denouncing and condemning the unbelief of the Jews: there is an undeniable anti-Jewish tendency peculiar to many Western readings. Positively, by insisting on the greatness and unity of the church, and on the authority of the apostles, and also simply by mentioning with predilection the grandeurs which separate Christianity from Judaism, that is to say, the Holy Spirit and Jesus as Christ and Lord.[85]

The rest of the study examined texts in which this tendency may be found, concluding that the Western text remains 'a valuable source of information on the first age of Christianity'.[86]

Fascher

E. Fascher's study of textual criticism as a hermeneutical problem was published in 1953.[87] Fascher wished to encourage textual critics to see copyists, not as corrupters of the text, but as the first interpreters of it. Scriptural interpretation in the church did not begin with the Fathers, but with the very early copyists of the generations between AD 50 and AD 125. In the circumstances of the period, though, the copyists who transcribed the works which have since become the New Testament did not separate commentary and text, but incorporated commentary into the text. We should value the work of these early copyists, and not dismiss it in the search for the 'original text'.[88]

Acts was a particularly fruitful field for the exercise of this type of approach. The writer of the longer, Western text clearly did not regard the book of Acts as in any sense unalterable. However, according to Fascher, the recasting of the text of Acts by the Western reviser was motivated more by literary than by theological considerations:

> In Acts it is a matter, not so much of theologically significant variants, as of psychological interpretations, which allow the narrative to take a more tangible form before the readers' eyes. [89]

Fascher would, then, have us see in the Western reviser a man who wanted to develop, not the theology of Luke, but his narrative. The Western reviser, in other words, was the interpreter of Luke the historian, rather than of Luke the theologian.

Epp

The most extensive attempt to analyse the textual characteristics of Acts made in the three decades after the War was that of E. J. Epp. While Epp expressed his debt to Fascher, he in fact developed the study of textual criticism as a hermeneutical problem in a different way. In 1962 Epp published a study of the 'ignorance motif' in Acts, based on part of his doctoral thesis submitted in 1961.[90] In 1966 a book based on the entire thesis appeared.[91] Epp's *The Theological Tendency* was the first book to have been devoted entirely to the text of Acts since the publication of Clark's *Acts* in 1933. Three streams of influence may be detected in Epp's work, which determined its general approach, its aim, and its scope respectively.

In common with most post-war studies, Epp's work repudiated any attempt to follow in the footsteps of Blass or Clark by constructing a comprehensive theory of the origins of Acts' textual peculiarities. He quoted as a warning B. H. Streeter's words that many a scholar 'has met his Waterloo in the attempt to account for, or explain away, the existence of the Bezan text'.[92] In general approach, therefore, Epp followed the pattern set in this post-war period.

In aim, Epp explicitly turned away from the pursuit of the original text. This is the second stream of influence to be detected in his work. Textual criticism, he argued, has as its goal, not merely the restoration of the original words of the author, but also the elucidation of the history of the text and its interpretation from the evidence of the variants. It is a valid task of textual criticism to approach textual history as a hermeneutical problem. Here the influence of Fascher is manifest, and also that of D. W. Riddle.[93]

The third stream of influence is to be found in the scope of the study, for Epp's major concern was with the 'anti-Judaic tendencies' of Codex D in Acts. The main section of the study investigates numerous readings of D – although their support in other witnesses is painstakingly recorded – with the aim of illustrating the tendency of the readings of D to exaggerate the distance of Jews from Christians, and of Judaism from Christianity.[94] In content, therefore, Epp's work is an extension of the brief observations made by Ropes on this subject, and of the more detailed study made by Menoud.[95]

We shall note below some of the criticisms of Epp's thesis which have appeared since the publication of *The Theological Tendency* (see pp. 25–7). It may also be said that his professed aim of studying the variants of D merely as a hermeneutical problem caused difficulties of method from the outset. For the variants of D could only safely be studied as hermeneutical problems, on the analogy of the redactional study of the use of Mark in Matthew and Luke, if it had first clearly been established that the variants being studied had entered the text by a later hand than that of the author. Epp assumed the existence of a Western reviser when he should have set himself to demonstrate it. The analogy of the Synoptic Gospels, after all, can be used against the idea that the Western text is a revision of the non-Western. B. H. Streeter, on the basis of his work on the Synoptics, was struck by the similarity between the extra material in the Western text of Acts and the extra material which Mark has in the passages where the three Synoptics are in parallel.[96] If it is accepted that Matthew and Luke used Mark, then it may be said that they frequently abbreviated Mark's material, in rather the way in which Clark suggested that the non-Western text was an abbreviation of the Western. The additional length of Matthew and Luke over Mark is made up by the incorporation of additional independent blocks of material, a feature which is lacking in the Western text of Acts, whose additional material is never independent of the other text. Epp's meticulous work on the variants of D was left highly vulnerable by the lack of any explanation of the origin of the D-variants. Redaction criticism of this sort cannot operate wholly independently of source-criticism.

Other studies

Epp's work was not alone in attempting to specify the nature of the Western readings in Acts. There were studies which set themselves to examine the role of Peter in the Western variants, and which concluded that one tendency of the text was to magnify Peter's importance.[97]

A study by W. Thiele (1965) was addressed to analysing the character of the Western variants in Acts.[98] Thiele reached the conclusion that while no witnesses to the Western text preserve it in its entirety – he alluded to von Soden's observation that the witnesses combine in a 'kaleidoscopic' manner[99] – the Western text is not merely the sum of the aberrations of particular manuscripts.[100] He also drew attention to the way in which Western readings often continue and exaggerate features which are already present in the other text.[101] The same observation has been taken up by subsequent studies of the text (see pp. 26f. below). There may be observable tendencies in the Western text of Acts, but they are related to tendencies which are generally thought to be Lucan. On internal evidence alone, Thiele argued, it would often be difficult to determine whether a Western or a non-Western reading was correct, but the case against the originality of the Western text becomes clear when one considers places, such as 7.55 and 15.5, at which the Western text has arisen from a misunderstanding of the non-Western.[102] Therefore, although his study maintained the prevailing view that the Western text is a later rewriting of the book of Acts by another hand than that of the author, Thiele opened up some questions which were to emerge with increased urgency from the mid 1970s, in particular, the extent of the 'Lucanism' of the Western variants.

A study by R. P. C. Hanson represented an ambitious attempt to

locate the provenance of the Western reviser.[103] Hanson maintained that, although more than one hand had been at work to
produce the Western text as we now have it, there was one
'interpolator' in particular who was responsible for most of the
characteristic Western readings.[104] Patristic evidence places this
interpolator in the early second century.[105] Some internal evidence
points to Rome as the place of writing: the interest in the figure of
Peter, the information on the Herods (which would be readily
available at Rome), and the reading *princeps peregrinorum* at
28.16.[106] Hanson combined this argument with a further one, that
Acts finishes where it does because the author was writing for a
Roman audience, whose local tradition would have been sufficient
to carry the narrative on.[107] The origin of the Western textual
tradition, Hanson then suggested, lay with a writer who, some
time in the period AD 120 to AD 150, prepared this work, which
originally had an intended Roman audience, for publication to a
wider readership.[108]

Hanson probably placed too much emphasis on the slender
evidence pointing to Rome as the place of origin of the Western
text. The only solid evidence in his argument was the reading at
28.16, and it is questionable whether the evidence will bear the
weight which he placed upon it.[109] Nor did Hanson establish at the
outset that the Western textual tradition is markedly un-Lucan.
Until that point is firmly established, any argument which proposes a Western reviser is open to the criticism of introducing an
unnecessary element. Hanson's study, though, rightly addressed
two problems which are too frequently neglected. Like Dibelius,
he attempted to explain why this book, more than any other in the
New Testament, should have undergone processes which have
resulted in divergent textual traditions. His postulation of a
Roman 'canoniser' was an attempt to explain this. The other
problem addressed by Hanson was the likelihood of an early
second-century reviser producing the sort of changes which we
observe in the Western text of Acts. Precisely because our knowledge of currents of thought in early second-century Christianity is
so scanty, it is possible to suppose that any tendencies detected in
the Western text of Acts could – or even must – reflect the thought
of the first half of the second century. But in his comments on the
place of Peter, for example, Hanson was doing what has not often
been done in this field, attempting to relate what is observed in
the Western text of Acts with what is known, or may be inferred

from other sources, about Christian thought in the early second
century.

Post-war eclecticism in retrospect

In an article of 1976 reviewing the course of work on all aspects of
Acts in the previous decade and a half, E. Grässer devoted
considerable attention to textual work.[110] His analysis of the
current state of text-research on Acts represents the majority view
at the end of the period which I have described as the post-war
period in the textual criticism of Acts. Grässer made the point that
recent discoveries of papyri suggest that the text of D and its allies
was only one among a profusion of texts which circulated in the
second and early third centuries.[111] Basing himself largely on
Haenchen, Grässer accepted that the 'Semitisms' of the Western
text in Acts could no longer be accepted as such, and that the
secondary nature of the Western readings, in their theological,
literary, and linguistic aspects, must now be accepted.[112] Epp's
work had usefully drawn attention to some anti-Judaic sentiment in
Western readings, but analysis of his cardinal texts revealed that it
would be an exaggeration to speak of an anti-Judaic tendency in the
Western text.[113] While Hanson was too precise in placing the
Western reviser, he was at least correct to observe that in this figure
we have to do with a man of the post-apostolic era, whose work
reflects the concerns of his day: universalism, interest in the
apostolic office, and so on.[114]

If Grässer's article expresses the majority opinion of the time, so
too in another way does the United Bible Societies' *Textual
Commentary on the Greek New Testament*, published in 1971.[115]
B. M. Metzger, who edited that volume, provided the *Commentary*'s section on Acts with a brief, but highly informative, Introduction outlining the problems posed by the text of Acts, and
surveying various of the attempts to resolve them.[116] At the
conclusion of this survey, Metzger turned to explain the method by
which the UBS Textual Committee had proceeded in its work on
Acts. Its approach was one familiar since the war-time articles of
Dibelius and Kilpatrick:

> Since no hypothesis thus far proposed to explain the
> relation of the Western and Alexandrian texts of Acts has
> gained anything like general assent, in its work on that
> book the Bible Societies' Committee proceeded in an

eclectic fashion, holding that neither the Alexandrian nor the Western group of witnesses always preserves the original text, but that in order to attain the earliest text one must compare the two divergent traditions point by point and in each case select the reading which commends itself in the light of transcriptional and intrinsic probabilities.[117]

True to this statement of intent, the *Commentary* contains discussions of variants of all types throughout the book of Acts. No explicit theory of the textual history of Acts is appealed to in the discussions of variants. However, Metzger recognised that a post-script to the statement quoted above was necessary:

> In reviewing the work of the Committee on the book of Acts as a whole, one observes that more often than not the shorter, Alexandrian text was preferred.[118]

This observation is an understatement. There is in fact no occasion on which the Textual Committee accepted a distinctively Western reading into its text, and only seldom was the 'Alexandrian' text deserted.[119] Nor does the *Commentary* preserve complete neutrality about the origin of the Western text: on several occasions it refers to the 'Western reviser'.[120]

The UBS Textual Committee was willing to concede that Western readings may on occasion contain factually accurate material, but ascribed this to the preservation of traditions which were only later incorporated into the text of Acts, in the same way in which Westcott and Hort also accounted for these passages.[121] It appears that the Committee was not united on this issue, since some of its members have expressed their positive evaluation of some Western variants,[122] while others have made clear that in their opinion there is little evidence of the hand of the author of Acts in the Western textual tradition.[123] Although the latter view prevailed in the establishment of the third edition of the UBS Greek New Testament (henceforth UBS[3]), the *Textual Commentary* makes clear that at several points the decision to reject a Western reading was not unanimous.[124]

The discussions which preceded the establishment of the text of UBS[3] were particularly significant because of the convergence of that text with the twenty-sixth edition of the Nestle–Aland Greek New Testament (henceforth N–A[26]) to form what is intended by its authors to be 'a new standard text'.[125] Since the UBS Textual

Committee did its work, the study of the text of Acts has taken a new direction, and indeed some of the members of the Committee have been instrumental in bringing this about. Not only the *Textual Commentary*, but also the text itself of UBS[3] and N–A[26] is a monument to the post-war period in the textual criticism of Acts. In the light of the new directions which the study of the text of Acts has taken since the mid 1970s, it is perhaps premature to describe UBS[3] and N–A[26] as the 'standard text' of Acts.

New directions: Luke and the Western text

Since the mid 1970s, work on the text of Acts has entered its third period, and has developed in two directions. In the first place, there has been criticism which has taken Epp's thesis as its starting-point.[126] This has gone beyond specific discussion of Epp's thesis to ask whether there is any tendentious purpose observable in the Western variants of Acts which could not be ascribed to the author of Acts. Attention has been drawn in this way to the 'Lucanism' of the theology of the Western variants. At the same time, the second direction taken by study of the text in this third period has been to assess the 'Lucanism' of the vocabulary and style of the Western variants in Acts. As a result of these studies, the 'Western reviser' has begun to appear an unnecessary entity, and the Occam's razor by which Ropes reduced to only one the writers responsible for the Western text has been turned against his own hypothesis that Acts was revised by someone other than the author.[127]

Reactions to Epp

Black

The work of Matthew Black on Semitisms in the Gospels and Acts, including the Western textual tradition of Acts was noted above (p. 13). In two subsequent articles, Black returned to the subject.[128] In them, Black has taken issue with Epp, in particular over the Western readings' portrayal of the Holy Spirit. There is, he has argued, no substantial difference between the portrayal of the Holy Spirit in the Western readings and the point of view of Luke himself. That is not to say that all Western readings are thereby shown to be authentic, but Black's work led him to suspect that anti-Montanist influence may have resulted in some more original

Western readings being toned down, producing a less 'enthusiastic' non-Western text. The non-Western (Old Uncial) text, rather than the Western, is the product of doctrinal tampering:

> On the whole, this review of the 'Holy Spirit' variants in Acts seems to me to point to a core of original Lucan tradition, not necessarily preserved in every case exactly as Luke wrote, but in line with the Gentile, anti-Jewish, and one must add, enthusiastic or charismatic character of the primitive text of Acts. It would seem not improbable that, at more than one point in the textual tradition, this 'spiritual' gospel has been pressed into the Procrustean mould of pro-Jewish and anti-Montanist Alexandrian scholasticism.[129]

Black's thesis represents a modified form of Clark's theory of the textual development of Acts, and significantly, Black has expressed cautious approval of Clark's work.[130] A further point of interest is the way in which Black has attempted to relate the textual history of Acts to known developments in the church, rather than, as is sometimes done, inferring these developments from the evidence of the Western text of Acts alone.[131]

Barrett

In a study published in 1979, C. K. Barrett specifically addressed the issues raised by Epp.[132] Barrett's study concluded that there is no new element introduced into the theology of Acts by Codex Bezae – limiting himself, as Epp had done, to that single witness to the Western text. Although a tendency to anti-Judaism may be found there, such a tendency already marked Luke's own work, and: 'The essential characteristic of this MS, or text, is to exaggerate existing tendencies.'[133] Barrett avoided discussion of the question of where and how the Western text originated. He suggested, however, that an answer may lie with the apocryphal Acts, which also exaggerate and enliven the stories of the apostles.[134] In the case of the Western text, though, Barrett concluded that the exaggeration followed lines already laid down in the other text.

Martini

From C. M. Martini's careful study of the possibly tendentious material in the Western text, several points of interest emerge.[135] First, Martini was impressed by the coherence of the Western text, both linguistically and in its attestation. He concluded that it is legitimate to speak of a Western text in the Acts.[136] Secondly, he did not detect a tension between the points of view of the two texts:

> I have scarcely found, in examining the different readings, any examples of real *polarity* between the alternative variants. In other words, it is almost always a matter of *more* or *less*, very seldom of *yes* and *no*, or of *for* and *against*.[137]

The only major exception to this observation is the existence of different forms of the 'Apostolic Decree' (15.20,29 and 21.25) in the two texts. In that instance, Martini allowed that a real divergence of understanding could be seen between the two texts.[138] In common with Thiele and Barrett, Martini noted that when a specific point of view is present in the Western text, it usually continues a line of thought already present in the non-Western text. Very seldom does the Western text have anything new to add, whether of ideas or of facts.[139] The third point of interest in Martini's study is his insistence, which he shares with Black, that developments in second-century Christianity cannot safely be inferred from the Western text of Acts alone. The opposite course must also be taken: to look first at the known concerns of the early second-century church, and then to see whether they are reflected in the Western readings.[140]

Martini did not attempt to answer the questions he raised about the origins of the text-forms of Acts beyond expressing a general agreement with Hanson in ascribing a date *c.* 120–50.[141] But Martini's work, together with that of Black and Barrett, suggests that one should not assume without any clear demonstration that there is a distance between the points of view of the Western and non-Western texts of Acts.

Linguistic Lucanism in the Western text

Concurrently with the renewed interest in the theological aspects of the textual problems in Acts, there has been a reawakening of interest in the stylistic and linguistic features of the problems. It is indeed in this field that the bulk of the new work on Acts has been done.

Wilcox

Wilcox's study of the Semitisms in Acts, including the Western textual tradition, has already been referred to (p. 13 above). A study by Wilcox of the linguistic traits of some Western readings, published in 1979, reached the conclusion that there was little in the readings investigated which told against Lucan authorship, and much which told in favour. In vocabulary and style, the readings were markedly Lucan.[142] From a linguistic point of view, Wilcox concluded, there is little reason not to ascribe these readings to the author of Acts, and 'What we have before us are probably two distinct revisions of one original Lukan work, which have had a somewhat separate development.'[143]

MacKenzie

R. S. MacKenzie published in 1985 a study of the language of some Bezan variants in Acts.[144] He identified several Bezan readings in missionary speeches as reflections of Lucan idiom, and therefore probably Lucan in origin. He proposed no overall thesis to account for them, although he suggested (following Wilcox) that there may have been two revisions of Luke's work, and concluded that 'the Bezan text of Acts may have preserved elements of a textual tradition, for these sermons at least, that is more Lucan than the present B textual tradition'.[145] His study was confined to the readings of D itself, and does not fully allow for the possibility that D's readings are sometimes late developments in the Western tradition. It is also perhaps prone to jump from the observation of Lucan style directly to the conclusion of Lucan authorship, but it none the less represents a further contribution to the reassessment of the Western text.

Delebecque

More extensive work on the language and style of the Western variants in Acts has been undertaken by E. Delebecque. In a series of articles which began to appear in 1980, Delebecque examined in considerable detail the vocabulary and style of a number of Western variants.[146] These studies came to a common conclusion: that both Western and non-Western readings exhibit the same ready facility with the Greek language of the day which is displayed by the author of Acts.

Delebecque's articles formed a preparation for the appearance in 1986 of his major work on the text of Acts.[147] In this work he argues that the stylistic features of the longer text throughout Acts demonstrate the same characteristics as are found in Luke's undisputed writings.[148] The longer text is also evidently secondary and a development of the shorter text.[149] The author of the longer text clearly had additional material at his disposal concerning the characters in the narrative of Acts, and concerning Paul above all.[150] From his analysis of the longer text's readings, Delebecque concludes that Paul is likely to have been the source of much of this material, and Luke, as Paul's companion, was himself responsible for incorporating it into his existing work.[151] The hypothesis to which Delebecque's observations lead is that Luke was the author of both the shorter and the longer text;[152] that the earlier, shorter text was composed while Paul was a prisoner in Rome;[153] that Paul was released after imprisonment in Rome, and undertook further travels in Spain and the Aegean terminated by a final Ephesian imprisonment during which Paul dictated 2 Timothy to Luke;[154] and that the long text of Acts represents Luke's revision of the work after Paul's death in Ephesus, probably shortly after AD 67.[155] 'The fact is', Delebecque maintains, 'that it is the death of the apostle which throws light on this new version. It is like a long reflection upon the second *Letter to Timothy*.'[156]

Delebecque's thesis has both strengths and weaknesses. He has taken a broader context of style than merely the New Testament as a background against which to judge the style of Luke and of the Western text. This is a strong point of his method. He has also drawn upon a mass of stylistic observations. But it might be argued that he weakens his case by an exclusive reliance on the linguistic and narrative aspects of the textual problem, without taking the theology of the variants into consideration. His thesis that Luke was the author of the longer text rests on a firmer foundation than his theory of how Luke wrote it. Delebecque's argument in this respect relies too heavily upon an assumption about the author of Acts, and upon a hypothetical reconstruction of the final years of Paul's life. The establishment of Delebecque's 'longer text' is also questionable. He recognises the existence of witnesses to the text other than D, but in practice uses D, supplemented by Clark's Z in the lacunae of that witness.[157] The form of Western readings requires closer attention than Delebecque has given.

However, none of these points effectively disposes of Delebecque's arguments, and his careful analysis of texts has provided the student of the text of Acts with a wealth of new perspectives on numerous variants.

Boismard and Lamouille

The two-volume work by M. E. Boismard and A. Lamouille, *Le Texte occidental des Actes des Apôtres* (1984) has to be classed with Ropes's and Clark's books as one of the most thorough studies of the text of Acts, and a major work of reference for any future studies.[158] Its approach and conclusions are as characteristic of the third period of the textual study of Acts as Ropes and Clark were for the first period, or Epp for the second.

Boismard had already signalled his interest in the text of Acts in a study written in 1978 and published in 1981: a detailed stylistic analysis of two units of variation in Acts 11.2 and 19.1.[159] He concluded that both textual versions were faithful to the vocabulary and style of the author, and hinted that a more comprehensive study would be necessary to uncover the complex tradition-history of the text.[160]

Le Texte occidental is the more comprehensive study suggested by the 1981 article. Boismard and Lamouille do what had not been attempted since Clark, that is, to offer a systematic interpretation of the textual history of Acts articulated around a hypothesis of the text's development. The hypothesis is presented relatively briefly, but the survey of witnesses in Volume I, and the analysis of stylistic evidence in Volume II, on which the work rests, are prodigious. The stylistic evidence is arranged in such a way as to demonstrate that both streams of textual tradition, the Western ('Texte occidental' = TO) and the Alexandrian ('Texte alexandrin' = TA), exhibit Lucan stylistic characteristics. It is also organised to show that TO is closer to the style of the Gospel than to that of Acts (TA): 'this fact', the authors comment, 'would favour the hypothesis of two redactions of Acts by Luke at some distance from one another'. [161]

The recovery of the true text of TO, though, is no easy matter. Boismard and Lamouille examine in detail the problems of the inner development of the Western text. They propose that the tradition stemming from the original TO has undergone a bifurcation: the original, and authentically Lucan, TO has given rise both to a relatively pure stream of tradition (TO^1), and to a degraded form (TO^2).[162] Study of the Western text has been hampered in the past by an over-reliance on D, which in fact is a representative of TO^2, and has suffered contamination from TA.[163] Because of the widespread and early influence of TA upon TO, it is necessary to seek the authentic TO readings even among rather scattered and diverse minuscule, versional, and Patristic witnesses.[164] Because of the importance which they attach to these witnesses, Boismard and Lamouille's description of witnesses, and their citation of them in the Apparatus, break new ground in several areas of study of minuscule, versional, and Patristic evidence (although an idiosyncratic system of sigla makes the Apparatus more difficult to use than might have been the case).

Once the original TO has been recovered, it is possible to say that it is 'an authentically Lucan text'.[165] TA also has its own internal history, and although B is likely to be the best representative, it does not always give the purest form of text.[166] But, as with TO, when the original form of TA is established, it too is authentically Lucan. The thesis which accounts for these phenomena is succinctly put:

> The solution which we discern would not be … exactly that of Blass, but a sort of synthesis between that of Blass and that of Pott:[167] that Luke wrote a first redaction of Acts, of which we find an echo in the Western text; that a certain number of years later he radically altered his initial work, not only from the stylistic point of view, as Blass had it, but also from the point of view of its content; that these two redactions were fused into one to give the present text of Acts, or more precisely, the Alexandrian text (in a purer form than that which we now have).[168]

We shall return at a later point to consider Boismard and Lamouille's work in detail.[169] They have taken up a task neglected since the War: the attempt, not merely to describe the textual peculiarities of Acts, but to account for them. In view of the renewal of interest in the text of Acts since the mid 1970s, it is understandable that the inadequacy of the post-war policy of neglect of this problem should have become clear. Whatever the

particular qualities of Boismard and Lamouille's work, it is at least
an indication that the larger questions, to which pre-war scholars
addressed themselves, are once again on the agenda of the textual
criticism of Acts.

The Western text as a post-Lucan phenomenon

The third and most recent period in the study of the text of Acts has
not produced a consensus view. General works on Acts, commentaries and other studies, continue to accept as a working basis the
outlook here characterised as the post-war approach. There have
also been textual monographs which continue the post-war
method: the studies referred to on pp. 25–32 above do not represent the sum total of textual studies of Acts in the period.[170] The
most thorough study to maintain the thesis of a post-Lucan origin
for the Western text has been that of B. Aland (1986).[171] Aland's
concern is with the Western text in the New Testament as a whole,
of which she takes the text of Acts to be an example.

From the evidence of groupings of readings she argues that we
may distinguish a definite 'Western main redaction': a redaction of
the text from which such witnesses as D have arisen. This redaction
represents a canalisation of a much freer text which circulated in an
early period. Glimpses of this pre-Western text may be seen in 614
and its allies, as well as in Irenaeus.[172] Aland gives considerable
attention to the text of Acts in Irenaeus, which was not, she
concludes, a 'thorough-going' Western text (*pace* Ropes), but
rather an example of the free text circulating in the second century
before the Western main redaction established itself.[173] From the
knowledge of Western readings shown by the Harclean Syriac
margin[174] and by Syrian Fathers, Aland locates the origin of the
Western main redaction in Syria. She is thus drawn to agree with
Ropes about the place of origin of the Western text as a redaction,
although she sees its nature differently, and places the date much
later, probably early in the third century.[175]

Aland has given a new precision to the term 'Western text',
distinguishing as she has done between the 'free text' of the second
century and the thoroughly 'Western' text to be found in the third
century. In her study, though, the secondary nature of the Western
text is taken as an established datum.[176] The problem which she
addresses is how to account for this secondary development within
the New Testament textual tradition. So, while she gives a critical

review of Boismard and Lamouille's work,[177] her own work does not seriously entertain the possibility that in Acts a substantial element of the Western text may have a Lucan base.

It may be possible to take issue with Aland's contention that Irenaeus is a witness merely for a 'free text', rather than a recognisably Western text. To take one small but telling instance: Aland is one of the very few scholars to draw attention to a minor agreement of Irenaeus with D in Acts 17.26, κατὰ ὁροθεσίαν for καὶ τὰς ὁροθεσίας. Here Irenaeus and D stand against all other witnesses. In Aland's view this is an intelligent clarification which D and Irenaeus (or their textual ancestors) could have arrived at independently.[178] The opposite view is not only possible, but likely: that this is a copyist's error which suggests some community of origin between D's text and that of Irenaeus. But even if, as Aland strongly maintains, the Western text as we know it from its later examples results from a third-century redaction, it is still possible to enquire into the elements from which the redactor drew his material. Aland's study has not, therefore, disposed of the need to investigate further the issues raised in the work of Wilcox, Delebecque, and Boismard and Lamouille.

The problem of the text of Acts today

In the light of the new directions taken since the mid 1970s the Western readings in Acts can no longer be lightly dismissed from consideration of Luke's work. The theological and linguistic gap between the major text-forms of Acts no longer seems as great as it once did. Neither the thesis of Blass nor that of Clark has been vindicated by recent work, but the observations on which their work rested have been brought under further scrutiny, and when their names are mentioned, it is no longer merely as curiosities of scholarship.

The large issues with which pre-war work on the text of Acts was concerned have been raised again: issues which had been put to one side after the War. The attempt to approach the Western text of Acts as a hermeneutical problem now appears to have been a premature essay in redaction criticism before secure source-critical foundations had been laid. It is these source-critical questions which emerge from recent work as the most pressing task for the textual criticism of Acts today.

One part of this task is an examination of the nature of the text-forms of Acts, and in particular an examination of the extent of the 'Lucanism' of each. In this examination, attention should be paid both to the theological and to the linguistic aspects of the problem. Recent studies have tended to be concerned with one or the other, but both are of equal significance. Another part of the task is an elucidation of the circumstances in which the text-forms we possess today could have arisen. The following chapters are an attempt to address this task. Only when it is done will it be possible to give an account of the history of the book of Acts which will explain the origins, and thus the nature, of the textual peculiarities of this work.

2

THE NATURE OF THE WESTERN TEXT OF ACTS

The Western text and the book of Acts

The first task to be tackled in attempting to discuss the textual peculiarities of Acts is to decide what the 'Western text of Acts' is. At the time that Blass wrote, for instance, it was still possible to assume that Codex D was, to all intents and purposes, the Western text. Discoveries of new MS material since that time, as well as a more sophisticated understanding of the processes by which the text types emerged, have made such a view rather obsolete. Even at the time of Blass, it was evident that a 'Western text' existed elsewhere in the New Testament, and that this fact would have to be taken into account in any satisfactory description of the Western text of Acts.

The problem today in seeking to analyse the Western text of Acts is, therefore, twofold. On the one hand there is the problem of locating the Western text of Acts: if the Western text is not merely the readings of Codex D, then where is it to be found? Is there, indeed, any homogeneous entity to be recognised as 'the Western text of Acts', or have we to do rather with ill-defined collections of readings which have been misleadingly called 'Western'? On the other hand there is the problem of relating the Western text in Acts to the Western text in the rest of the New Testament: is the Western text of Acts so distinctive as to deserve separate treatment? Is there, in other words, a problem of the Western text of *Acts* at all?

The homogeneity of the Western text

The Western text of the New Testament was a subject of considerable interest in the first half of the twentieth century.[1] Today it attracts less attention. This is largely because earlier in this century the Western text was thought to be a consistent textual tradition which might provide contact with a period before Alexandrian revision of the New Testament had taken place. Today, the Western text is often dismissed as a 'chimera'.[2] But such dismissal may be rash. There is, certainly, little reason to suppose that the Western text was current particularly, or exclusively, in the West.[3] Nor should we suppose that Codex D is always the best guide to Western readings. Although it is the major Greek representative of the Western text, it has a manuscript history of its own, and may not always give the earliest forms of Western readings. None the less, neither papyrus discoveries nor historical considerations can entirely rule out the possibility that there is a recognisable entity which may be called – conventionally, but misleadingly – the 'Western text'.

The unity of the Western text is a matter frequently touched on, but seldom, if ever, fully discussed. J. H. Ropes tentatively proposed the thesis that the Western text of the New Testament had been produced by a conscious ecclesiastical process, perhaps by the church in Antioch as part of the preparation of a primitive canon of Christian scriptures.[4] Ropes's proposal was very cautiously expressed, and was, as he was aware, far from proven. More recently, the unity of the Western text has been asserted by C. M. Martini,[5] and denied by E. Grässer.[6] But, as Plümacher has pointed out, the issue has never been fully discussed with extensive reference to texts.[7]

What degree of unity, then, does the Western text possess? There is certainly a group of Western witnesses with a large number of common readings, or at the least, readings with common features. These characteristic features include harmonisation (in the Gospels), addition of material in places (with occasional omission also), and alteration of style. The witnesses with common readings would appear to be related to one another. In that sense, the Western text can be seen to be carried in a 'family' of witnesses. But the Western text includes also witnesses with characteristic common features: certain *types* of reading which seem to have appealed to scribes. These features point, not so much to common ancestry among witnesses, as to a shared cast of mind among scribes – a liking for harmonisation, or stylistic emendation, for example.

It is possible to conclude that the Western text is not merely a heterogeneous collection of readings, yet without being as specific as Ropes about the time and place of its origin. There appear to be two levels of unity in the Western text. In the first place, there are groups of common readings, found as seams or strata in certain witnesses, which imply a common origin for the witnesses in which they are found. These seams or strata are not all from one point of origin. In this sense, it might be more appropriate to speak of Western *texts*, rather than of *a* Western text. In the second place, there is a unity of approach among Western witnesses, shown in the similar types of reading favoured by the copyists responsible for the Western witnesses. There is, in other words, a Western tendency shared by these witnesses. In this sense, it is legitimate to refer to *the* Western text, as long as it is understood that what is meant is a broad stream of textual tradition, and a way of handling the text, rather than a coherent recension of the text, created at a specific time.

The significance of Codex D is that it is the only Greek witness in which substantial numbers of the seams of Western material are present, and it is the major witness to the Western textual tendency. But it is not the only witness to that tendency, nor does it necessarily contain all the seams of Western material.

The significance of Western readings cannot be decided in advance, either by dismissing them as belonging to an aberrant stream of tradition, or by endorsing them as the only reliable form of the text. The attitude to the text which produced the Western textual tradition was prevalent until at least the late second century. The growing respect paid to primitive Christian literature, and the emergence of something like the concept of a 'New Testament' from the time of Irenaeus, are likely to have put an end to the tendency to 'improvement', which was the essence of the Western approach. During the period in which the Western text was being created, the various strata from which the text is composed will have been drawn from various sources. Each New Testament book has its own distinctive strata. A recent study of Codex D in Matthew, for example, has concluded that a major element of D's text in that book consists of the work of a second-century editor, who incorporated additional and alternative forms of the Matthean tradition.[8] Other books of the New Testament have a Western text of a different character. In Mark, harmonisation with the other Gospels appears to have played a major part in the formation of Western readings. In Luke it has been suspected that tendentious anti-Judaic material has been incorporated.[9]

Each Western reading, and each block of readings, should be

investigated on its merits. Such a reading may incorporate ancient material not originally in the text. There are several examples of this in the Gospels. One is the long section of extra material found at Matt. 20.28 in D, with support from Φ it syr[c.hmg]:

> But as for you, seek to increase from that which is small, and to be less from that which is greater. And when you go into a place, having been invited to dine, do not recline in the places of honour, lest a person more honourable than you should come, and the host should approach and say to you, 'Move farther down'; and you will be shamed. But if you recline in the lesser place, and someone lesser than you should come, the host will say to you, 'Go farther up'; and this will be beneficial to you.

This passage has clear links with Lk. 14.8–10. From its detail, though, it would not appear to be merely a borrowing from Luke, but rather an independent version of the same parable, placed here in the Western witnesses.[10] Another example is the celebrated *agraphon* found in D at Lk. 6.5:

> On the same day, when he saw a man working on the Sabbath, he said to him, 'Man, if you are aware of what you are doing, blessed are you; but if you are not aware, you are accursed and a transgressor of the Law.'

This passage, too, appears to be an example of floating tradition taken up by a Western witness. It was defended as an authentic pronouncement story by J. Jeremias,[11] although it has generally been regarded as inauthentic.[12] But it is in all probability an ancient piece of material.

The Western text appears to have been drawn together in an eclectic manner. Due attention should be paid to the various strata of which the Western text has been composed. Some strata may be early, and some may preserve authentic material. With these considerations in mind, it is now possible to examine the Western text in the book of Acts.

The Western text of Acts

The work of E. Haenchen on the text of Acts has, as noted above,[13] been remarkably influential. He has drawn attention to the existence of three levels of material within the text of Acts D. In the first level are the variants of a type common to the Western text elsewhere in the New Testament: 'a mass of small alterations intended to clarify and smooth'.[14] We may ascribe the material in this level to the general Western way of treating texts. The second level of material is more distinctive of the Western text of Acts. It consists of the alterations made to the text by a redactor: 'a meticulous, alert and erudite man, anxious to remove the faults in a book which strikes him as potentially valuable'.[15] We may identify this level of material as one of the strata or seams which characterise the Western text throughout the New Testament. The third level of material is peculiar to D alone. It consists of assimilations to the Latin of D (it[5]), and of scribal errors. It is this level which has most often provided the illusion that there has been some Semitic influence on the formation of the Western text of Acts. Wherever such influence appears detectable, it can usually be put down to simple error by the copyist of D.[16] Haenchen concluded that none of these levels reproduces an authentic text of Acts.[17]

Haenchen's analysis of the Western text of Acts is potentially very useful. Evidently, the Western text of Acts is related to the Western text elsewhere in the New Testament: it is found in a similar group of witnesses, and displays some similar characteristics. Yet at the same time, in Acts the Western text has distinctive features: it is, in particular, more extensive.[18] Both these aspects of the text can be accounted for by recognising that the Western text of Acts is a manifestation of the Western textual tradition found elsewhere in the New Testament, but that one of its most prominent features is a stratum of material peculiar to itself, which Haenchen ascribes to the work of a redactor. The particular problem of the Western text of Acts is to account for the existence of this stratum of material.

The difficulty is, in part, to distinguish this level of material from the type of material common to the Western text in the rest of the New Testament, and from the errors of D. Haenchen merely illustrated his points with a few examples. In order to make his analysis a useful basis for work, it would be necessary to draw up criteria for distinguishing these levels.

An example of the difficulty of analysing the Western text thoroughly in these terms is provided by Acts 17.26. Here every MS witness except D* reads: καὶ τὰς ὁροθεσίας. D*, though, reads κατὰ ὁροθεσίαν. This appears to be a clear instance of an error by a scribe of D itself (καὶ τάς – κατά). D* is deserted by the Latin of it[5] (*et determinationes*), and a corrector has even added interlined notes to bring the reading of D into accord with the Majority reading. However, the Latin of Irenaeus reads: *secundum determinationem*. Without the fortuitous support of Ir[lat] this reading would certainly look like an error of D – Haenchen's third level of Western readings. But unless the Latin of Irenaeus has been influenced by the very manuscript D itself, there must be more to the matter than merely an error in D alone. The reading certainly looks like a scribal error,[19] but on the principle that community of error implies community of origin, the reading may be more primitive than its present MS support would suggest.

Taking note of the warning provided by Acts 17.26, what criteria might be used to distinguish the different levels which make up the Western text of Acts, particularly as exhibited by its principal witness, D? In the first place, it must be asked whether a particular reading of D has any support from other witnesses, and whether it can be explained as a scribal error or as an assimilation to the Bezan Latin. If it is without support, and if it can be explained in these ways, then there must be a suspicion that it is part of Haenchen's third level – a reading produced merely by the inner development of Codex D. In the second place, it must be asked whether a reading is simply a clarification or smoothing of the text, of a sort found throughout the Western text, or whether its contribution is more substantial. This distinction – between Haenchen's first and second categories – is a very difficult one to make, but it may be possible to make it in many instances.

The material which cannot be discounted in either of these ways has a claim to be regarded as part of the stratum of readings which makes up the distinctive element in the Western text of Acts.

The distinctive Western stratum of Acts

Several studies of the text of Acts have attempted to characterise the Western text.[20] But one feature of the distinctive Western stratum of Acts which has not received the attention it deserves is its commentary-like character. In one sense, the entire Western text of the New Testament is a form of commentary, which illustrates the way in which copyists in an early period thought that the text should be recast. In Acts, though, the distinctive Western stratum can particularly frequently be read as a commentary by a reader who has thought about the difficulties of the text.

The function of the Western text as a form of commentary has been noted briefly by several scholars. W. M. Ramsay suggested that the Bezan text be read as a sort of second-century commentary on Acts; although he also thought that several Majority readings resulted from the incorporation of marginal notes and glosses.[21] Lake and Cadbury described the Western text as often 'the earliest and in many ways the best commentary'.[22] Haenchen has described the postulated Western redactor as 'Acts' earliest commentator'.[23]

If the Western text of Acts is read as a commentary, then it can be seen to have several typical features.

Narrative commentary

One typical feature of this Western commentary material is the introduction of small scenes which help the main narrative. A particularly clear example is found in 10.25. Here the majority of witnesses narrate Peter's arrival at Cornelius' house in this way: Ὡς δὲ ἐγένετο τοῦ εἰσελθεῖν τὸν Πέτρον, συναντήσας αὐτῷ ὁ Κορνήλιος. D, though, has Προσεγγίζοντος δὲ τοῦ Πέτρου εἰς τὴν Καισαρείαν προδραμὼν εἷς τῶν δούλων διεσάφησεν παραγεγονέναι αὐτόν. Ὁ δὲ Κορνήλιος ἐκπηδήσας καὶ συναντήσας αὐτῷ. D has substantial support here from it[51] syr[hmg] and cop[G67].[24] If this is an addition to the text, the motive seems quite clear: to explain how it was that Cornelius knew that Peter was near.[25]

Another example is the comment at the end of 14.2 that after the Jews had stirred up trouble for Paul and Barnabas at Iconium ὁ δὲ κύριος ἔδωκεν ταχὺ εἰρήνην (D (E) it[5.(50).51.54.58.59.(61).63.] vg[1260 al.] syr[hmg] cop[G67] nedl[2] ger[tepl] prov; Cass Bede). This looks like a comment intended to explain why Paul and Barnabas, troubled in 14.2, are able to carry on their mission work at Iconium 'for a substantial time' in 14.3.[26]

At 16.30 D it[5] and syr[p.h**] (the Syriac with a minor variation) describe the Philippian goaler's sensible precaution: after the earthquake he spoke to Paul, but only τοὺς λοιποὺς ἀσφαλισάμενος. The additional material seems designed to answer a reader's possible query by introducing a small retrospective scene.

At 18.12 a similar participial retrospect is given by D it[5.55] (with partial support from syr[h**] sah): συνλαλήσαντες μεθ' ἑαυτῶν ἐπὶ τὸν Παῦλον καὶ ἐπιθέντες τὰς χεῖρας. This reading explains how it was that the Jews appeared before Gallio, leading Paul with them.[27]

The text of Acts 21.16f. has received considerable attention. It presents difficulties because D has been mutilated at this point and part of the reading must be reconstructed.[28] The two texts give the following readings (taking Ropes's reconstruction of D):

N–A[26]	Codex D[vid]
συνῆλθον δὲ καὶ τῶν μαθητῶν	
ἀπὸ Καισαρείας σὺν ἡμῖν	ἐκ Κεσα[ραίας σὺν ἡμεῖν·
ἄγοντες παρ᾽ ᾧ ξενισθῶμεν	οὗτοι δὲ ἤγαγον ἡμᾶς
	πρὸς οὓς ξενισθῶμεν.
	καὶ παραγενόμενοι εἴς
	τινα κώμην ἐγενόμεθα
Μνάσωνί τινι Κυπρίῳ	παρὰ Νάσωνί τινι Κυπρίῳ
ἀρχαίῳ μαθητῇ.	μαθητῇ ἀρχαίῳ.
Γενομένων δὲ ἡμῶν	Κἀκεῖθεν ἐξιόντες
εἰς Ἱεροσόλυμα . . .	ἤλθομεν εἰς Ἱεροσόλυμα . . .

om. συνῆλθον δὲ καὶ τῶν μαθητῶν: D it⁵
οὗτοι δὲ ἤγαγον ἡμᾶς D it⁵ (ἄγοντες ἡμᾶς: sah arm)
πρὸς οὓς . . . Ἱεροσόλυμα: D it⁵ syr^hmg

> (it⁵ gives *apud quem* for
> πρὸς οὕς)

Some commentators have held that the Western text, in placing Mnason's dwelling between Caesaraea and Jerusalem, is merely making plain what is already implied in the other text.[29] The majority, though, has concluded that the Western text has arisen from a misunderstanding of the other text.[30] Whether or not the Western text rests on a misunderstanding, it shows something of the way that the Western additional material often provides small scenes which help the narrative. Here the problem is that a reader of the shorter text might suppose that the journey from Caesaraea to Jerusalem was undertaken in one stage. The Western reading indicates that it was broken at least once,[31] and this is certainly more credible for a journey of at least sixty miles. Lake and Cadbury reached an unwarranted conclusion in assuming that this reading pointed to a Palestinian origin for the Western text:[32] after all, an attentive reader with no more knowledge of Palestine than he had gleaned from the book of Acts might notice that Claudius Lysias' troops when travelling in the opposite direction broke their journey at Antipatris (Acts 23.31f.). Whatever the value of the

Western material here as information, it gives an indication of the sort of concern which lies behind the text.

A further example of the retrospective explanation is found in several Western witnesses at 27.15 (257. 614. 876. 913. 1518. 1611. 1765. 2138. 2147. 2401. 2412. syr^h** Cass Bede: D is not extant here). The Majority text has: Συναρπασθέντος δὲ τοῦ πλοίου, καὶ μὴ δυναμένου ἀντοφθαλμεῖν τῷ ἀνέμῳ, ἐπιδόντες ἐφερόμεθα. The Western witnesses have a more extensive version: . . . ἐπιδόντες τῷ πλέοντι καὶ συστείλαντες τὰ ἱστία ἐφερόμεθα. Syr^h continues: 'as chance would have it'. In the narrative, the boat containing Paul and his companions is being forced to run before the wind, and the Western reading reassures the reader that the crew at least furled the sails. It is a common-sense deduction of what is likely to have happened, and is remarkable only for the unobtrusive way it is fitted into the narrative as a participial retrospect.

Another feature of Western material read as commentary is a concern with the entrances and exits of characters in the narrative.

The entry of characters on to the scene of action is made more explicit in several places:

5.21
συνεκάλεσαν τὸ συνέδριον: Maj.
ἐγερθέντες τὸ πρωὶ
καὶ συνκαλεσάμενοι τὸ
συνέδριον: D it⁵ cop^G67

5.22
οὐχ εὗρον αὐτοὺς ἐν
τῇ φυλακῇ: Maj
καὶ ἀνοίξαντες (D
ἀνύξαντες) τὴν φυλακὴν οὐκ
εὗρον αὐτοὺς ἔσω: D 876.
1611. (2138) it^5.54.(61).69 syr^h** cop^G67

11.28
ἀναστὰς δὲ εἷς ἐξ
αὐτῶν: Maj
ἦν δὲ πολλὴ ἀγαλλίασις.
συνεστραμμένων δὲ ἡμῶν ἔφη
εἷς ἐξ αὐτῶν: D it^5.54.58.62. vg^1259*.1260.1277.1282
cop^G67; Aug.

16.35
ἀπέστειλαν οἱ στρατηγοί: Maj
συνῆλθον οἱ [D οἷς]
στρατηγοὶ ἐπὶ τὸ αὐτὸ
εἰς τὴν ἀγορὰν καὶ
ἀναμνησθέντες τὸν σεισμὸν
τὸν γεγονότα ἐφοβήθησαν καὶ
ἀπέστειλαν: D syr[hmg]

Just as the entry of characters is made more explicit in Western readings, so too the exit of characters receives attention:

5.18
— :Maj
καὶ ἐπορεύθη εἷς ἕκαστος εἰς τὰ ἴδια: D it[5] cop[67]

12.23
γενόμενος σκωληκόβρωτος: Maj
καταβὰς ἀπὸ τοῦ βήματος γενόμενος σκωληκόβρωτος:
D it[5] (cop[G67])

14.18
— : Maj
ἀλλὰ πορεύεσθαι ἕκαστον εἰς τὰ ἴδια: C 6. 33. 36. 81. 88.
104. 257. 307. 383. 431. 453. 467. 614. 1175. 1799. 2138.
2147. 2298. 2412. al. it[55] (*et di[miserun]t eos ab se*) syr[hmg]
arm.

28.29
— : p[74] ℵ A B E Ψ 048 33. 81. 181. 1175. 1739. 2464. lec[6]
it[50.53.59] vg[gk629] syr[p.h] cop arm geo eth[mss]
καὶ ταῦτα αὐτοῦ εἰπόντος ἀπῆλθον οἱ Ἰουδαῖοι πολλὴν
ἔχοντες ἐν ἑαυτοῖς συζήτησιν: Maj
it[6.51.54.61] vg[231a.1266.1700.]
vg[(cav.tol.1199.1213.1259*.1260.1282.1897.)] syr[h**]
ndl[1.2] prov eth[ms]; Cass.

Some Western readings make changes of scene explicit:

3.11[33]
κρατοῦντος δὲ αὐτοῦ τὸν Πέτρον καὶ τὸν Ἰωάννην: Maj
ἐκπορευομένου δὲ τοῦ Πέτρου καὶ Ἰωάνου συνεξεπορεύετο κρατῶν αὐτούς: D it[5.55.] cop[G67]

19.28
ἔκραζον: Maj
δραμόντες εἰς τὸ ἄμφοδον ἔκραζον: D (καὶ δραμόντες
κτλ: 383. 614 in 614 εδ φοδον for ἄμφοδον) it⁵ syrʰᵐᵍ.

Other Western readings demonstrate the same concern for the
movement of characters by including additional information:

8.1
πλὴν τῶν ἀποστόλων: Maj
πλὴν τῶν ἀποστόλων οἳ ἔμειναν ἐν Ἰερουσαλήμ: D*
(+ μόνοι 1175) it⁵·⁵¹·⁵²·⁵⁵·⁵⁶ vgᴹᴹ sah copᴳ⁶⁷ prov¹ ethᵐˢˢ;
(?Ps-)Augᶜᵃᵗʰ BarS

14.7
— : Maj
ὁ δὲ Παῦλος καὶ Βαρνάβας διέτριβον ἐν Λύστροις: D
E it⁵·⁵⁰·⁵⁴·⁵⁵·⁵⁸· vg¹²⁶⁰· ¹²⁶⁶ gerᵗᵉᵖˡ copᴳ⁶⁷; Bede

15.34³⁴
— : Maj
ἔδοξε δὲ τῷ Σειλέᾳ ἐπιμεῖναι αὐτούς (αὐτοῦ: C D it⁵)
C D 33. 36. 88. 181. 242. 257. 323. 383. 431. 453. 467. 522.
536. 614. 915. 945. 1108. 1175. 1522. 1611. 1739. 1799.
1891. 2147. 2298. 2412. pc. it⁵·⁶·⁵¹·⁵⁸·⁶¹·⁶²·⁶³·⁶⁷· vgᴮᴳ·ᶜᵃᵛ·ᵗᵒˡ·
¹²⁶⁰·¹²⁶⁶·¹²⁷⁶·¹⁷⁰⁰·ᵍᵏ⁶²⁹· syrʰ** sah bohᵐˢˢ arm geo nedl gerᵗᵉᵖˡ
prov eth; Cass Ephr (?Ps-)Oec Theoph
μόνος δὲ Ἰούδας ἐπορεύθη: D it⁵·⁶·⁵¹·⁵⁸·⁶¹·⁶²·⁶³·⁶⁷·
vgᴮᴳ·ᵗᵒˡ·¹²⁶⁰·¹²⁶⁶·¹⁷⁰⁰· armᵒˢᶜ nedl prov; Cass
add: to Jerusalem: it⁵⁸ armᵒˢᶜ; Cass

18.2
— : Maj
οἳ καὶ [κε: D] κατῴκησαν εἰς τὴν Ἀχαΐαν: D it⁵·⁵⁵·
syrʰᵐᵍ

20.15
— : p⁷⁴ ℵ A B C E 33. 36. 431. 453. 522. 1175. 1739. 1891.
pc. vg boh
καὶ μείναντες ἐν Τρωγυ(λ)λίᾳ: D Maj it⁵·⁵¹· syr sah.

Only occasionally does additional information of this sort add anything new to the narrative. When it does so, as at 20.15, the Western material has been regarded with greater favour by several critics than has the mass of the Western text.[35] However, notices such as that at 20.15 should be compared with similar passages in the Western text of Acts dealing with the movement of characters in the narrative. Such small notes are characteristic of the Western text of Acts, and clear reasons would have to be given to justify treating 20.15, for instance, differently from those other notes.

The notices of movement are an indication of the meticulous quality of the Western text in Acts to which Haenchen referred.[36] The material can be read as a commentary whose purpose is both to make what is happening more explicit and to tidy up the narrative.

The Western readings also appear to attempt to clarify the narrative by supplying motives for actions. There are several examples:

11.25f.
ἐξῆλθεν δὲ εἰς Ταρσὸν ἀναζητῆσαι Σαῦλον, καὶ εὑρὼν ἤγαγεν εἰς Ἀντιόχειαν: Maj
ἀκούσας δὲ ὅτι Σαῦλός ἐστιν εἰς Θαρσὸν ἐξῆλθεν ἀναζητῶν αὐτόν, καὶ ὡς συντυχὼν παρεκάλεσεν ἐλθεῖν εἰς Ἀντιόχειαν: D it[5.(51.54*.62mg)] (syr[hmg]) cop[G67]

The Western additional material explains why Barnabas should have gone to Tarsus to look for Saul, and how it was that he was able to bring him to Antioch – he entreated Paul to come. The Western reading at 11.25f. should be compared with the Western reading at 18.27. In the latter passage, Apollos is the subject:

18.27
Βουλομένου δὲ αὐτοῦ διελθεῖν εἰς τὴν Ἀχαΐαν, προτρε- ψάμενοι οἱ ἀδελφοὶ ἔγραψαν τοῖς μαθηταῖς ἀποδέξα- σθαι αὐτόν: Maj
Ἐν δὲ τῇ Ἐφέσῳ ἐπιδημοῦντές τινες Κορίνθιοι καὶ ἀκούσαντες αὐτοῦ παρεκάλουν διελθεῖν σὺν αὐτοῖς εἰς τὴν πατρίδα αὐτῶν. συνκατανεύσαντος δὲ αὐτοῦ οἱ Ἐφέσιοι ἔγραψαν τοῖς ἐν Κορίνθῳ μαθηταῖς ὅπως ἀποδέξωνται τὸν ἄνδρα: D it[5] (syr[hmg])

The fuller Western version of this passage explains what lay behind Apollos' desire to go to Greece, and explains also the writing of the Ephesians' letter.

A Western additional passage in 13.8 gives the motive for Elymas' concern to turn Sergius Paulus away from the faith:

13.8
— : Maj
ἐπειδὴ ἥδιστα ἤκουεν αὐτῶν: D*(ἐπιδή) (E) it⁵·⁵⁰· syrʰ**
copᴳ⁶⁷; Bede

Other examples of the Western concern to provide motive are:

18.21
δεῖ με (δὲ D*; om. με vg²³¹ᵃ) πάντως τὴν ἑορτὴν (+ ἡμέραν D) τὴν (om. D) ἐρχομένην ποιῆσαι εἰς Ἱεροσόλυμα: D H L P Ψ Maj. it⁵·⁵¹·⁵⁸·⁵⁹·⁶¹·⁶³· vg⁽²³¹ᵃ·⁾· ¹²⁶⁶·¹⁷⁰⁰·ᵍᵏ⁶²⁹ syr ndl gerᵗᵉᵖˡ prov ethᵐˢˢ; Cass Chr Theoph

19.1³⁷
Ἐγένετο δὲ ἐν τῷ τὸν Ἀπολλῶ εἶναι ἐν Κορίνθῳ Παῦλον διελθόντα τὰ ἀνωτερικὰ μέρη κατελθεῖν εἰς Ἔφεσον: Maj.
Θέλοντος δὲ τοῦ Παύλου κατὰ τὴν ἰδίαν βουλὴν πορεύεσθαι εἰς Ἱεροσόλυμα εἶπεν αὐτῷ τὸ πνεῦμα ὑποστρέφειν εἰς τὴν Ἀσίαν. διελθὼν δὲ τὰ ἀνωτερικὰ μέρη ἔρχεται εἰς Ἔφεσον: p³⁸ᵛⁱᵈ D it⁵ syrʰᵐᵍ; Ado Ephrᶜᵃᵗ

23.25
— : Maj
ἐφοβήθη γὰρ μήποτε ἁρπάσαντες αὐτὸν οἱ Ἰουδαῖοι ἀποκτείνωσιν καὶ αὐτὸς μεταξὺ ἔγκλημα ἔχῃ ὡς εἰληφὼς ἀργύρια: p⁴⁸ (614). 2147. 2412. it⁶·⁵¹·⁵⁴·⁶¹·⁶²·⁶³· vg¹⁷⁰⁰ (syrʰ**) geo ndl prov

24.24
[Drusilla] who wished that she might see Paul and hear the word. Wishing therefore to satisfy her [Felix sent for Paul]: syrʰᵐᵍ (boh bohem); Cass

26.14
— : Maj
διὰ τὸν φόβον: 614. 1611. 2147. 2401. 2412. it⁵¹ (syrʰᵐᵍ) sahᵐˢ bohᵐˢˢ ethᵐˢ

Theological commentary

In the readings mentioned above, the Western material aids the narrative, and can be read as a commentary on the work of Luke the historian. There are other readings, though, which can be read as a commentary on the work of Luke the theologian. Several studies have been devoted to the search for recognisable theological tendencies in the Western material in Acts.[38] Whatever specific tendencies may inform the Western text, it is hard to deny that Western readings have often an edificatory content. It is this unexceptionable emphasis on edification which provides one of the strongest arguments for maintaining that the Western is later than the alternative text. It would be hard to imagine the author or a later scribe omitting this material if it were originally present.

Among the the most prominent forms of edificatory material is the pious expansion of the titles of Jesus. One of the first reactions to Blass's publication of his hypothesis was the catalogue drawn up by T. E. Page of the pious expansions of the titles of Jesus and other edificatory material in Blass's β-text (the Western text).[39] Page's observation remains a strong argument against the view that the Western text is prior to the non-Western.

Boismard and Lamouille have attempted to argue that the multiplication of edificatory material is a feature only of the degenerate form of the Western text as it is found in, for example, D. They maintain that the original Western text, TO, contained *fewer* Christological titles than the alternative Alexandrian text (TA).[40] According to Boismard and Lamouille, the textual stream flowing from TO has divided into two courses: a relatively pure stream (TO[1]) lies behind the the distinctive Greek text of E and behind the text of it[55], but the stream represented by D syr[hmg] and cop[G67] (TO[2]) is a 'degenerate' form of text.[41] One of the forms of degeneration to which TO[2] has been subject is the introduction of Christological titles.[42]

The major difficulty with Boismard and Lamouille's attempt to rehabilitate the Western text in this way is the elusiveness of the original TO. To take the additional Christological titles as the clearest type of edificatory additional material in the Western tradition: Boismard and Lamouille argue that in several places the original TO did not have certain Christological titles which are now found in the great majority of witnesses.[43] But in each of the cases cited the evidence is drawn from relatively minor Western witnesses, typically from one or two minuscules, Patristic citations, a few Vulgate MSS, or from Dutch, Sahidic, or Ethiopic witnesses. No doubt an original Western reading may be preserved in any of these witnesses, but the more scattered and marginal the witnesses are, the less certainty one can have that they are pointing to a common lost original, and that they are not merely a collection of random and unrelated errors and alterations. The argument is also in danger of becoming circular: copyists are more likely to add Christological titles, some Western witnesses do not have certain Christological titles, therefore these witnesses give the original Western readings, and therefore the Western text originally had fewer Christological titles. But the possibility should be maintained that the Western tradition has degenerated through random omissions, as well as through pious expansions.

There is also the question of whether Boismard and Lamouille's distinction between TO[1] and TO[2] will hold good. The phrase ὁ κύριος ʼIησοῦς Χριστός is a particular favourite of D (16 times,[44] and ὁ κύριος ἡμῶν ʼIησοῦς Χριστός three times[45]). On each occasion D is supported by other Western witnesses. The phrase ὁ κύριος ʼIησοῦς Χριστός has only one certain occurrence in Acts (11.17), as does also ὁ κύριος ἡμῶν ʼIησοῦς Χριστός (15.26). Boismard and Lamouille ascribe each occurrence of ὁ κύριος (ἡμῶν) ʼIησοῦς Χριστός to the degenerate TO[2], either explicitly or by implication. But it is important to note the way that it[55] keeps company with D in these readings. D and it[55] agree on the three occasions on which D reads ὁ κύριος ʼIησοῦς Χριστός in passages where it[55] is extant (5.42, 6.8, 14.10). At 18.5, where D has διαμαρτυρόμενος . . . εἶναι τὸν Χριστὸν (+ κύριον) ʼIησοῦν, it[55] omits the entire phrase.[46] At 18.8 there is another divergence: D reads τοῦ κυρίου ἡμῶν ʼIησοῦ Χριστοῦ, and it[55] *Iesu Christi*.[47] There is sufficient agreement between the two witnesses, though, at 5.42, 6.8 and 14.10 to make it questionable whether it[55] really witnesses to a text which avoided the sort of Christological titles for which D shows a preference.

The tendency of it[55] to prefer explicit Christological titles is manifest elsewhere, also: 3.13 ʼIησοῦν (+ Χριστόν) D and it[55]; 4.10 *in nomine (+ domini) Iesu Christi* it[55] against D; 7.55 ʼIησοῦν (+ τὸν κύριον) D and it[55]; 9.20 *(+ dominum) Iesum*: it[55] (D not extant).

Boismard and Lamouille allow that even it[55] must be regarded as having suffered 'contamination' from TO[2],[48] but when the main witness to TO¹ shows the same tendencies as the supposedly degenerate TO², then it becomes increasingly difficult to be certain that TO¹ actually existed. Certainly, the Western textual tradition developed in a number of directions, and it is quite likely that one of these directions was the multiplication of the titles of Jesus: it is highly unlikely that in every case the most elaborate expression is the most primitive form of the Western text. Nevertheless, it is hard to maintain a clear distinction between two recognisable streams of tradition in the early witnesses, and still harder to maintain that one stream is relatively less corrupt than the other. The evidence suggests that additional Christological titles were, at the least, an early component of the Western tradition, quite as much in Boismard and Lamouille's TO¹ as in TO².

The treatment of the name of Jesus was only one of the ways in which the Western readings demonstrate a concern for the reader's edification. The same concern is exhibited in several readings which stress the act of believing as the point of entry into the Christian community:

2.41

οἱ μὲν οὖν ἀποδεξάμενοι τὸν λόγον αὐτοῦ ἐβαπτίσθησαν: p⁷⁴ ℵ A B C 81. 1175. 1739. pc. vg sah boh eth

οἱ μὲν οὖν ἀσμένως ἀποδεξάμενοι τὸν λόγον αὐτοῦ ἐβαπτίσθησαν: Maj syr[p.h]; Bede Chr

οἱ μὲν οὖν πιστεύσαντες τὸν λόγον αὐτοῦ ἐβαπτίσθησαν: D it⁵

(ἀποδεξάμενοι . . ἐπίστευσαν καὶ ἐβαπτ.: (E) it[(50).54.61.62] syr[hmg] cop[G67]; Aug Ps-EusV)

4.31

καὶ ἐλάλουν τὸν λόγον τοῦ θεοῦ μετὰ παρρησίας: Maj.

καὶ ἐλάλουν τὸν λόγον τοῦ θεοῦ μετὰ παρρησίας παντὶ τῷ θέλοντι πιστεύειν: D E it[5.50.61.62] vg[MM.1213.1259.1266.1277.1282] ndl[ms]

prov¹ cop[G67]; Bede Iren (Aug) Ephr

8.37

See below, pp. 69–77.

11.17
ἐγὼ (δὲ) τίς ἤμην δυνατός κωλῦσαι τὸν θεόν: Maj (?Ps-)Did
ἐγὼ τίς ἤμην δυνατός κωλῦσαι τὸν θεόν τοῦ μὴ δοῦναι αὐτοῖς πνεῦμα ἅγιον: 467 it⁵⁴·⁶² Aug (BarS).
ἐγὼ τίς ἤμην δυνατός κωλῦσαι τὸν θεόν τοῦ μὴ δοῦναι αὐτοῖς πνεῦμα ἅγιον πιστεύσασιν ἐπ᾿ αὐτῷ:D it⁵
(ἐγὼ ... πιστεύσασιν ἐπὶ τὸν κύριον Ἰησοῦν Χριστόν: it⁽⁶¹⁾·⁶³ vg⁽⁴⁹³⁾·¹²⁶⁶ bohem ndl² gerᵗᵉᵖˡ prov syrʰ**).

(The Latin witnesses and the versions dependent on the Latin in this reading vary between *in nomine Iesu Christi* and *in dominum Iesum Christum*. This variation is evidently due to an error in the Latin (*in nom ... /in dom ...*)

18.8 See below, pp. 154–6.

Other edificatory material is found throughout the Western text of Acts. The following are a few examples:

4.32
— : Maj
καὶ οὐκ ἦν διάκρισις ἐν αὐτοῖς οὐδεμία: D it⁵; Cyp
Zeno (καὶ οὐκ ἦν χωρισμὸς ἐν αὐτοῖς τις: E it⁵⁰·⁶² copᴳ⁶⁷; Ambr Bede)

5.15
— : Maj
ἀπηλλάσσοντο γὰρ ἀπὸ πάσης ἀσθενείας ὡς εἶχεν ἕκαστος αὐτῶν: D
(καί for γάρ: it⁵·⁵⁴ copᴳ⁶⁷); (?Ambr) Chrom
καὶ ῥυσθῶσιν ἀπὸ τῆς ἀσθενείας αὐτῶν.
it⁽⁵⁰⁾·⁵⁸·⁶¹·⁶²·⁶³·²⁶² vgᵃᵐ·ᵗᵒˡ·ᴹᴹ·²³¹ᵃ·⁽⁴⁹³⁾·¹²⁶⁶·¹⁷⁰⁰·ᵍᵏ⁶²⁹
ndl prov ethᵐˢˢ; Lucif

9.22
Χριστός] + ἐν ᾧ ὁ Θεὸς εὐδόκησεν: it⁵¹·⁵⁴·⁵⁵·⁶⁷ copᴳ⁶⁷ (D def)

9.40
ἀνάστηθι] + ἐν τῷ ὀνόματι τοῦ κυρίου ἡμῶν Ἰησοῦ

Χριστοῦ: it$^{51.54.57.(61.).63.67.}$ vg$^{(493)}$ syr^{h**} cop^{G67} sah; Ambr Ps-Aug^{sol}

Ps-Aug^{Spec} (om. τοῦ κυρίου ἡμῶν: sah^{ms} geo eth^{ms}; Cyp Cass) (D def).

The Western text's treatment of Luke's work

The Western text of Acts can, therefore, be read as a commentary on both the theological and the narrative content of the book. It is perhaps better to regard the Western additional material as commentary than as interpolation because of a marked feature of the Western readings in Acts: that although they are widespread and frequent, they have a peculiarly restricted nature. As Ropes expressed the point:

> If a reviser had had the Old Uncial text of Acts at his disposal, and had wished to rewrite it so as to make it fuller, smoother, and more emphatic, and as interesting and pictorial as he could, and if he had had no materials whatever except the text before him and the inferences he could draw from it, together with the usual religious commonplaces, it must be admitted that moderate ingenuity and much taking of pains would have enabled him to produce the 'Western' text.[49]

All Western readings in Acts are related to the non-Western text. They clarify and smooth the other text, they recast certain scenes, they add details, they explain, and sometimes they correct. But they do not add wholly new material.

Passages which one might expect to have become growth points in the text have not done so. If the distinctive stratum of the Western text of Acts was produced in the early second century, several features of the text are hard to explain.

The treatment of the end of the book is one such feature. The endings of several New Testament works have attracted the attentions of improvers. The ending of Romans presents a group of problems for the textual critic. The final chapter of John appears to be a later addition to the Gospel. The ending of Mark at 16.8 prompted at least two efforts at improvement. It is understandable that the ending of a work should attract the addition of material, especially if, as in the case of Mark, matters are not brought to a resolution at the close. It is notable, then, that the ending of Acts has not been filled out by the Western text, if it is the work of a second-century reviser. The narrative is left where the author left it, with Paul in prison, the outcome of his trial still unknown. This is all the more surprising when it is considered that Paul's martyrdom was a major focus of second-century interest in him.[50] The Western text betrays no knowledge of Paul's martyrdom, or of concern with it, beyond Luke's own presentation.

Attempts to characterise the *Tendenz* of the Western text have claimed to have discovered theological concerns in the text which must be ascribed to a later period than that of Luke. However, the procedure usually followed in such studies has been to begin with minute study of the Western text, to determine its characteristic emphases, and then to assume that these emphases – anti-Judaic, anti-feminine, and so on – must have been the concerns of the early second century. It is equally necessary, though, to begin with the known concerns of the second century, and to ask whether the Western text of Acts in fact reflects them.[51]

One might have expected the portrayal of the apostles in the Western text to show evidence of second-century attitudes, if the text were essentially a second-century product. The hagiography of the Western text is, though, very muted.

Some commentators have detected an elevation of Peter in some readings.[52] But the degree to which this has taken place is very modest. The difference between Mark 8.29f. and Matthew 16.16–20 is far greater than that between any of the 'Petrine' Western readings in Acts and their non-Western counterparts.

There are Western readings which emphasise the wisdom, authority, and power of the apostolic figures in Acts, among which are the following:

5.15
See above, p. 51.

6.10f.
καὶ οὐκ ἴσχυον ἀντιστῆναι τῇ σοφίᾳ καὶ τῷ πνεύματι ᾧ ἐλάλει: Maj
    ... οὐκ ἴσχυον ἀντιστῆναι τῇ σοφίᾳ τῇ οὔσῃ ἐν αὐτῷ καὶ τῷ πνεύματι τῷ ἁγίῳ ᾧ ἐλάλει, διὰ τὸ ἐλέγχεσθαι αὐτοὺς ἐπ᾽ αὐτοῦ μετὰ πάσης παρρησίας. μὴ δυνάμενοι οὖ[ν] ἀντοφθαλμεῖν τῇ ἀληθείᾳ ... : D it[5.55] (E it[50.56.61] vg[am.1266.] syr[hmg] cop[G67] bohem ndl ger[tepl] ; Bede Did Jul)

9.22
ἐνεδυναμοῦτο] + (ἐν) τῷ λόγῳ: C (E) 467 it⁵⁰·⁵⁴·⁵⁵·⁶⁷
cop^G67 (D def)

But essentially the Western text does nothing more than continue Luke's own portrait of the figures in Acts. In contrast to the
honorific titles of Jesus, there is no increase in honorific titles for
the apostles, in spite of the second-century tendency to speak of
them with reverence.[53]

Undoubtedly there was interest in the apostles in the second
century, and the stories will already have been circulating which
were to be incorporated into the literature of the apocryphal *Acts*.
However, we should note Streeter's observation that the Western
additional material in Acts scarcely looks like units of independently circulating tradition.[54] It should also be remembered that the
interest of early second-century writers in the apostolic age was a
quite practical one. They were principally concerned with the
problems and events of their own day, and with the apostolic age
only as it gave guidance and support for the positions held in their
own day. What was important in the second century was not so
much tradition *about* the apostles, as tradition *of* the apostles.

Traditional stories and reminiscences of the apostles clearly did
survive well into the second century. This interest, though, appears
to have been of two types. On the one hand there was the
hagiographical concern of the Christian communities. This concern
provided the seed bed for the growth of the apostle-legends which
underlie such collections as the *Acts of Paul*. In contrast to this
'popular' interest in the apostles was a more 'theological' appeal to
the apostles as legitimators of tradition and practice. So Clement
and Ignatius appeal to apostolic precedent for their church order.[55]
Later in the century, apostolic authority was invoked in the
Quartodeciman controversy.[56] That the two types of interest lay
close together is shown by Irenaeus' story of John's encounter with
Cerinthus at the baths.[57] The point of the story was to show that the
apostle was engaged in the same struggle against Gnosticism as
Irenaeus himself. In the second century the apostles were put to
work in the service of the contemporary church.

There is little evidence in the Western text of Acts of concern
with the known problems of the second-century church, particularly Gnosticism in its various forms. At one time Rendel Harris
thought to have found an anti-Montanist emphasis in the Western

text, but this suggestion has found little support.[58] It has been suggested that the Western text of Acts should be regarded as a sort of forerunner of the apocryphal *Acts*, prefiguring the apocryphal books' concern to make the stories of the apostolic age more readable and acceptable to a later era.[59] But there is a clear divide between the treatment of the apostles in the the Western text of Acts and in the apocryphal *Acts*. In the latter, the *Acts of Paul* in particular, the apostles are brought firmly into the writers' own age: Paul refutes Gnostic heresy,[60] encourages martyrdom,[61] and teaches clearly the custom of delaying baptism.[62]

The Western text does not exhibit the second-century tendency to use the apostles to legitimate contemporary practice. One prominent possible exception to this might be the eunuch's profession of faith at 8.37. Here, so it has been argued, is clear evidence that the Western text has used Acts to legitimate contemporary baptismal practice. The passage 8.37–9 will be discussed more fully below (pp. 65–77), but one observation may be made about 8.37 at this point: if the dialogue is the work of a second-century interpolator, why has he placed it precisely here in the narrative? Why has he made the relatively obscure Philip responsible for the paradigmatic formula, rather than Peter or Paul, who also baptised candidates precipitately (Peter 2.41, Paul 16.15,33). The baptism of John's disciples by Paul in 19.5 would have given an interpolator an excellent opportunity to show that this was the formula used by Paul himself when baptising 'in the name of the Lord Jesus'. Peter and Paul were for second-century Christians the twin pillars of apostolic authority, while Philip, by contrast, was better known to the post-apostolic generations as the father of his daughters (Papias in Eusebius, *HE* 3.39.9). The attribution of the formula to Philip by a second-century interpolator would represent a missed opportunity. The Western text's treatment of the Apostolic Decree of 15.20,29 and 21.25 has also been regarded as conforming Luke's work to second-century tendencies in the church. The Decree will be discussed below (pp. 87–105), and, to anticipate the conclusion of that discussion, it may be argued that the Western form of the Decree can be understood against the background of Luke's own day. For all its deviations from the alternative text, the Western text leaves the apostles as Luke left them, facing the problems of the first, rather than the second, century.

The hagiography of the Western text of Acts is also muted, when compared with the developments in popular piety of the second century. The Western text has virtually nothing new to add to the narrative. It is wholly subordinate to the existing text in a way in which the *pericope de adultera* (John 7.53–8.11) or the Marcan endings, for example, are not. If it is secondary to the alternative text, and the edificatory material in it suggests that it is, then its aim is to elucidate the existing text. It is in this respect quite different from the apocryphal *Acts*, whose purpose was to concentrate attention on the figures of the apostles.

Further, if the Western text of Acts is a second-century production, then it was made in a period when Acts, as far as may be seen, was largely neglected. The first certain evidence for the use of Acts comes in Irenaeus. Before him the evidence amounts to little more than a scatter of possible allusions.[63] The book of Acts fell in the gap between Gospel and Apostle, and its importance does not seem to have been recognised until Irenaeus pointed out how significantly it filled that gap for the purposes of anti-Gnostic polemic.[64] When Irenaeus rescued Acts from oblivion, it was precisely because it served the needs of his own day. Yet if the Western text of Acts were produced in the early second century, then it would have been produced in a period when the book was neglected, and without making use of the text to confront the issues of the day.

The Western text of Acts shows a meticulous interest in the details of Luke's narrative: it is precisely this interest which distinguishes the Western text of Acts from any other pre-Irenaean evidence we have. But the Western text of Acts also shows a lack of imaginative freedom which distinguishes it from the later apocryphal *Acts*. In view of these considerations, the assumption of a second-century origin for the Western text of Acts needs a firmer base than it has customarily received, if it is to succeed in providing an account of the text's origins.

3

LUCANISM AND THE WESTERN TEXT
OF ACTS

Introduction

A major element in the recent attempts to rehabilitate the Western
text of Acts has been the detection of 'Lucanisms' in the text. In the
face of studies which have argued that there is a gap between the
outlook and language of Luke and those of the Western text of
Acts, several recent writers have maintained that there is no
appreciable difference between them, and that the case for Lucan
authorship of the Western text is therefore a strong one.[1]

Martini's work (see p. 27 above) demonstrates that it is possible
to recognise a strongly Lucan character in the Western text, and yet
to conclude that the Western readings are later developments.[2]
This should make it clear from the outset that the detection of
Lucanisms in the Western text cannot necessarily by itself demonstrate that the text is Lucan in origin. However, it is important to
describe the literary characteristics of the text as clearly as possible,
not only for the possible positive indications of Lucan authorship,
but also because un-Lucan characteristics, if found, would provide
strong evidence that Luke was not responsible for the Western text
of Acts.

Lucanisms are of two types: linguistic and theological. Studies of
the language of Luke have been made by several scholars.[3] Since
the advent of redaction criticism, studies of the theological
emphases of Luke, in the Acts as well as in the Gospel, have also
become numerous.[4] We are well served, therefore, by comparative
material against which to assess the faithfulness of the Western
readings to the expression and outlook of Luke.

This chapter will first examine the Lucanism of the Western text
in Acts in general, and will then investigate three conspicuous
Western readings. The readings to be examined have frequently
been regarded as departing from Luke's outlook, and will in

consequence be test-cases for the Lucanism of the Western text in Acts.

Language

The linguistic characteristics of the Western text of Acts have played a particularly prominent part in discussions of the Lucanism of the Western text of Acts. In part, this is because linguistic phenomena are not dependent on subjective decisions, in the way in which arguments from an author's theological emphases are bound to be. They are also quantifiable. Linguistic data can be analysed and presented in statistical tables, a process which gives the evidence an appearance of objectivity. Statistics, of course, must always be treated with caution, but it is understandable that critics should choose methods which appear to offer the promise of certain results.

Linguistic evidence has been used since the very origins of the textual criticism of Acts. Leclerc argued in 1684 that certain passages in D are likely to be stylistic improvements, and Simon in 1689 that the Greek of D is too accomplished, in Acts as elsewhere, to have been the work of the apostles.[5]

Almost all critics who have discussed the textual problems of Acts from the time of Blass onwards have referred at some point to the linguistic evidence provided by the Western readings: either, with Blass, Zahn, and more recently, Delebecque, in order to demonstrate the faithfulness of the Western text to the usage of Luke; or with Ropes, Knox, and others to demonstrate its departure from Luke's usage; or, with Kilpatrick, to employ Lucan usage as the test of the authenticity of readings.

None of these critics, however, attempted the analysis of the evidence in a systematic fashion. They used material drawn from various parts of the text, or referred to linguistic points as they occurred in the course of a commentary, but none attempted the tabulation and analysis of all the linguistic data in order to achieve a comprehensive picture of the evidence. Boismard and Lamouille's work represents a new departure in this area largely because of the very comprehensiveness of its approach. It offers, not merely a few comments on the Lucanism of particular variants, but a detailed analysis of the linguistic character of the Western and non-Western texts in Acts as a whole.

The conclusion of Boismard and Lamouille that the Western text in its original form (TO) is authentically Lucan[6] is based, not principally on the relatively few texts considered in Volume I of the work, but mainly on the discussion of the entire text in the Critical Apparatus, and on the tables of stylistic characteristics, in Volume II.

Fundamental to Boismard and Lamouille's findings are two methods: a method of determining the original state of the Western text, and a method of analysing the linguistic character of the original Western text. In order to arrive at the most likely original form of the Western text, Boismard and Lamouille investigate individual variants as they occur, although their discussion of variants is informed by the theory of textual development which they explain in Volume I.[7] In order to specify what constructions and items of vocabulary are distinctively Lucan, Boismard and Lamouille have formulated canons for placing material into categories, reflecting the various degrees to which the material conforms to Luke's usage elsewhere. The Lucan character of material in categories A, B, and C is established by reference to the entire New Testament. In category A is material for which 100 per cent of occurrences in the New Testament are in Luke–Acts, in category B material for which 99.99–80 per cent of the occurrences are in Luke–Acts, and in category C the material for which 79.99–60 per cent of the occurrences are in Luke–Acts. Categories D and E are established by reference to the Gospels and Acts. In D is the material for which 100 per cent of the occurrences in the Gospels and Acts are in Luke–Acts, and in E material for which 99.99–75 per cent of the occurrences are in Luke–Acts. Boismard and Lamouille also distinguish between material which is paralleled only in Acts in Luke's work (designated by a), and material which is found in the Gospel and Acts (designated by b).[8]

Boismard and Lamouille classify material in both 'Alexandrian' and Western texts which falls into these categories, first in alphabetical order, then by frequency of occurrence, and finally arranged verse by verse.[9] This massive presentation of evidence lends considerable weight to the authors' contention that *both* forms of the text have substantial authentically Lucan characteristics of style, and therefore deserve to be considered as Lucan in origin.[10] The authors consider the possibility that TO has been constructed in conscious imitation of Luke, but reject it, because the relationship between TO and the style of Luke is too close. An imitator would betray his hand, particularly in long passages such as 11.2.[11]

All that is lacking from the presentation is some form of résumé and analysis of the lists, which would enable the reader to appreciate at a glance the significance of the material. Table 1 attempts to provide such a résumé.

The figures suggest that in general the authors' description of the Western text as 'un texte authentiquement lucanien'[12] is borne out by the linguistic evidence. It is particularly noticeable that the more decidedly Lucan categories A and B register an increase in the number of Lucan characteristics found in TO when compared with TA, while the less Lucan category C registers a decrease. The increase is more marked if the particle τε is taken out of consideration, as is probably justified in view of the difficulties which this word provides for the textual critic.[13] Similarly, the less Lucan category E shows a greater net omission of Lucanisms than the relatively more Lucan category D. The conclusion appears to be that TO shows a marked preference for the peculiarities of Luke's linguistic idiom.

There are some points to consider, however, which tell against drawing any oversimplified conclusions even from a study as thorough as that of Boismard and Lamouille. In the first place, the selection of the New Testament as a standard against which to judge what is distinctively Lucan is rather arbitrary. The reasons for taking the New Testament as a standard are clear: there is the very practical point that the basis for comparison is set out most helpfully in concordances, and there is the more general point that the New Testament is a collection of books roughly contemporary with one another, and with a great deal of common subject-matter. But with a basis of comparison as narrow as the New Testament books, relatively small peculiarities of vocabulary can assume an unwarranted significance. So Luke, for instance, uses a certain amount of vocabulary to do with sea travel, uniquely among New Testament writers. This vocabulary might appear particularly Lucan, if the rest of the New Testament were to provide the basis of comparison. In fact, though, this vocabulary is suggested by the subject-matter, and it would be misleading to think that it is in any significant sense a peculiarity of Luke's style. Delebecque has in large part avoided this difficulty by putting Luke's style against the background of Hellenistic usage.[14] This is a more realistic approach, even though it does not lead to the sort of statistical results found in Boismard and Lamouille's work. None of this means that comparison between Luke's usage and the usage of the

Table 1. *Boismard and Lamouille's stylistic characteristics*

	A	Aa	Ab		B	Ba	Bb
1.	A	Aa	Ab		B	Ba	Bb
2.	1152	655	497		946	186	760
3.	1109	623	486		941	164	777
4.	+43	+32	+11		+5	+22	−17
5.	+3.88	+5.14	+2.26		+0.53	+13.41	−2.19
6.	191	114	77		132	30	102
7.	148	82	66		127	8	119

	C	Ca	Cb
1.	C	Ca	Cb
2.	1210	278	932
3.	1258	269	989
4.	−48	+9	−57
5.	−3.82	+3.35	−5.76
6.	119	44	75
7.	167	35	132

	D	Da	Db		E	Ea	Eb
1.	D	Da	Db		E	Ea	Eb
2.	264	111	153		785	80	705
3.	276	119	157		953	69	884
4.	−12	−8	−4		−168	+11	−179
5.	−4.35	−6.72	−2.55		−17.63	+15.94	−20.25
6.	39	21	18		58	17	41
7.	51	29	22		226	6	220

N.B. The figures for Bb and Eb are significantly affected by the lower frequency of τε in TO. If τε is taken out of consideration, the figures are:

	B	Bb	E	Eb
1.	B	Bb	E	Eb
2.	946	760	754	674
3.	877	713	809	740
4.	+69	+47	−55	−66
5.	+7.87	+6.59	−6.80	−8.92
6.	132	102	58	41
7.	63	55	113	107

Note: The rows in this table are numbered as follows:

1. The designations of the categories of stylistic characteristics (Boismard and Lamouille, *Texte occidental*, II, pp. 194f.). Column A represents the aggregate of Aa and Ab, B the aggregate of Ba and Bb, and so on.
2. The number of stylistic characteristics occurring in TO.
3. The number of stylistic characteristics occurring in TA.
4. The net increase of stylistic characteristics in TO.
5. The increase of stylistic characteristics in TO as a percentage of the stylistic characteristics in TA.
6. The number of stylistic characteristics in TO, but not in TA.
7. The number of stylistic characteristics in TA, but not in TO.

rest of the New Testament is entirely worthless, but it suggests that the limitations of such comparisons should always be borne in mind.

In the second place, a just picture of the Lucanism of the Western text of Acts should look, not merely at the positive aspect of specifically Lucan words and idioms used in the Western readings, but also at the possibility of non-Lucan traits in the text. Boismard and Lamouille enable the reader to do this to a certain extent, by including reference to places at which TO does not have Lucan stylistic characteristics which appear in TA. From Table 1 it may be seen that there are 719 instances in which Lucan stylistic characteristics present in TA are not present in TO (542 if the occurrences of τε are not included). These instances exceed the instances in which TO has stylistic characteristics not present in TA (539). In addition, Boismard and Lamouille do not consider whether TO uses words or idioms which Luke appears to avoid. There are examples of such usage in TO. At 10.30 TO has the word ἄρτι, which not only does not appear elsewhere in Luke–Acts, but which Luke apparently avoids in passages where Matthew's parallels have it (Matt. 11.12 – Lk. 16.16; Matt. 23.39 – Lk. 13.35; Matt. 26.29 – Lk. 22.25). In 1.2, TO uses the word εὐαγγέλιον as a description of the Christian message (κηρύσσειν τὸ εὐαγγέλιον). Luke uses the word only twice elsewhere, and in both instances it is qualified (ὁ λόγος τοῦ εὐαγγελίου, 15.7; τὸ εὐαγγέλιον τῆς χάριτος τοῦ Θεοῦ, 20.24). TO also shows a preference for θέλω which exceeds the normal frequency of this verb in Luke–Acts (x28 in Luke, x14 in Acts, x11 in additional material of TO). In order to establish the Lucan nature of Boismard and Lamouille's TO, it would be necessary to consider also any un-Lucan stylistic characteristics present in it. They may not be sufficient to alter the general picture, but they are part of the evidence, and deserve to be considered.

In a detailed review of the work of Boismard and Lamouille, F. Neirynck and F. van Segbroeck have argued that Boismard and Lamouille's establishment of Lucan stylistic characteristics needs refinement. In Acts we may be reasonably certain that we have to do with Luke's own style. But in the Gospel of Luke, we must take into account the effect of Luke's use of sources. When Luke has simply borrowed his language from Mark or from another source, then it is misleading to take this language as characteristic of Luke himself. Neirynck and van Segbroeck point out that Boismard and

Lamouille's study would increase in value if the influence of source material were taken into consideration in the establishment of Lucan stylistic canons.[15] They also point out that Old Testament citations are another possible source from which material alien to Luke may be incorporated into the work. Boismard and Lamouille recognise this, but appear to be inconsistent in their treatment of the problem.[16] Neirynck and van Segbroeck make clear that it is important to distinguish additions in TO from substitutions. A word or phrase which appears in Boismard and Lamouille's Index of Stylistic Characteristics, and which thus appears to have a Lucan character, may in fact be replacing a more strongly characteristic element in the alternative text. Neirynck and van Segbroeck give several examples of this.[17]

A final point which suggests caution in the employment of stylistic arguments is the problem of identifying the Western text of Acts. It has become clear that the Western text does not simply equal the text of D.[18] Boismard and Lamouille have consciously reconstructed what they consider to be the earliest and most authentic recoverable version of the Western text (TO), and have attempted to distinguish it from the secondary stream of Western development (TO^2). Some such reconstruction of the text is inevitable, given the state of the witnesses. Boismard and Lamouille's TO, like Blass's β and Clark's Z before them, is a constructed text which depends at numerous points on the judgement and opinions of the editors. Because of this it is bound to be disputed by the judgement and opinions of others. TO is thus a debatable base from which to argue for the Lucanism of the Western text, particularly so when Boismard and Lamouille on occasion choose between variants within the Western tradition by deciding for the variant which is judged the more Lucan.[19]

The search for linguistic Lucanism has been helped forward by the work of Boismard and Lamouille, and this work points to some definite results. The Western text of Acts does not depart strikingly from the linguistic traits of Luke, and includes much that, judged against the usage of the rest of the New Testament, looks characteristic of the author. But this does not by itself establish Lucan responsibility for the Western text of Acts. The most that can be said with certainty is that the linguistic evidence does not rule out the possibility that Lucan material exists in the Western text of Acts. On the linguistic evidence alone, it would be rash to draw any much firmer conclusions.

Theology

Early studies

Parallel with the investigation of the language of the variants of Acts has gone an investigation of the theological outlook of the text; a form of redaction criticism of the Western text. Here criticism has been less inclined to discover evidence of Lucanism in the text. Indeed, the outlook implied by the Western text has often been thought to betray a complete break with that of Luke.

W. L. Knox believed that one of the main characteristics of D was to bring the work of Luke into agreement with the presuppositions and concerns of a later period, and that the reviser who produced the text of D thereby obscured and obliterated many of Luke's specific points.[20] P.-H. Menoud went further than these general observations in his study published in 1951.[21] Menoud detected in the Western readings an overall tendency to emphasise the newness of the Christian faith by criticising Judaism and exalting the church and its leaders. Like Knox, Menoud was suggesting that the setting of the Western text is to be found in an age later than that of Luke.

Epp and after

The most thorough-going example of such tendency criticism of the Western variants in Acts is E. J. Epp's *The Theological Tendency of Codex Bezae*.[22] Epp proposed that very many of the variants in the Western tradition in Acts witness to a particular tendency. This tendency may be described, briefly, as anti-Judaic: 'Codex Bezae in Acts, where it represents (as is so often the case) the distinctive 'Western' text, shows a decidedly heightened anti-Judaic attitude and sentiment.'[23] Epp regarded this tendency in the same light as Menoud, that is, that it served to highlight the authority and importance of the new faith.[24] Epp consciously avoided the question of the likely origin of the Western text of Acts[25], but he noted that:

> The D-text is both considerably more consistent in delineating its special viewpoint and somewhat more abundant in its evidence than might reasonably be expected of an aberrant textual tradition.[26]

This comment implies that in Epp's view the Western text of Acts is the product of a reviser other than the author of Acts, and that this reviser has betrayed his existence by the tendentious nature of his alterations to the text.

The important question, however, is not merely whether any point of view is discernible within the Western readings, but to what extent this point of view diverges from that of Luke. Barrett has argued that Epp has not established sufficiently strongly that there is any appreciable gulf between the interests and outlook of the Western text in Acts, and those of Luke himself.[27] Whatever tendencies exist in the Western readings continue those already present in the alternative text. Black has examined the treatment of the Holy Spirit in the Western text of Acts, and has concluded that the Western tradition is in fact more Lucan than the Alexandrian.[28] Martini, too, although maintaining that the Western text is a later production, did not find, in general, any real tension between the two text forms of Acts.[29]

In the face of this disagreement over the theological Lucanism of the Western text of Acts, it might be instructive to take as test cases three passages in which a gap between the outlook of Luke and that of the Western text has been detected. These three passages (8.37–9, 11.2, and the 'Apostolic Decree' of 15.20,29, 21.25) each contain significant variants between Western and non-Western texts. Examination of the passages should help clarify the extent to which each text-form is faithful to the thought and expression of Luke, and may provide some indication of the characteristics of the text-forms.

Acts 8.36–9

Acts 8.36–9 contains two major textual problems. The first is the inclusion in some Western witnesses of the material in 8.37. The second is the presence of a longer reading at Acts 8.39 in some witnesses, Western witnesses among them. It should not be assumed, however, that both readings have the same origin, and it is therefore necessary to examine each in turn before considering the longer and shorter texts of Acts 8.36–9 as a whole.

Acts 8.39

πνεῦμα κυρίου ἥρπασεν τὸν Φίλιππον: Maj; Did Jer (1/2)
πνεῦμα ἅγιον ἐπέπεσεν ἐπὶ τὸν εὐνοῦχον, ἄγγελος δὲ κυρίου
ἥρπασεν τὸν Φίλιππον: A 36. (88). 323. 453. 467. 876. 913. 945.
1739. 1765. 1891. 2298. pc.
it[54.58.61.67.] vg[1213.1260] syr[h**] cop[G67] geo
arm; (?Ps-)Aug[cath] (?BarS) Cass Ephr Fulg Jer (1/2) (D def)

The longer reading at Acts 8.39 is generally taken to be an
addition to the text. Metzger's *Textual Commentary* gives three
reasons for this opinion. In the first place: 'scholars have been
impressed by the weight of attestation supporting the shorter text'.
In the second place, it seems probable that the words were added
'in order to make explicit that the baptism of the Ethiopian was
followed by the gift of the Holy Spirit'. Thirdly, it is suggested that
the extra material was added 'to conform the account of Philip's
departure to that of his commission (by an angel of the Lord, ver.
26)'.[30]

The case against the longer text appears to be a strong one, but
each of the points made above is open to criticism. In addition, the
Commentary's case is weakened by a failure to examine the shorter
text and its own claim to authenticity. When that text is examined,
it appears that its own claim is by no means secure.

The *Commentary*'s first point, the weight of attestation in favour
of the shorter text, cannot be a decisive argument. The longer text
has considerable support, Greek and versional, manuscript and
Patristic: enough, at least, to suggest that it should be considered
on its merits. The real question to ask is whether it or the shorter
text has a greater claim to be regarded as the author's work.

This question is not answered by the *Commentary*'s remaining
points. The second point could indeed be used as an argument in
favour of the reading's authenticity, for if the shorter text were
original, this would be the only place in Acts at which baptism is not
associated with the reception of the Spirit. Black was willing to
argue that this was a point in favour of the longer text.[31] Similarly
with the third point: the longer text clearly does conform the
account of Philip's departure with that of his arrival, but this
aptness of the reading to its context could betray the mind of the
author quite as easily as that of a copyist, as has been argued by
Black and by Boismard and Lamouille.[32]

The *Commentary*'s remarks might provide corroborative evidence that the longer reading is an addition to the text, but they do not demonstrate this when taken by themselves. The intrinsic probability of each reading must be examined if a judgement is to be formed about the likely original reading of the passage.

It has not often been noted that the shorter reading here contains an uncharacteristic phrase. Πνεῦμα κυρίου is not typical of Luke's style. Apart from this passage, it is used twice in Luke–Acts: once in the direct quotation of Is. 6.1 at Lk. 4.18, and once at Acts 5.9 in what is probably an adaptation of Exodus 17.2. It might be argued that in Acts 8.39, as at Lk. 4.18, Old Testament influence has prompted the author to use an untypical expression. We might suspect the influence of 2 Kgs. 2.16–18 in particular, and perhaps also 1 Kgs. 18.12, Ezek. 3.12, 8.3, 11.1, and 11.24.[33] Once again, however, what applies to the author might well apply to a copyist. A copyist whose eye jumped from πνεῦμα to κυρίου would be able to continue reading without difficulty.[34] Indeed, the existence of Old Testament parallels would help to conceal the mistake, once made. On the basis of this evidence, then, we could say that πνεῦμα κυρίου is unusual for Luke, although not wholly inexplicable here, but that on the other hand a copyist may have produced this reading by the accidental omission of the material in the longer reading. It is to be noted, though, that in view of the author's preferred usage, there is a presumption against πνεῦμα κυρίου.

A further question arises: is the author more likely to have written πνεῦμα κυρίου or ἄγγελος κυρίου? We might attempt to answer this question by comparing the ways in which Luke portrays the operation of πνεῦμα κυρίου and ἄγγελος κυρίου.

The Spirit in Luke always acts through human agents, and never as a physical agent in his own right. This is exemplified by the contrast between Mk. 1.12 and Lk. 4.1:

> Mk. 1.12 καὶ εὐθὺς τὸ πνεῦμα αὐτὸν ἐκβάλλει εἰς τὴν ἔρημον.
> Lk. 4.1 Ἰησοῦς δὲ ... ἤγετο ἐν τῷ πνεύματι ἐν τῇ ἐρήμῳ.

Luke's version avoids any possible interpretation by which the Spirit might be thought physically to force Jesus into the wilderness. There is a similar contrast in the following parallels:

> Matt. 1.18 εὑρέθη ἐν γαστρὶ ἔχουσα ἐκ πνεύματος ἁγίου.
> Matt. 1.20 τὸ γὰρ ἐν αὐτῇ γεννηθὲν ἐκ πνεύματός ἐστιν ἁγίου.

Lk. 1.35 πνεῦμα ἅγιον ἐπελεύσεται ἐπὶ σὲ καὶ δύναμις ὑψίστου ἐπισκιάσει σοι· διὸ καὶ τὸ γεννώμενον ἅγιον κληθήσεται υἱὸς Θεοῦ.

By using one of his more normal expressions for the coming of the Spirit, Luke avoids the more explicit language of Matthew about the role of the Spirit in the conception of the child. Therefore, while stylistically πνεῦμα κυρίου is unusual for Luke, theologically it is quite without parallel for him to portray the Spirit as a physical agent, in the way in which the shorter text of Acts 8.39 does. Indeed, he appears to avoid doing so.

Luke uses ἄγγελος κυρίου quite differently. Whereas πνεῦμα κυρίου appears only twice in Luke–Acts, ἄγγελος κυρίου is used on six occasions (Lk. 1.11, 2.9, Acts 5.19, 8.26, 12.7, 12.23). In contrast to the Spirit, 'an angel of the Lord' does appear in Acts as an agent in the accomplishment of the miraculous. At 5.19 'an angel of the Lord' opens the prison doors and frees the apostles. At 12.7 'an angel of the Lord' wakes Peter and brings him out of prison. At 12.23 'an angel of the Lord' strikes Herod dead. It would be more in keeping with Luke's outlook for him to have written of 'an angel of the Lord' snatching Philip away than to have made the Spirit do so.

If it is argued that the longer text at Acts 8.39 is an interpolation, it must also be argued that the interpolator has chosen a point at which the author has used an untypical expression, πνεῦμα κυρίου, and at which he has written of the Spirit in an uncharacteristic way. By inserting the extra material, the interpolator would have created a reading thoroughly in keeping with the author's language and assumptions about the Spirit and about the 'angel of the Lord'. His interpolation would also have destroyed the parallel with 2 Kgs. 2.

These phenomena are readily explained, though, if the longer reading is taken to be original and the shorter as secondary. Such an understanding of the passage would also explain the neatness of the relation between the two texts. Interpolations often, though not invariably, require some revision of the surrounding text to take account of the new material. An omission by parablepsis, however, can leave little trace if grammatical sense is maintained. For these reasons, it is more likely that the longer reading at Acts 8.39 represents what the author wrote than that the shorter text is original. The parallel with 2 Kgs. 2 and other Old Testament passages served probably to create, and certainly to perpetuate, the error of omitting it from the text.[35]

Acts 8.37

The text

Εἶπεν δὲ αὐτῷ [+ ὁ Φίλιππος: E] εἰ [ἐὰν: E 629] πιστεύεις ἐξ
ὅλης τῆς καρδίας σου [om. σου· 323 pc.] ἔξεστιν [σωθησει: E.
om.: 629 it⁵¹].
᾿Αποκριθεὶς δὲ εἶπεν πιστεύω τὸν υἱὸν τοῦ Θεοῦ εἶναι τὸν
᾿Ιησοῦν Χριστόν [πιστ. εἰς τὸν Χν τὸν υἱὸν τοῦ Θεοῦ: E].
om. vs.: Maj.
add vs.: E 36. 242. 257. 323. 453. 467. 522. 629. 876. 913. 945. 1522.
1739. 1765. 1891. 2298. pc.
it⁶·⁵⁰·⁵¹·⁵⁴·⁵⁶·⁵⁷·⁵⁸·⁵⁹·⁶¹·⁶²·⁶³·⁶⁷·
vgᵃᵐ·ᴹᴹ·ᵗᵒˡ·ᵛᵃˡⁱᶜ·²³¹ᵃ·²⁴³·⁴⁹³·¹²⁶⁶·¹³⁹⁶·ᵍᵏ⁶²⁹· syrʰ**
copᴳ⁶⁷ arm geo nedl gerᵗᵉᵖˡ prov ethᵐˢ; Ambstr Aug
Ps-Augᴰˢ Bede Chrom Cyp Fulg Iren (?Ps-)Oecum Pac Theoph

The problem

The Western variant at Acts 8.37 is one of the most theologically
significant in the entire work. It has been seen either as authentic,
and therefore 'the earliest baptismal ritual', [36] or, more usually, as
not original, and therefore 'a baptismal formula of a later generation'.[37] In spite of the significance of the reading, it has been the
subject of remarkably little textual examination, probably because
it has appeared to most critics to be an obvious pious expansion of
the text. It has been argued that Acts 8.37 must have been added in
order to demonstrate that Philip did not baptise the Ethiopian
eunuch without a profession of faith.[38] Since no motive for the
omission of the passage is apparent and no other New Testament
writing gives evidence of profession of faith being required before
baptism, the reading is generally assumed to be a second-century
addition to the text.

   In fact, however, there may have been good reason for a
second-century reader to take offence at such a scene as that
described in Acts 8.37. One of the commonest criticisms of the
second-century church was its secrecy, especially the secrecy which
surrounded its rites. To Pliny, the church seemed a sort of secret
society, and one of the main accusations dealt with by the apologists was that of dreadful crimes committed at the closed meetings
of the Christians.[39] In general the apologists revealed very little of

what did happen in the meetings to which, by common consent, the uninitiated were not admitted.[40] The secretiveness of Christians was a major part of Celsus' attack on the church of his day.[41] Origen found it hard to refute. He resorted to saying that the basic facts of Christian belief were known and open to all, but that the Christians had certain esoteric teachings of necessity because persecution had made them cautious and because there were some people who were not able to take the solid food of advanced teaching.[42] In any case, Origen added, there were good precedents among philosophical sects for keeping back esoteric teachings from public view.[43]

Celsus' criticisms and Origen's reply probably give a fair picture of the way Christians appeared in the late second and early third centuries. Christians were quite open about their exoteric teaching, summarised in the Rule of Faith as it is found, for instance, in Irenaeus or Tertullian.[44] But Celsus' charge had an element of truth, that: 'Christians perform their rites and teach their doctrines in secret.'[45] There was an esoteric dimension to second-century Christianity which should not be ignored. Even by the time of the *Didache* the dominical saying 'Give not that which is holy to the dogs' (Matt. 7.6) was being applied to sacramental discipline.[46]

There was in this period no consistent *disciplina arcani*. While all seem to have agreed that baptism and eucharist were reserved for those who showed they were worthy of them,[47] there may have been a difference of opinion about the amount which might be revealed to outsiders concerning the nature of Christian worship. Justin, for example, was able in mid-century to describe the rites of the Christians with considerable candour.[48] The Christians known to Celsus, though, appear to have been less forthcoming. While secrecy was not of the essence of Christianity, as it was of Gnosticism, it remained an undeniable feature of the church as it developed in the course of the second century.

It would have been quite possible, therefore, for some second-century readers to have found Acts 8.37 too candid in its description of the pivotal rite of the church, admission to fellowship. Not even Justin spoke as frankly as this about the examining of baptismal candidates. Some readers, of course, did not object to it, and Irenaeus cites the passage with approval. But not only is it possible to see why the passage might have been removed by a cautious second-century scribe, it is harder to see why such a uniquely revealing glimpse of the testing of a baptismal candidate should have been added during a period when such rites were being surrounded by an increasing veil of secrecy.

Acts 8.37 cannot therefore be dismissed as an obvious example of pious expansion in the text. Given the possible motive for removing it, if genuine, its internal characteristics deserve investigation.

Language

(a) εἰ [ἐὰν: E 629] πιστεύεις ἐξ ὅλης τῆς καρδίας σου

To what sort of Christian environment might the phrase 'to believe with the whole heart' belong?

It may be an unselfconscious use of a Semitic idiom (see Dt. 4.29, 6.5 etc., Matt. 22.37, Mk. 12.30,33, Lk. 10.27). Or it may be a self-conscious imitation of biblical style by a Christian writer, perhaps one of that category of idioms described by Wilcox as 'liturgicalisms'.[49]

Paul's words in Rom. 10.9f. suggest that the pattern 'believing in the heart – confessing Jesus', found in Acts 8.37, had parallels in the earliest years of the Christian church. It may even be that this passage from Romans has affected the reading of E, which in place of ἔξεστιν has σωθήσει.

The opening section of Acts 8.37 is therefore set in a Semitic idiom for which there are parallels within the New Testament. This at least raises the question of whether we have here to do with a piece of primitive material.

(b) ἔξεστιν

It has already been noted that the alternative reading σωθήσει for ἔξεστιν can be accounted for by the influence of Rom. 10.9f. But the copyists who altered ἔξεστιν to σωθήσει were right to observe that ἔξεστιν is an unusual word to find in a Christian context. It is possible that it was originally absent from the text (it is omitted by 629 and it[51]). But given its widespread presence in the witnesses, the reading of 629 and it[51] seems to be due to accidental omission.

Cullmann took ἔξεστιν to be a technical term in early Christian baptism, a sort of *nihil obstat* pronounced over the baptisand.[50] Cullmann did not appeal to any other passages than this one, but he might have mentioned two second-century texts which have a bearing upon it. The first is Ignatius, *Smyrneans* 8.2: οὐκ ἐξόν ἐστιν χωρὶς τοῦ ἐπισκόπου οὔτε βαπτίζειν οὔτε ἀγάπην ποιεῖν. Ignatius' words, though not dealing with the fitness of candidates, at least show that by an early stage in the second century, there was concern to administer baptism according to what is 'proper' (ἐξόν). Somewhat later are the words of Justin, *Apology* 66.1: καὶ ἡ τροφὴ αὕτη καλεῖται παρ᾽ ἡμῖν εὐχαριστία, ἧς οὐδενὶ ἄλλῳ μετασχεῖν ἐξόν ἐστιν ἢ τῷ πιστεύοντι ἀληθῆ εἶναι τὰ δεδιδαγμένα ὑφ᾽ ἡμῶν. From this one could argue that ἔξεστιν is likely to have been used by the church in the early second century with particular reference to the proper and fitting administration of the sacraments. On such a view, Philip's comment εἰ πιστεύεις … ἔξεστιν would be a natural expression of sacramental discipline in the early second century. That, at least, is one interpretation of the evidence, but other possibilities should be considered.

The term ἔξεστιν also had a setting within Judaism. The sense 'what is permitted by the Law' predominates in the Gospel accounts of Jesus' disputes with the representatives of Pharisaic Judaism (Mk. 2.24 par., 3.4 par., etc.). This use of the word did not pass easily into the Christian church. Paul's attitude πάντα μοι ἔξεστιν, ἀλλ᾽ οὐ πάντα συμφέρει (1 Cor. 6.12, 10.23) seems to have predominated in Christian ethical thinking.

In Christian sacramental usage, though, ἔξεστιν may have had a history which in some circles stretched back well beyond the time of Ignatius. In order to illustrate this, we might consider the parallels between Acts 8.36–9 (longer text) and the account of Jesus' baptism in Matthew.

Matthew 3.14–16	Acts 8.36–9
	καί φησιν ὁ εὐνοῦχος·
	Ἰδοὺ ὕδφρ,
῾Ο δὲ ᾽Ιωάννης διεκώλυεν	τί κωλύει με βαπτισθῆναι;
αὐτὸν λέγων·	εἶπεν δὲ αὐτῷ
᾽Εγὼ χρείαν ἔχω ὑπὸ σοῦ	εἰ πιστεύεις ἐξ ὅλης τῆς
βαπτισθῆναι	καρδίας ἔξεστιν.
καὶ σὺ ἔρχῃ πρός με;	
ἀποκριθεὶς δὲ ὁ ᾽Ιησοῦς εἶπεν	ἀποκριθεὶς δὲ εἶπεν
πρὸς αὐτόν·	πιστεύω τὸν υἱὸν τοῦ Θεοῦ
ἄφες ἄρτι	εἶναι τὸν᾽Ιησοῦν Χριστόν.
οὕτως γὰρ πρέπον ἐστὶν	
ἡμῖν πληρῶσαι πᾶσαν δικαιοσύνην.	
τότε ἀφίησιν αὐτόν.	καὶ ἐκέλευσεν στῆναι
	τὸ ἅρμα καὶ κατέβησαν
	ἀμφότεροι εἰς τὸ ὕδωρ
	ὅ τε Φίλιππος καὶ
	ὁ εὐνοῦχος

Matthew 3.14–16	*Acts* 8.36–9
βαπτισθεὶς δὲ ὁ Ἰησοῦς	καὶ ἐβάπτισεν αὐτόν.
εὐθὺς ἀνέβη ἀπὸ τοῦ ὕδατος·	ὅτε δὲ ἀνέβησαν ἐκ τοῦ
	ὕδατος
καὶ ἰδοὺ ἠνεῴχθησαν αὐτῷ	
οἱ οὐρανοί,	
καὶ εἶδεν τὸ πνεῦμα τοῦ Θεοῦ	πνεῦμα ἅγιον
καταβαῖνον ὡσεὶ περιστερὰν	ἐπέπεσεν
καὶ ἐρχόμενον ἐπ᾽ αὐτόν.	ἐπὶ τὸν εὐνοῦχον,
	ἄγγελος δὲ κυρίου
	ἥρπασεν τὸν Φίλιππον.

Three points of similarity stand out in these passages. In the first place there is the hindrance to baptism to be dealt with. As Cullmann noted, κωλύειν/διακωλύειν is used, and seems to have a technical meaning in both cases. In the second place is the overcoming of the hindrance to baptism by a formula which allows baptism to take place (πρέπον ἐστίν: Matt., ἔξεστιν: Acts). The terms used are different, but similar in form and identical in effect. Thirdly, there is the importance placed on the ascent from the water as the moment of the descent of the Spirit. Luke, in his account of the baptism of Jesus, links the descent of the Spirit with Jesus' prayer (Lk. 3.21f. cf. Matt. 3.16 and Mk. 1.10). Daube has argued that this emphasis on the moment of rising from the water was carried over from Judaism into the church. In Rabbinic thought, he wrote, new birth occurs at this point in proselyte baptism.[51]

The ἔξεστιν of Acts 8.37, therefore, far from necessarily pointing to a mid second-century context, is one of a series of features in 8.36–9 which suggest a setting closer to Matthew's Gospel than to Justin Martyr, and to a community in touch with Judaism. These features seem to indicate a likely origin for this reading in primitive times, and perhaps in Syria or Palestine.[52]

(c) ἀποκριθεὶς δὲ εἶπεν

The construction ἀποκρίνεσθαι (participial) + λέγειν, which is generally recognised as a reflection of Semitic idiom, occurs frequently in the Gospels. On seventeen occasions Luke eliminates it when it is present in parallel passages.[53] He cannot, however, be said to have an aversion to it, because he retains it on 5 occasions when it occurs in parallels,[54] he has it on 9 occasions when parallel passages do not have it,[55] and it occurs on 21 occasions in material peculiar to Luke.[56]

The phrase does not belong to any one Semitic language exclusively, and it cannot be used to demonstrate that Acts 8.37 is primitive, since the influence of the Septuagint may account for its presence here. None the less, the fact that it is present points to the possibility that this passage may have had its origin in a Semitic-speaking milieu. In particular one may note that one of the few passages in which ἀποκρίνεσθαι + λέγειν is given by all three Synoptists is in the account of Peter's confession (Matt. 16.16 – Mk. 8.29 – Lk. 9.20). It may be suspected that the account of the eunuch's confession in Acts 8.37, like that of Peter in the Gospels, has its origins in a primitive setting.

The confession

There are two principal questions to be asked about the eunuch's confession: in the first place, is it necessarily later than the first century, and in the second place, if it could be primitive, could it have been put into the text of Acts by the author?

(a) Dunn has pointed out that there is, apart from Acts 8.37, 'no firm association between baptism and confessional formulae in the New Testament'.[57] Before we follow Dunn in dismissing this passage on these grounds, we need to ask whether confession of faith before baptism could have taken place in the apostolic age, and if it could, whether it is likely to have taken the form: πιστεύω τὸν υἱὸν τοῦ Θεοῦ εἶναι τὸν Ἰησοῦν Χριστόν.

Dunn notes the similarity between the Ethiopian's confession and Romans 10.9f.[58] Confession of faith as a specific act is presupposed in several other New Testament passages (Matt. 10.32, Lk. 12.8, Jn. 9.22, 1 Tim. 6.12, Heb. 3.1, 4.14, 10.23, 13.15). Confession of faith has a particular significance in the Johannine literature. Important confessions are made in John's Gospel at 1.34,41,45,49, 4.42, 6.69, 9.35–8, 11.27, 20.28. There is a close parallel between the Ethiopian's confession and 1 Jn. 4.15: ὃς ἐὰν ὁμολογήσῃ ὅτι Ἰησοῦς ἐστιν ὁ υἱὸς τοῦ Θεοῦ ὁ Θεὸς ἐν αὐτῷ μένει καὶ αὐτὸς ἐν τῷ Θεῷ. The words spoken by the Ethiopian are reminiscent also of the concluding words of John 20: ταῦτα δὲ γέγραπται ἵνα πιστεύσητε ὅτι Ἰησοῦς ἐστιν ὁ Χριστὸς ὁ υἱὸς τοῦ Θεοῦ, καὶ ἵνα πιστεύοντες ζωὴν ἔχητε ἐν τῷ ὀνόματι αὐτοῦ (Jn. 20.31; cf. Jn. 11.27). To believe that Jesus is Christ and Son of God was, for the Johannine tradition, fundamental.

This double confession of Jesus was important also for the circle of Matthew. The ideal confession made by Peter at Matt. 16.16 has a double-membered form, σὺ εἶ ὁ Χριστὸς ὁ υἱὸς τοῦ Θεοῦ τοῦ ζῶντος, which the parallels in Mark and Luke do not (Mk. 8.29: σὺ εἶ ὁ Χριστός: Lk. 9.20: τὸν Χριστὸν τοῦ Θεοῦ).

Even if, though, it is granted that several New Testament writers attach importance to the profession of faith in Jesus in terms similar to those of Acts 8.37, it could still be argued that Acts 8.37 runs counter to the rest of the New Testament by associating a declaratory statement of faith with baptism. But in fact, Acts 8.37 is the climax, in the Western text, of a catechetical scene in which the significance of the Isaiah passage has been explained. It is not part of the baptismal scene, which consists of the baptism and the descent of the Spirit. Its setting is in catechesis, rather than in baptism itself.

Its simplicity of expression may suggest a primitive date, but does not demand it, since credal formulae in Christological, binitarian, and trinitarian forms continued to exist simultaneously in the second-century church.[59] We cannot, then, propose a progression of credal confessions from simple to complex, assuming that the simple disappeared as the complex arose, and then hope to place Acts 8.37 at an early point in the development. The most that can be said with regard to the eunuch's confession is that in its content it is not anachronistic as a part of Acts.

(b) Two features of the eunuch's confession make it unique in Luke–Acts, and have as a consequence been taken as evidence that it cannot be Lucan. The first is that the phrase ὁ' Ιησοῦς Χριστός is not Lucan. Metzger takes this as evidence against the authenticity of the reading.[60] In the second place, this is the only point at which a convert expresses the content of his faith at conversion.

The first of these features demonstrates only that the reading is not a free composition of Luke. If he were reproducing a received formula, the objection would lose some of its force. In any case, A. Souter thought it likely that Irenaeus' text had only 'Ιησοῦς,[61] and this is the reading accepted by Boismard and Lamouille in their reconstruction of the original TO.[62]

The second observation is a stronger objection to the Lucan authorship of this verse. Is there any reason why a convert should at this point alone in Acts express the content of his faith? An answer to this question may be suggested by a comparison between the story of the eunuch and the preceding story of Simon Magus. Luke appears to place the two men deliberately in parallel. They are the two specific examples of the work of Philip 'the evangelist' (21.8).

Both men stand in the margin of Judaism to which the Hellenist mission is directed. Both are great men in their own land (οὗτός ἐστιν ἡ δύναμις τοῦ Θεοῦ ἡ καλουμένη Μεγάλη, 8.10; ὃς ἦν ἐπὶ πάσης τῆς γάζης αὐτῆς, 8.27).

But the two men are also contrasted: the one an unstable convert, the other exemplary. While Simon's conversion was the result of seeing 'signs and great wonders', the Ethiopian's faith was based on an explanation of the prophetic scriptures (8.13,30–5; compare 8.30–5 with Lk. 24.25–7). Simon did not receive the Spirit, but the Spirit fell on the eunuch immediately at his baptism (8.15f.,39 longer text). The hollowness of Simon's faith soon became evident, but the eunuch 'went on his way rejoicing' (8.18–23,39). Luke seems to be following the pattern of pairing which he uses elsewhere in his work in order to make theological or didactic points.[63] For this reason, it may be suspected that there is a reason for his placing an ideal confession of faith in the mouth of this ideal baptisand.

Conclusion

It has been argued here that the longer text of Acts 8.39 is the original reading, the text in most witnesses having been accidentally shortened by scribal error.

Acts 8.37 contains elements which also appear to indicate authenticity. The lingustic style and content are consistent with Lucan authorship, and may suggest the use of primitive material drawn perhaps from a Syro-Palestinian source. A reason has been suggested for Luke's including a confession of faith at this point (see pp. 75f. above). There are clear connections of style and narrative between Acts 8.37 and its context.

The greatest obstacle to accepting this reading as authentic has always been the assumption that the scene it depicts would have been regarded by copyists as merely an edifying addition to the story. The balance of motive seemed to weigh heavily in favour of addition rather than deletion. But in view of the secrecy with which second-century Christians surrounded their rites (see pp. 69–71 above), the balance of motive moves in favour of deletion. It is more likely that a second-century scribe, conscious of the need for reticence about the rites of admission to fellowship, removed this passage than that a scribe in this period should have added such a uniquely revealing glimpse of the preparation of a baptismal candidate. Acts 8.37 therefore provides one piece of evidence that the non-Western text contains at least some conscious editing.

Acts 11.1–3

The text

N–A[26]	Codex D
1. ἤκουσαν δὲ οἱ ἀπόστολοι καὶ οἱ ἀδελφοὶ οἱ ὄντες κατὰ τὴν Ἰουδαίαν ὅτι καὶ τὰ ἔθνη ἐδέξαντο τὸν λόγον τοῦ Θεοῦ.	ἀκουστὸν δὲ ἐγένετο τοῖς ἀποστόλοις καὶ τοῖς ἀδελφοῖς οἳ ἐν τῇ Ἰουδαίᾳ ὅτι καὶ τὰ ἔθνη ἐδέξατο τὸν λόγον τοῦ Θεοῦ.
2.	ὁ μὲν οὖν Πέτρος διὰ ἱκανοῦ χρόνου ἠθέλησαι πορευθῆναι εἰς Ἱεροσόλυμα καὶ προσφωνήσας τοὺς ἀδελφοὺς καὶ ἐπιστηρίξας αὐτοὺς πολὺν λόγον ποιούμενος διὰ τῶν χωρῶν διδάσκων αὐτούς·
ὅτε δὲ ἀνέβη Πέτρος εἰς Ἰερουσαλήμ,	ὃς καὶ κατήντησεν αὐτοῖς καὶ ἀπήγγιλεν αὐτοῖς τὴν χάριν τοῦ Θεοῦ.
διεκρίνοντο πρὸς αὐτὸν οἱ ἐκ περιτομῆς λέγοντες ὅτι	οἱ δὲ ἐκ περιτομῆς ἀδελφοὶ διεκρίνοντο πρὸς αὐτὸν λέγοντες ὅτι
3. εἰσῆλθες πρὸς ἄνδρας ἀκροβυστίαν ἔχοντας καὶ συνέφαγες αὐτοῖς.	εἰσῆλθες πρὸς ἄνδρας ἀκροβυστίαν ἔχοντας καὶ συνέφαγες συν αὐτοῖς.

1. ἀκουστὸν ... ἐν τῇ Ἰουδαίᾳ: D (τοῖς ἐν τῇ Ἰ. corr.D) it[5] (syr[p])
   After τὸν λόγον τοῦ Θεοῦ add καὶ ἐδόξαζον τὸν Θεόν: it[51.54(2).58.(59).63.67]. vg[BG.MM.1260.1266.gk629] (syr[h**]) (cop[G67]) nedl[1.2]. ger[tepl] prov[1]; Aug
2. ὁ μὲν οὖν ... διδάσκων αὐτούς: D it[5.54.58.62]. vg[1213.1259.1260.1277.1282]. (syr[h**], but προσφωνήσαι for προσφωνήσας, and καὶ ἐδίδασκεν for

πολὺν λόγον … διδάσκων αὐτούς) cop^{G67} ger^{tepl} prov^1. NB: after ἐπιστηρίξας αὐτούς add ἐξῆλθεν/ἐπορεύθη: it$^{54.58.62.}$ vg$^{1213.1259.1260.1277.1282.}$ cop^{G67} prov^1.

ὅς καὶ … τοῦ Θεοῦ: D it^5 cop^{G67}.

οἱ δὲ ἐκ περιτομῆς ἀδελφοί: D it^5 (it$^{54.58.67.}$ cop^{G67} sah eth^{mss}.)

3. εἰσῆλθες … συνέφαγες: p^{74} ℵ A D E H P 242. 945. 1739. 1891. 2298. Maj. it$^{51.54.67.}$ Vg syr^{hmg} sah boh cop^{G67} eth. εἰσῆλθεν … συνέφαγεν· p^{45} B (L) 33. 36. 257. 431. 453. 467. 522. 614. 1108. 1175. 1518. 1611. 2138. 2412. syr^{p,h}

The problem

The text of Acts 11.1f. has been the subject of a considerable amount of scholarly discussion. The greater part of this discussion has concluded, or often assumed, that the textual problem of these verses is to explain the origin of the longer readings given by several Western witnesses. It is generally supposed that the shorter readings here are clear in their meaning, and unexceptionable in their Lucanism. A closer investigation of the text, though, reveals that this is not the case, and that the shorter reading requires explanation, quite as much as does the longer.

Most of the scholars who have discussed this passage have taken the view that the Western readings here have arisen from the non-Western. The opposite view was maintained by Blass and Clark. Here, as elsewhere, Clark detected the omission by homoeoteleuton of several στίχοι when 'the eye of a copyist passed from τοῦ Θεοῦ at the end of v. 1 to τοῦ Θεοῦ later on'.[64] Metzger is justified in remarking that this does not explain all the differences between the Western and non-Western texts in Acts 11.1f.[65] Nevertheless, Clark's proposal has the advantage of not taking the non-Western text as its point of departure, and of allowing that the non-Western text may need explanation quite as much as does the Western. When the Western text in these verses is read without the influence of the non-Western on the mind of the reader, it may be seen that there are strong suggestions that the non-Western reading may not be Luke's work.

The Western readings

The Western readings in these verses have clearly undergone a process of development, and it is important to attempt to reconstruct this process, distinguishing earlier from later features in the readings. Four questions in particular arise. In the first place, what is the status of the reading καὶ ἐδόξαζον τὸν Θεόν, given by some witnesses in 11.1? Is it a primitive Western reading, even though absent from D? Secondly, in 11.2 has ἐξῆλθεν been omitted by D and Teplensis, or has it been added by those versional witnesses which have a verb here? Thirdly, what is the status of the passage ὃς καὶ ... τὴν χάριν τοῦ Θεοῦ: is it an addition to an originally shorter Western reading, or has it been omitted by most Western witnesses? Finally, is the reading of D in 11.2, κατήντησεν αὐτοῖς, tolerable, or does it call for emendation?

(a) Ropes considered that καὶ ἐδόξαζον τὸν Θεόν in 11.1 was a true Western reading, because of the range of witnesses which have it.[66] Boismard and Lamouille ascribe it to the secondary Western stream, TO².[67] It is difficult to reach a firm conclusion on the question of whether this phrase is a primitive element in the Western text, or a late accretion. Conceivably, the similarity between this phrase and the preceeding one (καὶ ... ἐδέξατο ... τοῦ Θεοῦ) may have caused its omission, but equally possibly, the phrase may have been 'borrowed' from 11.18 or 21.20.

(b) The second problem concerns the wording of the longer text in 11.2. At the beginning of the passage Peter was, it is to be assumed, still in Caesaraea (10.48). In the longer text, the aorist participles προσφωνήσας ... ἐπιστηρίξας lead the reader to expect a finite verb stating that Peter actually set out for Jerusalem. There is such a verb in all witnesses except D and Teplensis.[68] In D, the text moves to another participial construction, in the present tense, implying that Peter had left Caesaraea and was travelling διὰ τῶν χωρῶν, presumably towards Jerusalem. The sense, therefore, appears to demand a verb here. The most likely explanation is that a verb originally present in the longer reading has dropped out of D and Teplensis by accidental omission.

(c) The third question concerns the status of the passage ὃς καὶ ... τοῦ Θεοῦ. Since it is attested only by D and partially by cop^G67, is it likely to be a relatively late expansion of the text?

When the Latin and Syriac witnesses, together with the Provençal and Teplensis, reach διδάσκων αὐτούς, they continue with the phrase ὅτε δὲ ἀνέβη Πέτρος εἰς ᾿Ιερουσαλήμ. Codex D has ὃς καὶ ... τοῦ Θεοῦ at this point, and cop^G67 appears to show knowledge of both forms of text: 'and he came to Jerusalem, and spoke to them of the mercy of God. But when Peter went up to

Jerusalem'.[69] If the reading of the Latin and Syriac witnesses is the more original, why should a reviser have taken exception to it, and have produced the awkward reading now in D? But if the reading of D is the more original, then the versions may be seen as giving two ways of dealing with its awkwardness. The Latin and Syriac have taken ὃς καὶ ... τοῦ Θεοῦ as parallel to ὅτε δὲ ... Ἰερουσαλήμ, as have most modern commentators, and have substituted the latter for the former. Cop[G67] has here conflated the Western and non-Western accounts. Here, then, D appears to give the earliest Western form of the reading.

(d) The final point concerns κατανταν: does it demand emendation? Four answers to this question are possible.

(i) Metzger's argument is that κατανταν construed with the dative is found nowhere else in Acts; it is, moreover, intolerable Greek; it is original to the reading here, and the reading as a whole, therefore, cannot be the work of the author of Acts.[70]

(ii) Delebecque agrees that the phrase κατήντησεν αὐτοῖς is original, but by arguing that αὐτοῖς is 'a dative of interest of a sort which is common in better Greek', concludes that it is not evidence against Lucan authorship of this passage.[71]

(iii) Zahn believed emendation to be necessary, and suggested that αὐτοῦ should be read in place of αὐτοῖς.[72] Ropes at one point appeared willing to accept this,[73] but proposed an alternative explanation of his own (see iv below). Boismard has followed Zahn's suggestion, adducing also the reading of cop[G67], 'and he came to Jerusalem', as evidence for a text behind the Coptic which read αὐτοῦ.[74]

(iv) Ropes thought that here as elsewhere the Greek of D has been affected by the Latin, which gives *obviavit eis*.[75] If this is correct, then the simple dative may have replaced a prepositional phrase, perhaps κατήντησεν εἰς αὐτούς.

Two points depend on the interpretation of this phrase. There is first the question of style: whether Luke could have written the passage in which it occurs. The other, and less frequently noticed, concerns the narrative. The reading with αὐτούς/-οῖς implies Peter's arrival, not necessarily in Jerusalem, but among the brethren in Judaea. With this reading, Acts 11.1–18 may not refer to an incident in Jerusalem at all, but to an incident, or series of incidents, in the course of a journey through Judaea. This would alter the significance of the entire narrative in 11.1–18.

Proposal (i) is justified in drawing attention to the difficulty of the

reading, although the usage can be paralleled in the papyri.[76] It is
not, however, justified in assuming that this form is original to the
reading. Indeed, bearing in mind the laxity of the scribe of D, it is
quite possible that it is not original. Proposal (ii) would be stronger
if examples from the New Testament, and from the work of Luke
in particular, could be shown. Proposal (iii) is open to similar
criticism. From the normal adverbial use of αὐτοῦ in the New
Testament, one might expect it to be used of a verb of rest, rather
than motion (Matt. 26.36, Lk. 9.27, Acts 15.34 Western, 18.19,
21.4, but see Mk. 6.33D and see Kilpatrick's comment, n. 75
above). The Coptic evidence is a doubtful support for this proposal;
the scribe may have brought in the reference to Jerusalem to clarify
αὐτούς quite as easily as αὐτοῦ. Proposal (iv), though, fits what is
known of the scribe of D and his writing habits, and appears to be
the most likely explanation of the origin of the reading. The
implications of this conclusion will be of importance for an understanding of the language of the longer text and for that of its
narrative.

Language

The studies by Wilcox, Boismard, and Delebecque have all been
concerned with the linguistic traits of the material in the longer text
of Acts 11.1f.. Each has also been concerned with the question of
whether these traits may point to the possible Lucan authorship of
this material.

Wilcox's study investigated the 'Lucanisms' of this longer,
Western text in 11.2, according to the canons developed by J. C.
Hawkins and H. J. Cadbury. Wilcox found five 'Lucanisms' in Acts
11.2D: ἱκανός, προσφωνεῖν, κατάνταν, μὲν οὖν, χάρις. The
word ἐπιστηρίζειν is also typically Lucan. This amounted to 17.85
per cent of the text (21.42 per cent including ἐπιστηρίζειν), which
may be compared with an average incidence of 9.15 per cent of
'Lucanisms' in the text of Acts as a whole. His conclusion was that:
'If such a high concentration of Lukan traits were found in a verse in
the ordinary (B) text of Acts, the inference of Lukan editorial
activity would be hard to avoid.'[77]

Boismard carried out a thorough phrase-by-phrase analysis of
the longer text of Acts 11.2, basing the work on a form of text which
included ἐξῆλθεν and κατήντησεν αὐτοῦ. He concluded that the
author of this version imitated the style and vocabulary of Luke

without a slip. In *Texte occidental*, Boismard and Lamouille refer to the stylistic faithfulness of this passage to the usage of Luke as a principal piece of evidence for the Lucan character of TO.[78] Delebecque included Acts 11.1 in his work on this passage. Here he noted the Septuagintal style of ἀκουστός + γίνεσθαι and that the adjective ἀκουστός is found in good Hellenistic authors. Luke, a good Hellenist in style, influenced also by the LXX, could have written Acts 11.1D.[79] As noted above (p. 80), he also gave cautious endorsement to Wilcox's conclusions about Lucan editorial activity in 11.2.

These three scholars have made a strong case for the Lucan character of the Western readings in Acts 11.1f. A few further observations should be made, though, and of these, while most tell in favour of their conclusions, there is also some contrary evidence which should be taken into account.

Ropes and Delebecque were impressed by the 'Semitic' or 'Septuagintal' quality of ἀκουστὸς δὲ ἐγένετο.[80] Ropes was so impressed, indeed, that he was willing to accept it as one of the few places in Acts at which the Western text gave the original reading. But the UBS Textual Committee was more impressed by the observation that the word ἀκουστός occurs nowhere else in the New Testament.[81] In favour of the phrase, however, it should be noted that Luke in Acts is fond of the parallel form γνωστός (x10 in Acts, x2 in Luke, x3 in the rest of the New Testament; γνωστός + γίνεσθαι x4 in Acts, x0 in the rest of the New Testament).

Another phrase of interest is πολὺν λόγον ποιούμενος. Luke uses λόγος on occasion as a virtual synonym for φήμη (Lk. 5.15, Acts 11.22) or διήγησις (Acts 1.1). It appears that this is the sense of λόγος in Acts 11.2D. The parallel with Acts 1.1 is striking (Τὸν πρῶτον λόγον ἐποιησάμεν ...), and so is the parallel with Acts 13.44D, where the reference is to Paul giving a full account concerning the Lord (πολύν τε λόγον ποιησαμένου περὶ τοῦ κυρίου). At Acts 11.2, then, πολὺν λόγον ποιούμενος means 'giving a full account', and not merely 'speaking much', as Metzger translates.[82] The apostles and brethren in Judaea had heard something of what had happened at Caesaraea (11.1). According to the Western text, Peter took advantage of his journey to Jerusalem to give them a full account of what had happened. This is quite in accordance with Luke's usage.

The phrase κατήντησεν αὐτοῖς might tell against Lucan authorship of this reading. Even if some conjectural emendation is made, it remains the case that Luke's normal use is καταντᾶν + preposition + place name. This phrase is not paralleled elsewhere in the writings of Luke, or indeed in the New Testament.

The linguistic features of the longer readings in Acts 11.1f. are strong evidence for the possibility of Lucan authorship of the material. These features, though, cannot by themselves demonstrate Lucan authorship, particularly in view of the doubtful κατήντησεν αὐτοῖς. The Lucan character of the language in these variants raises questions which can only be resolved when the narrative of the variant is considered.

The narrative

The most important point to establish about the content of the longer readings in Acts 11.1f. is what they say about Peter's movements. Most commentators understand the reading of 11.2 to describe a journey in three stages: (1) Peter called together the brothers at Caesaraea, and strengthened them, then set out; (2) Peter went on a teaching journey through the country; and (3) Peter arrived at Jerusalem. Most agree that stage 3 of the narrative is, in Clark's words, 'indispensable to the sense'.[83] But it was argued above (pp. 79f., points (c) and (d)) that Codex Bezae is most likely to represent the earliest form of Western text here, and that according to Bezae the events of 11.2–18 took place not in Jerusalem, but in the course of a journey towards Jerusalem. In other words, the three-stage journey Caesaraea – Judaea – Jerusalem is the result of conflating the Western and non-Western readings. A few commentators have noted that the Bezan narrative does not explicitly bring Peter to Jerusalem.[84]

Delebecque has called attention to two awkward points in the narrative of Bezae. In the first place, ὃς καί is separated by a considerable distance from its antecedent Πέτρος. In the second place, in the phrase διδάσκων αὐτούς, the word αὐτούς refers to the people of the country through which Peter is passing, but the reference changes without explanation to the Jerusalem church in the next clause, κατήντησεν αὐτοῖς.[85] Both these features can be explained, once it is accepted that the Western text does not narrate Peter's arrival in Jerusalem. On this interpretation, the clauses πολὺν λόγον ... διδάσκων αὐτούς and ὃς καί ... τὴν χάριν τοῦ Θεοῦ would be two versions of the same information.[86] They should be understood in this way: what happened at Caesar-

aea became known to the apostles and brethren in Judaea, so
Peter, who had intended for some time to go to Jerusalem, having
called together the brethren (at Caesaraea) and strengthened
them, *either* [he arrived among them] giving a full account, teaching
through the country places, *or* he arrived among them, and
announced to them the grace of God.

On this reading of the text, then, Acts 11.1–18 concerns Peter's
relations with 'the apostles and brethren in Judaea', and not
specifically with the church in Jerusalem. The narrative of chapter
11 thus becomes less clearly an anticipation of the Jerusalem
Council which is to take place in chapter 15.

There are also indications in the non-Western reading that its
own account of Peter's movements is less coherent than that of the
Western reading.

The non-Western text relates a direct journey to Jerusalem, and
an encounter there with 'those of the circumcision'. But this would
be beside the point in the circumstances: Luke would not have
explained how the 'apostles and brethren in *Judaea*' learned from
Peter of what had taken place at Caesaraea. Why should he have
introduced these groups, if he was going to overlook them immediately? Elsewhere he distinguishes Jerusalem from Judaea (Lk.
21.21, Acts 1.8, 8.1), and if he wished to say that Peter's Caesarean
ministry became known in Jerusalem, why did he not say so? (cf.
11.22).

If Luke intended Acts 11.3–18 to be an account of a confront-
ation in Jerusalem, then he has portrayed it in an uncharacteristic
way. The imperfect verbs διεκρίνοντο and ἐξετίθετο in verses 2 and
4 are an indication that Luke may not have envisaged a single
controversy scene here. While the tense may have an inceptive
force, it remains the case that in the Gospel Luke habitually
narrates controversy stories in the aorist, even when this means
altering the tense from that in Mark.[87] In Acts, too, apologetic
speeches are introduced by the aorist, with the exceptions only of
this passage and 26.1.[88]

Acts 11.3–18 is also uncharacteristic of Luke's portrayal of the
Jerusalem church. In Luke's view, the church at Jerusalem always
deliberated and acted in a controlled manner. Important issues
were always dealt with, this passage apart, by the apostles or elders,
or both (Acts 1.15, 6.2, 9.27, 15.6, 21.18) or by the church as a
whole (Acts 11.22). The direct discussion bewteen Peter and 'those

of the circumcision' in Acts 11.3–18, if it is envisaged as taking place in Jerusalem, introduces a note of anarchy into the working of the mother church which is out of keeping with the picture Luke wishes to portray elsewhere. The apostles and elders in Jerusalem acted as a tribunal in any important matter, and yet in the Majority text of Acts 11.1–18 they take no part in a highly significant debate. It seems reasonable to conclude that, despite the statement of the non-Western text that Peter went to Jerusalem, Luke envisaged that the challenge and apologia of 11.3–18 took place, not in Jerusalem, but in Judaea, and not once, but repeatedly. If we are to look for a parallel with Acts 15, it is with Paul in 15.3, travelling through the country districts, and telling of the conversion of the Gentiles, rather than with him in 15.4ff., facing his opponents in Jerusalem.

The Western reading of Acts 11.2 therefore fits the context better than does the non-Western. It states that Peter, in the course of a journey to Jerusalem, gave the apostles and brethren in Judaea a fuller account of the episode at Caesaraea. The Western narrative was set out in two versions or drafts. According to one version, Peter went through αἱ χῶραι[89] and gave the 'full account' (πολὺς λόγος), which appears in verses 5–17. According to the other version, Peter arrived among 'them' (the apostles and brethren in Judaea: v. 1), and announced to them the 'grace of God', apparently an oblique way of referring to God's acceptance of the Gentiles (see Acts 11.23). On this journey, the circumcised brethren[90] on several occasions upbraided Peter (διεκρίνοντο), and Peter on those occasions gave his defence (ἐξετίθετο).

Conclusion

The assumptions commonly made about the longer text of Acts 11.1f. deserve to be questioned. Once it is accepted that the Western reading does not refer to Peter's arrival in Jerusalem, then much of the case for a tendentious purpose behind the narrative is undermined.

The assumption that the longer text grew out of the shorter text also should be called into question. If a scribe faced with the shorter text produced from it the text as it is in Codex D, then one would have to say that he exchanged clarity of narrative for obscurity, that none the less he produced a text which is better suited to its context than the original had been, that he broke the parallels with 15.1–6, and that in all this, he expressed himself in language which is largely characteristic of the author.

If one supposes, however, that a copyist had a text like that of D before him, the origin of the shorter text, and of the intermediate forms, can be explained. A copyist who could not make sense of the passage ὁ μὲν οὖν Πέτρος . . . τὴν χάριν τοῦ Θεοῦ, but who noticed that it at least stated that Peter wished to go to Jerusalem, might decide to cut the Gordian knot by substituting a clause expressing what he understood the passage to mean: ὅτε δὲ ἀνέβη Πέτρος εἰς Ἰερουσαλήμ. After all, had not Paul gone up to Jerusalem in similar circumstances? But 'the apostles and brethren in *Judaea*' in verse 1 and the imperfect tenses in verses 2 and 4 remained as evidence that he had mistaken the author's meaning.

Copyists who became aware of both forms of text were faced with a choice between fulness with obscurity or brevity with apparent clarity. Several compromised, producing the readings which substitute ὅτε δὲ . . . Ἰερουσαλήμ for ὃς καὶ . . . τοῦ Θεοῦ. In D alone was the reading preserved in something near its original form, although cop[G67], by conflating the readings rather than making a substitution, remains close to it.

There is therefore a strong case for believing that the Western reading at Acts 11.1f. is Lucan, and that the non-Western reading in verse 2 at least is an attempt by a later copyist to make sense of an admittedly muddled passage. If authentically Lucan here, the Western text suggests that Luke did not understand Acts 11.1–18 as an anticipation of the discussion of 15.5–29, as the non-Western text implies. In the Western text, the rejoicing of 11.18 is the rejoicing of the Judaean congregations to whom Peter had spoken, and in no sense represents an official sanction for the Gentile mission by the Jerusalem church, whose suspicion remained (see 11.22), and was only to be relieved by the Jerusalem Council. This conclusion calls into question source-critical hypotheses which suggest that Acts 11 is an alternative account of the Jerusalem debate of Acts 15, which Luke has separated. If the Western text of Acts 11.2 is Lucan, then for Luke the events of chapter 11 were part of the progression towards those of chapter 15, and not an uneasy anticipation of them.

But if the Western reading of Acts 11.2 is original, then Luke's text here was more in the nature of a rough draft than a polished and complete piece of work. This observation may be one piece of evidence to help unravel the enigma of the origin of Acts' textual peculiarities.

Acts 15.20, 29 and 21.25: the 'Apostolic Decree'

The forms of the Decree

There is a more extensive literature on the text of the 'Apostolic Decree' than on any other textual problem in the book of Acts.[91] This interest stems from the fact that the Decree is directly relevant to the problems raised by the place of the Law, not only in the book of Acts, but in the primitive church. When it is also observed that the different textual forms of the Decree appear to give different interpretations of the place of the Law, then the textual study of this passage has implications both for the understanding of Luke's thought and for the conditions of the church from which Luke drew the Decree.

The Decree appears three times in Acts: once in the apostolic letter (15.29), once in James's speech before the writing of the letter (15.20), and once at a later point, when James reminds Paul of the contents of the Decree (21.25). In addition to this, the witnesses to the text give six different forms. Study of the Decree should begin, then, by identifying the forms in which the Decree occurs. When that has been done, it is possible to examine the problems posed by the text, and to consider what is the most likely original form of the text.

Table 2 sets out the forms in which the text of the Decree occurs. It does not deal with alterations in the order of the terms of the Decree.[92] It also omits from consideration the phrase φερόμενοι ἐν τῷ ἁγίῳ πνεύματι, which several Western witnesses have in 15.29. P.-H. Menoud and E. J. Epp attribute considerable significance to this phrase, seeing in it the key to the anti-Judaic meaning of the Decree in its 'D-version'.[93] The key to understanding the Decree will here be looked for in the text of the Decree itself.

The problem

Text-critical research on the Decree has concentrated on finding the form of text which both fits the context best and most adequately explains the origin of the other forms. No complete consensus has emerged, and although an influential body of schol-

Table 2. *Text-forms of the Apostolic Decree*

	15.20	15.29	21.25
1. Omit πορνεία without Golden Rule	p[45] arm eth[mss] Didasc	(p[45] lacking) vg[1396] eth[ms] ?Clem (Or) ?CyrJ	(p[45] lacking)
2. Four prohibitions without Golden Rule	ABCE Maj. lat[maj] syr[p.h(text)] boh geo ConstAp PsAug[Spec] Chr	ABCE Maj. lat[maj](inc it[51]) syr[p.h(text)] boh geo Amph App Ps-Aug[Spec] Chr Clem ConstAp CyrJ Didasc Epiph PsEusV Gaud Hes Or Theod	All MS witnesses except those in category 4/5 below
3. Four prohibitions with Golden Rule	242.323.522. 536.945.1522. 1739.1891. 2298 sah (eth) it[61]	242.323.522.536. 614.945.1522. 1739.1799. 1891.2298.2412. it[54.58.61] it[63.67] vg[1213.1258.] vg[1260.1266.] vg[1277.] syr[h] sah (eth) ger[tepl] prov ?Evag ?AuctPel	
4. Omit πνικτόν without Golden Rule	it[51] ndl[1] Ephr	Ambstr Aug (?Ps-)Fulg Jer Pac Tert	D it[5.51] geo(Garitte) Aug Ps-Aug[Spec]
5. Omit πνικτόν with Golden Rule	D it[5] (it[67] lacking) Ir[lat + gk]	D it[5.67] Eth[mss] Ir[lat + gk] Cyp Ephr	
6. Omit αἷμα without Golden Rule	—	2495. sah[ms] Or Meth	—

arly opinion judges form 2 to be the original, this opinion has never been without critics, and is open to question at a number of points. Of the two most poorly attested forms, form 6 is universally taken to be an aberration, largely because of its weak attestation, but form 1 has had some advocates. In a note published in 1934, M. J. Lagrange argued that this could be the original form of the Decree, since there is a recognised tendency to add to the text of Acts, a tendency most clearly seen in the Western text.[94] Lagrange's suggestion was taken further by Menoud in 1951 (see p. 18). He also argued that a code such as that of the Decree is likely to have been elaborated in the course of transmission. Tentatively, he suggested that the original text lacked πνικτόν, πορνεία, and the Golden Rule. Since no witness has such a text, though, he was willing to identify form 1, without πορνεία or the Golden Rule, as the likely original. Boismard and Lamouille suggested that TA (the archetypal non-Western text) should have exhibited form 1 at 15.20.[95] This approach has the advantage of reducing the Decree to a food law, a restriction which is appropriate if table fellowship was the issue which prompted its formulation.

W. G. Kümmel brought three arguments against Menoud's proposal. In the first place, the textual evidence is not strong. Origen's citation, p[45], and the Ethiopic are not reliable witnesses.[96] Secondly, Menoud based his argument on a defective method, since the earliest form of a tradition is not necessarily the shortest: 'in a living tradition, both growth *and* contraction of a text will have to be taken into consideration'. [97] Thirdly, one should not assume that the Decree need concern only food regulations: table fellowship was not the issue in 15.1.[98] Kümmel's points are cogent. The additional witnesses to this form of the text which he does not cite (see Table 2) do not materially affect his point about the weakness of its attestation. A further point is the question why πορνεία should have been added, and added consistently, in witnesses which have otherwise had a very diverse history. For these reasons, therefore, form 1 is not to be accepted as original.

The choice between the remaining forms (2–5) is generally expressed as that between an 'ethical' and a 'ritual' understanding of the Decree. Since the beginning of the critical debate over the text of the Decree in the last century, it has been recognised that three of the terms of the Decree can bear more than one meaning. The term εἰδωλόθυτον can refer to the eating of meat sacrificed to idols – this would be the 'ritual' sense – or it could have the 'ethical' sense of idolatry in general. Αἷμα could refer to the eating of blood ('ritual'), or to the shedding of blood ('ethical'). So, too, πορνεία could refer to fornication ('ethical'), or to infringement of a ritual code, such as the Levitical purity laws. Only πνικτόν does not have this ambiguous quality, and seems to point to a 'ritual' interpretation alone, while conversely, the presence of the Golden Rule at the end of the Decree seems to indicate a 'moral' understanding of the Decree.

The most influential study of the Decree's text in recent years has been that of Kümmel. Kümmel accepts this distinction between an 'ethical' and a 'ritual' form of the Decree. He therefore argued that form 3, because it has πνικτόν and the Golden Rule, is a mixed form of text.[99] Form 4 is more perplexing. Tertullian is the major witness to this form. His citation of the Decree occurs in *De Pudicitia* 12.4. Kümmel noted that Tertullian would not have needed to refer to the Golden Rule in order to make his point in the argument he was following in *De Pudicitia* 12. When it is noted that Tertullian also had the 'Christianising addition' φερόμενοι ἐν τῷ ἁγίῳ πνεύματι, then it is quite possible that he also had a text with the Golden Rule, even if he did not actually cite the Rule. Tertullian would thus become a witness for form 5 of the text, and form 4 could be seen as an accidental aberration from form 5.[100]

In this way, Kümmel reduced the decision to a choice between forms 2 and 5. He drew attention to the way in which, in form 5, the omission of πνικτόν is accompanied by the Golden Rule, and by the phrase φερόμενοι ἐν τῷ ἁγίῳ πνεύματι. These three alterations point to a single *Tendenz*: a desire to turn a Decree which arose in particular historical circumstances into a regulation having validity for Christians of all times.[101] Kümmel's reconstruction of the text's history is that form 2 stood in the original text of Acts. Form 5 was an early 'improvement' of the original, making a universally valid moral rule out of a context-bound ritual decree. Form 3 is a mixture of forms 2 and 5. The remaining forms, 1, 4 and 6, are accidental and occasional aberrations. Form 2 is to be preferred, both because it fits the context best, and because it best explains the origin of the other forms.

Kümmel's arguments and his conclusions represent the majority opinion of textual critics today on the text of the Decree. Epp, while intending not to discuss the origin of the D-text, but only its meaning, took it as 'obvious' that the B-text was composed of a ceremonial part and a moral part, while the D-text was composed of a moral part alone:

> This ethical emphasis in the D-text, over against the largely ceremonial stress of B, is clear, and shows that once again the D-text reveals its distance from the Judaising viewpoint and, by so doing, its distance from the viewpoint of Judaism itself, at least in its ritual and ceremonial emphasis; and it was this emphasis, after all, which occasioned the 'apostolic decree' in the first place.[102]

The same assumption that the forms of the Decree can ultimately be reduced to an 'ethical' and a 'moral' type is to be found also in Metzger's *Textual Commentary*:

> It therefore appears to be more likely that an original ritual prohibition against eating foods offered to idols, things strangled and blood, and against πορνεία (however this latter is to be interpreted) was altered into a moral law by dropping the reference to πνικτοῦ and by adding the negative Golden Rule, than to suppose that an original moral law was transformed into a food law.[103]

This quotation from Metzger also indicates another assumption which appears in arguments over the history of the text of the Decree: that it is more likely that a ritual injunction would be transformed in Christian circles into a moral law than that the opposite should be the case.

There has long been a minority opinion which has favoured form 4 as the most likely original form of the Decree. The most extensive study of the Decree yet undertaken is that of G. Resch.[104] Resch argued that Patristic evidence showed the Fathers to have maintained an ethical interpretation of the Decree, and that this interpretation was essentially correct: the Decree was 'the shortest sytematic compendium of the Christian ethic'.[105] The Decree in its 'extra-canonical', that is, three-membered form without πνικτόν, retains the original ethical emphasis of the Decree. In Alexandria, though, fear of demonic contamination from eating the blood of sacrificial victims led to the addition of πνικτόν to the Decree.[106] Resch persuaded Harnack of the correctness of this view,[107] and also Kirsopp Lake.[108]

Ropes reached the same conclusion: indeed, this was the most

notable point at which he was willing to depart from the text of B to
follow a Western reading.[109] T. Boman has argued that an original
ethical Decree without πνικτόν was first misunderstood as a ritual
prescription, and then altered by the addition of πνικτόν in order to
secure the ritual interpretation.[110]

Y. Tissot introduced a new refinement into discussion of the
Decree by drawing attention to possible distinctions between the
original form of the Decree before its incorporation into Acts, and
the form (or forms) in which Luke originally cited it in his work.[111]
Tissot postulated an original four-membered Decree, which Luke
incorporated in its full form in Acts 15.29, but in 15.20 he removed
πνικτόν, because it is not found in the Law, to which James is
referring.[112] Of our witnesses, it[51] thus preserves the original text.
However, in the 'Eastern' textual tradition 15.20 was conformed to
15.29,[113] while in the Western tradition a reviser, δ[1], took exception
to the Judaising emphasis of the four-membered Decree, and
removed πνικτόν from the two references in which it rightly
belonged, 15.29 and 21.25.[114] Later, a second reviser, δ[2], added the
Golden Rule – a revision which Tissot considers 'gauche'.[115]

S. G. Wilson has also argued, tentatively, for form 4 as the
original state of Luke's text. He has begun by examining the
meaning of the Decree in Luke's work, and has concluded that an
ethical interpretation is likely to be Luke's own understanding of it,
although Wilson leaves open the possibility of a different understanding of the Decree in its pre-Lucan history. Bearing in mind the
semantic and textual difficulties raised by πνικτόν, Wilson has
concluded that Luke may well have had an original three-part
Decree, to which he attached an ethical significance.[116]

Few critics, even among those who favour an 'ethical' interpretation of the Decree, have been willing to accept the Golden Rule as
part of the original text. F. Manns has argued that the background
to the Decree lies in Jewish proselyte instruction.[117] It was the
custom to begin such instruction with the essentials, and the
Golden Rule often played a part in this.[118] Form 5 represents a
basic minimum required of Christian converts at a time before
church and synagogue had moved finally apart, and the four-
membered Decree, shorn of the Golden Rule, represents a later
reinterpretation in a 'ritual' sense, by a church which no longer
understood the Decree's true original function.[119] Boismard and
Lamouille accept the Golden Rule as part of TO at 15.29, but
regard it as a harmonisation by TO[2] at 15.20.[120]

The interpretation of the Decree

Two issues are raised by the various approaches to the interpretation of the Decree. The first concerns the contrast which is commonly drawn between 'ethical' and 'ritual' understandings of the Decree. Is it right to begin with a sharp contrast between 'ritual' and 'ethics': is it clear that these are two distinct and opposed categories? And in addition to this: is it self-evident that there would be a drift from a 'ritual' to an 'ethical' interpretation of the Decree in second-century Christianity? The second issue concerns the term πνικτόν: is its setting really in the Jewish environment of the mid first century, or does it belong more firmly to the increasingly Gentile church of the second century?

Kirsopp Lake long ago pointed out the difficulty with the basic assumption in Kümmel's case, the absolute antithesis between 'ritual' and 'ethical' prescriptions. He made his point by reference to the American law of prohibition: 'that is a food law, but in the minds of those who assent to it, its justification is that it is wrong to touch alcohol'.[121] To someone who assents to that way of seeing the world, ritual defilement is morally wrong. Only if one does not accept the wrongness of, say, eating blood can one put it in a different category from, for example, hating one's neighbour. For someone who accepted a value-system in which eating blood was wrong, there would be nothing incongruous about placing such a prescription alongside the command to love one's neighbour. 'Ritual' can only be separated from 'ethics' in someone else's value-system.

Some second-century Christians drew a distinction between 'ritual' and 'ethical' commands. This distinction certainly informs the interpretation of the Old Testament in the epistle of Barnabas, for instance. It cannot, though, be assumed that all Christians would draw the distinction at all times, or that all would draw the distinction at the same points.

It has often been taken as axiomatic in debate on the textual history of the Decree that 'ritual' prescriptions would be turned into 'ethical' ones in the course of the development of early Christianity. So Haenchen asserts:

> a later reinterpretation [of the Decree] in a 'ritual' sense, in which πνικτόν was added, may be considered out of the question. Readily understandable, on the other hand, is a

later reinterpretation in a 'moral' sense, in which πνικτόν had to be dropped and the 'golden rule' added.[122]

In a general sense this assertion may be true, that the Christian church became less concerned with ritual purity than had been the Jewish communities out of which it sprang. Or at least, that its concerns with purity were expressed in a different manner. It would be naive, though, to interpret this as the replacement of 'ritual' with 'ethics'. Lake saw this when he protested against the assumption that Jewish Christians would place more emphasis on 'ritual'. This assumption, he maintained, was part of Christian prejudice towards Judaism.[123] Although the early church did not take over the value-system of the Jewish communities, it none the less drew lines of purity of its own.

Food laws, with which the Decree is concerned at least in part, are an example of this. R. M. Grant has traced in the food laws of three communities of the ancient world, Pythagoreans, Christians, and Jews, a development towards reinterpreting or explaining away food laws as moral or philosophical injunctions. The history of the interpretation of the Decree, he argues, precisely illustrates this trend.[124] Grant's evidence for Christian and Jewish attitudes, though, is drawn largely from Alexandrian sources: the epistle of Aristeas, Philo, 4 Maccabees, and Origen. Elsewhere, there is evidence that the church in the second century maintained a ban on the consumption of blood, even though other food laws were abandoned.

No New Testament writer explicitly sanctions the eating of blood. In several passages the thought is expressed that 'nothing is unclean of itself' (Mk. 7.19, Acts 11.8f., Rom. 14.14). But this refers to the distinction between clean and unclean animals as food. This important element in the value-system of Judaism was abandoned at an early point, and apparently without a great deal of contention. One of the few echoes of controversy is the treatment by Mark of Jesus' saying in Mk. 7.15. Jesus' saying on the inner springs of evil is made by Mark (or his source) the basis of an extended exegetical passage, in which it is interpreted as effectively abolishing the distinction of clean and unclean foods (Mk. 7.17–23). But even if the point was contentious in Mark's own time, the conclusion which he drew was early and widely accepted: there was no type of food which was unclean for the Christian. Even groups such as the Ebionites, who apparently upheld vegetarianism as part of the higher righteousness,[125] did not maintain the distinction between clean and unclean animals of the Levitical code.

Blood, however, was treated differently. Regrettably, no full study of food laws in the early church has appeared since that of Böckenhoff in 1903, but his conclusion seems correct, that the prohibition on blood was regarded in early Christianity as an element of Old Testament law which had been newly reinforced by the apostles.[126] Although the Apostolic Fathers and the Apologists have nothing to say about the eating of blood, there is evidence from the late second and early third centuries that Christians abstained from blood. This abstention could be used to make an apologetic point: Christians could not be guilty of the crimes attributed to them, because they did not even consume the blood of irrational animals (*Ep.Ecc.Lug. & Vienn.* in Eusebius, *HE* 6.1.26), or: the high moral scruples held by Christians about the shedding of human blood are demonstrated by their abstention from animal blood in their meals (Minucius Felix, *Octavius* 30.6). The prohibition on blood is to be found in the Pseudo-Clementines (*Hom.* 7.4.2–3, 7.8, 8.23.1, 9.23.2), in the *Sibylline Oracles* (2.96), in Clement of Alexandria (*Paed.* 2.7; *Strom.* 4.15), and in Tertullian (*Apol.* 9.13; *De Pud.* 12.4; *De Mon.* 5). The evidence of Tertullian is particularly interesting. His reference to abstention from blood in *De Monogamia* illustrates the way in which 'ritual' prohibitions could be upheld even by a thinker who maintained that there was a clear distinction between the dispensation of Christ and that of Moses:

> In Christ all things are recalled to their initial state, so that faith is turned back from circumcision to wholeness of the flesh, just as from the beginning there was freedom in the matter of foods, with abstinence from blood alone.

The Mishnah tractate *Hullin* may have what is an incidental reference to Christian observance of abstention from blood in the second century when it enjoins that no one should make a hole in the public street for blood to run into 'lest he confirm the heretics in their ways' (*Hullin* 2.9). This may mean that the 'heretics' – which often indicates Christians – were in the habit of disposing of blood in this way.

It is, then, by no means 'out of the question' that a reinterpretation of the Decree in a 'ritual' sense could have taken place in the second century. To see the development of early Christian thought as a drift from 'ritual' to 'ethics' is an oversimplification. It was quite possible for early Christian teaching to include elements which might be described as 'ritual' alongside those which might be called 'ethical'. The *Didache* includes not only teaching on the 'Two Ways' (2–5), but also clear instruction on not eating food offered to idols (6). The *Apology* of Aristides (15) has a similar juxtaposition of 'ethical' and 'ritual' precepts in its description of Christians. Aristides states that: 'whatever they [the Christians] do not wish that others should do to them, they do not practise towards anyone, and they do not eat of the meats of idol sacrifices, for they are undefiled'. It evidently did not seem incongruous to Aristides to place the negative Golden Rule alongside 'ritual' prescriptions. Something similar can be said of the teaching of the Pseudo-Clementines. The catechism found in *Hom* 7.4.2–4 is strongly reminiscent of the Apostolic Decree with the Golden Rule.[127] It demonstrates that it was possible to combine the Golden Rule with something very like the Decree, without the latter losing its 'ritual' sense.

The consequence of the argument we have followed so far is that much of the textual work on the Decree has begun by casting the problem in the wrong terms. When a decision has to be made between forms 2–5 of the Decree one cannot begin by classifying them as 'ritual' or 'ethical', nor can one assume that the 'ritual' is more likely to be primitive. Each of the forms has to be examined without this prejudgement.

It is a common observation also, if one begins by setting 'ritual' and 'ethical' forms of the Decree in antithesis, that Luke cannot have been responsible for both.[128] However, if it is accepted that there is no absolute antithesis between these forms of the Decree, this objection loses its force.

τὸ πνικτόν in the Decree

It is widely accepted that the Decree is to be understood against the background of the laws of Lev. 17 and 18. There may also be a reference to the Noachic commands of Genesis 9. These points have been made by several scholars.[129] Lev. 17 and 18 is the only substantial body of law which applies to the προσήλυτος (which in the LXX represents the Hebrew *ger*) as well as to the Israelite.[130] This relationship is reinforced when it is noticed that the decree in 15.29 and 21.25 appears to deal with the stipulations in the same order as they occur in Leviticus: Lev. 17.1–9 εἰδωλόθυτον, 17.10-12 αἷμα, 17.13–16 πνικτόν, 18.1–23 πορνεία.

As Wilson has observed, though, there is difficulty in fitting τὸ πνικτόν into this scheme.[131] Lev. 17.13–16 deals with animals in two categories: those taken in hunting, and those which die from natural causes or are killed by wild beasts, but there is no specific reference to strangulation or to suffocation. Although Judaism had the technical terms *n^ebelah* and *t^erepah* to denote an animal that died from natural causes, and one killed by wild beasts respectively (rendered in the LXX θνησιμαῖον and θηριάλωτον), it had apparently no general term to cover animals which died by strangulation or suffocation.[132] The Mishnah tractate *Hullin* has one reference to choking: 'All may slaughter and at any time and with any implement except with a reaping-sickle or a saw or with teeth or with finger nails, since these choke (*hanaq*)' (*Hull.* 1.2). This is a curious statement, though, because all the implements named are for cutting, not for strangulation. It has been suggested that this is a metaphorical use of *hanaq*, 'to cause agony as by choking'.[133] Alternatively, the meaning could be that these implements do not produce the clean incision of windpipe and artery required by correct methods of slaughter. The serrated edges would tear instead of cutting. Despite this reference *Hullin* does not set up a category of 'strangled meat'. It maintained the Jewish and scriptural distinction between *n^ebelah* and *t^erepah* which was characteristic of Judaism.[134] It is possible to regard πνικτόν in Acts as a collective term for *n^ebelah* and *t^erepah* as Strack-Billerbeck explictly does, but it is important to note that in this respect at least, it is those witnesses to the text of Acts which have the word πνικτόν which show, in Epp's words, 'distance from the viewpoint of Judaism itself, at least in its ritual and ceremonial aspects'.[135] This is because the word πνικτόν not only introduces a term not found in Lev. 17, but blurs a distinction made in Leviticus, and carefully maintained in Judaism.

The term πνικτόν also raises semantic problems. Molland made an important observation when he drew attention to the 'lapidary' nature of the Decree.[136] The Decree gives the reader remarkably little help in defining its terms, hence the wide variety in its interpretation. When speaking of the 'meaning' of the Decree, commentators have usually meant the process of identifying the referent of each term, the object or activity to which each term refers. But words have also an affective or emotive element, which expresses the user's feelings towards the subject of which he is speaking. In the Decree, the affective element is as significant as the referential element of the terms. In the case of the three terms εἰδωλόθυτον, αἷμα, πορνεία, the referent is difficult to identify, but the affective element is strong and unambiguous. In the case of πνικτόν, though, the opposite is true.

The letters of Paul reveal the difficulty of identifying the referent of the term εἰδωλόθυτον. One man might refer to a piece of meat as εἰδωλόθυτον, while to another it was simply βρῶμα (1 Cor. 8.1–13, 10.14–33). Might those in Corinth who had 'knowledge' have said that in eating things bought in the meat market (1 Cor. 10.25) they could not be eating εἰδωλόθυτον, 'for we know that an idol has no real existence' (1 Cor. 8.4)? If the Decree were known in Corinth,[137] there would be at least three ways of interpreting this term of the Decree: that no meat sacrificed to idols should be eaten (so those without 'knowledge', perhaps prompted as Barrett suggests by Peter); that since there was no reality to an idol, then εἰδωλόθυτον was a word without a referent, and any meat could be eaten (so those with 'knowledge'); and that although idols have no real existence, yet as long as there are those who believe there to be such things, then idol-meat should be avoided, for the sake of these people, and not because of the idol (Paul). Yet, for all this diversity, none of these positions flatly opposes the Decree. It is a peculiarity of the word that no one would say that they ate εἰδωλόθυτον. The pagan would say that he ate ἱερόθυτον, recognising the polemical element in the word εἰδωλόθυτον (see 1 Cor. 10.28). The Christian (or Jew) would say either that he ate no meat which had been contaminated by sacrifice, or that no such contamination was possible.

Similarly, the term αἷμα had a high affective value in Jewish circles, but the referential element was less clear. Αἷμα was to be avoided, but did this mean not drinking blood (as in some pagan sacrificial customs), or not eating meat with blood in it, or not shedding human blood? The uncertainty existed already in scripture: in the Noachic commands respect for blood is shown both by not eating blood (Gen. 9.4), and by not shedding human blood (Gen. 9.5f.). In the community of the Pseudo-Clementines, αἷμα could refer both to murder and to forbidden food.[138] Among Christians, too, Tertullian shows how the prohibition on blood could cover two referents when he argues: 'For if blood is forbidden, how much more do we understand human bloodshed to be forbidden' (*De Pud.* 12.5).

B. J. Malina has made a study of the use of the word πορνεία in the New Testament.[139] His work makes it clear that we should not look for precision in the referential aspect of this term. Its most significant feature is that it acts as a term of disapprobation concerning sexual conduct. It does not refer consistently to the same kind of conduct in all cases. In this context, he suggests that the background is Leviticus 18, and that πορνεία refers to 'the deviant lines of conduct listed in Lev. xviii,6–23'.[140] Malina's study indicates why attempts to identify the 'meaning' of this word (so significant for the 'Matthean exceptions') are difficult to bring to a satisfactory conclusion. While πορνεία has a very imprecise referential element, it has a highly charged expressive or affective element. Its use reminds us again of the 'lapidary' nature of the Decree.

The word πνικτόν is different. Its precise referent is hard for a modern reader to establish,[141] but it presumably would have been clear to contemporaries. As Burkitt observed: 'The word is technical and unfamiliar outside the poultry-shop and the kitchen.'[142] In comparison with the other terms, the referential value is narrow and precise, but it seems to have carried little or no expressive element in Judaism. Unlike 'idol-meat', 'blood', and 'fornication', 'things strangled' were not an object of concern, still less of revulsion, in Jewish circles. Πνικτόν is precisely the sort of word which might be used to define a less precise word, such as αἷμα .

The meaning of the Decree

To summarise the observations made so far: the contrast of 'ethical' and 'ritual' categories implies a judgement of value which may be foreign to the point of view of first- and second-century Christianity. It has been seen that moral teaching in the second-century church included elements which to a present-day observer appear both 'ethical' and 'ritual'. Contemporaries would not have made this distinction. The history of the text of the Decree cannot therefore be understood purely as the drift from an original 'ritual' sense to a later, second-century 'ethical' sense. The word πνικτόν does not fit a Jewish background as well as is sometimes supposed, and is a different type of word from the other terms of the Decree. For these reasons, the commonly accepted view of the text, which takes form 2 as the original, is questionable and the history of the text's development requires reconsideration.

The history of the text

Why should πνικτόν have been removed from the text, if it were originally present? We have no evidence of Christians in the second century objecting to food laws which proscribed the meat of strangled animals, and some evidence that they observed such proscriptions (see pp. 93–6 above). Moreover, the term occurs in Christian writings on food laws from the late second century, but not in Jewish treatments of improperly slaughtered meat, which were based on the categories found in Leviticus 17 (see pp. 96–9 above). It is more likely, then, that πνικτόν would be used in the Christian circles of the second century than in the Jewish environment of the first century which is the historical background of the Decree.

Tertullian's statement in *Apol* 9.13 may give the explanation of how this word entered the text of the Decree:

> Your error with regard to the Christians is shameful. We do not indeed eat blood in our meals, and moreover abstain also from strangled meat and carrion, so that we may by no means be contaminated by blood or that which lies between the viscera.

It was a desire to explain more clearly the prohibition on blood which led to the addition to the Decree of the prohibition on strangled meat. Origen had τὸ πνικτόν in his text, but believed that it was there in order to safeguard the blood-prohibition (*Contra Cels.* 8.30). Ambrosiaster was convinced that πνικτόν was a thoughtless addition to the Decree made by Greek copyists. No one, he argued, who knew Roman law would need to be told to abstain from murder, so αἷμα must have referred to the consumption of blood. But:

> Greek sophists, not understanding these things, but knowing that we should abstain from blood, adulterated the scripture, adding a fourth command, that we should also abstain from strangled meat. (*In Gal.* 2.2)

The question was evidently asked whether the prohibition on blood in the Decree meant only drinking blood, or whether it meant only bloodshed. The answer given by Tertullian, and written into the Decree, was that the consumption of blood took place if one ate meat from an animal which had been killed by strangulation or suffocation. The term used to express this conviction was taken, not from Judaism, but from the church's own teaching on the meaning of the blood prohibition.

It is difficult to give a date to this alteration. It had entered the text used by Clement of Alexandria, but must have been added at some time after the blood prohibition had become the subject of exegesis and comment. The first Christian writer after Luke to mention the prohibition on blood is Justin, who refers to it in the context of the Noachic commands (*Dial.* 20). The policy of pursuing 'safety at all costs' seems to have been characteristic of the second-century church in the matter of things sacrificed to idols.[143] Tertullian's comments suggest that a similar attitude existed towards the consumption of blood. In all probability, therefore, πνικτόν entered the text early in the second century.

The development of the text is mirrored in the witnesses. Forms 4 and 5 preserve the original three-membered Decree. In some texts, explanatory comments were added to clarify the point that the Decree forbade the consumption of animals killed by strangulation or suffocation, hence Gaudentius' 'from blood, that is, from strangled meat'.[144] Some copyists substituted πνικτόν for αἷμα, giving form 6 of the Decree. The most satisfactory way of emending the text, though, proved to be the addition of καὶ τοῦ πνικτοῦ as a fourth clause. The result was forms 2 and 3 of the Decree.

The Golden Rule in forms 3 and 5 of the Decree is usually taken to be self-evidently secondary. In fact, it raises three distinct but related problems. The first is whether it is likely that the Golden Rule would have been deleted if it had originally been present. The second problem has to do with its aptness: did it make sense to settle the Gentile controversy at Antioch by an appeal to the Golden Rule? The third problem arises from the observation that the Golden Rule may alter the Decree from a 'ritual' to an 'ethical' formula. Each of these problems seems to render it impossible that the Golden Rule stood in the author's text, while taken together the case against the Rule appears unanswerable. But there are indications that the presence of the Rule in Luke's text, if not in the Decree before its incorporation in Acts, is not as inept as is often supposed.

To take the third problem first: it has here been maintained that neither the absence of πνικτόν nor the presence of the Golden Rule necessarily alters the Decree from a 'ritual' to an 'ethical' code. The evidence we have from the second century suggests that the stipulations of the Decree were observed in their 'ritual' sense, even by people who knew the Decree in the supposedly 'ethical' forms 4 and 5. Tertullian would be an example of this attitude to the Decree.

Certainly 'ethical' justifications for the Decree were found in Christian thought from a very early point, just as 'ethical' justifications for Jewish practices are to be found. In both cases, this was an attempt to justify what was no longer self-justifying. In the case of the Decree, it was an inevitable result of the attempt to abstract certain provisions only from the body of Levitical purity laws. Taken in isolation from the wider corpus of which they were a part, the stipulations of the Decree were no longer elements with their place in a system;[145] they were an anomaly. They lacked a basis, and an alternative basis had to be found. Paul, it appears, pointed one way to finding such a basis. For εἰδωλόθυτον and πορνεία, this basis was found in responsibility to one's brother (1 Cor. 8 and 10; 1 Thess. 4.6). When Tertullian interpreted the blood-prohibition as including murder, he was continuing Paul's approach (*De Pud.* 12.4f.). Other ways of justifying the prohibitions were also found, however. The *Didache* and Clement of Alexandria enjoined abstinence from things sacrificed to idols because of the fear of eating the food of demons.[146] Alexandrian Christianity continued this type of justification (Origen, *Contra Cels.* 8.30). There were also Christians who continued to interpret the Decree within the framework of a wider corpus of laws of uncleanness. These groups did not need to justify the prescriptions of the Decree, because the regulations fitted into a coherent system. Such were the members of the community of the Pseudo-Clementines, who understood πορνεία, in a way quite consistent with the Levitical purity laws, to refer to the emission of sexual fluids.[147]

It is only with some reservations, therefore, that one can assent to Barrett's observation: 'Jewish Christianity [in the matter of things sacrificed to idols] triumphed, though Jewish Christians became less important in the church.'[148] Second-century Christians observed the regulations of the Decree, but their reasons for doing so varied. Some found ways of justifying their observance which owed nothing to Jewish Christianity. It is their attempts to justify their observance which have led their modern interpreters to suggest that the Apostolic Decree became an 'ethical' code in the course of the second century. But, as Grant has noted, people may continue to observe regulations when the justification for them has altered.[149] It was the fate of the Decree to become in the second century a practical code in search of a theological basis.

The motive for the prohibitions, as they appear in Acts, is fear of pollution. The term ἀλίσγημα (cf. Dan. 1.8), found in 15.20, probably expresses something of Luke's own understanding of the purpose of the Decree. The examples of Aristides and the Pseudo-Clementines, though, show that the Golden Rule could be combined with a list of 'ritual' precepts without the precepts losing their 'ritual' nature.[150] The Golden Rule, therefore, need not have turned the Decree into a moral code, and there is no unbridgeable gap between those forms of the Decree which have the Rule and those which do not.

A better way of understanding the significance of the Golden Rule's being attached to the Decree might be to begin with Manns's observation of the importance of the Rule in the instruction of converts to Judaism. From this he drew the conclusion that the forms of the Decree which have the Rule show a greater awareness of Jewish customs and are more likely to be original.[151] Manns drew attention to the celebrated story of R. Hillel in TB *Shabbat* 30a. Yet the Golden Rule was used also in the instruction of Christian converts.[152] It had an honoured place in the church's teaching, as is clear not only from the New Testament references (Matt. 7.12, Lk. 6.31), but also from the numerous citations of it in both its positive and negative forms in Christian writers of the early centuries.[153] Its presence in the Decree does not, then, necessarily point to a Jewish context, but it may be seen as transforming the Decree from an historical document relating to a particular problem (15.23) into an instrument of instruction having a wider significance. The Golden Rule changes the setting and not the sense of the Decree. It takes it from the specific circumstances of Antioch into the general διδαχή of the church.

This observation directly raises the second problem to do with the Golden Rule in the Apostolic Decree: its suitability to context. It made little sense to attempt to settle the questions raised in 15.1 by reference to the Golden Rule.[154] Although this observation is justified, it should also be noted that Luke himself did not believe that the use of the Decree was confined to the settlement of the Antioch controversy. The very fact that he has placed it here, at the centre and focal point of the book, suggests strongly that he believed that the Decree had a continuing importance for his readers.

The Decree had a twofold significance for Luke. It was, on one level, a product of specific circumstances (15.1). Luke recognised that it had an original audience in a particular and limited area (15.23). He narrates the promulgation of the Decree to this original audience (15.30f.). He also believed, though, that the Decree possessed a wider significance not merely as a document to settle a specific controversy, but as an instrument of instruction for converts. He demonstrates this not only by including it on three occasions, but by including a scene in which it is used beyond the confines of 'Antioch, Syria and Cilicia' (16.4f.). In Lycaonia, and perhaps beyond, Luke envisaged the decisions of the Council being handed on (παρεδίδοσαν 16.4). He does not mention the reading of the letter, as he did at Antioch (15.30f.), suggesting that Christian teachers using the Decree would not simply read the text, but give an exegesis of the Decree. Luke has himself given an example of how the Decree might be explained, by including the speech of James (15.13–21). Luke believed that the original purpose of the Decree was to quieten controversy in Antioch, and that it succeeded (15.31), but that it also had a wider function among churches beyond the original addressees, and that if it was made known and expounded among the churches at large, it would serve to strengthen them in the faith (16.5).

Kümmel observed rightly that the Western version of the Decree (form 5) expressed a desire to make the Decree into a regulation having validity for Christians of all places and in all times.[155] But this is precisely Luke's own desire. It would be quite in accordance with Luke's understanding of the present-day function of the Decree, as opposed to its original purpose, for him to have included the Golden Rule as a supplement to it.

The remaining problem is that it is hard to see why an originally present Golden Rule should have been omitted by scribes. It could be understood as a marginal note, appended to 15.29 to indicate something of the way in which the Decree was used in the instruction of converts, as described in 16.4. From there, it entered the text, first of 15.29, and then of 15.20.[156] If some copyists incorporated the note, while others omitted it, then two streams of textual tradition would arise.

The Apostolic Decree: conclusion

Both Western and non-Western textual traditions of the Decree have undergone addition. The original form is unlikely to have included πνικτόν. The term πνικτόν is probably an exegetical addition made in the second century to explain the meaning of αἷμα. Its presence in the non-Western textual tradition is therefore a later development. The presence of the Golden Rule in the Western tradition is also a development, but it is a development in a direction with which Luke was fully in sympathy.[157]

Two observations may be made on the basis of the argument followed here. The first is that the Apostolic Decree does not exist in two mutually exclusive forms – 'ethical' and 'ritual' – as is often supposed. Martini argued that the Decree was the only point at which there was a 'polarity' between the Western and non-Western texts of Acts.[158] It has here been argued, though, that the difference between the original Western form (5) and the original non-Western (4) is the difference between a Decree suited to its original purpose, and one suited to its contemporary function.[159] Both forms would express Luke's own convictions about the Decree. The second observation is that the Golden Rule could be well understood as an annotation to the text made by the author himself. The study of 11.1f. has brought up indications of an original text of Acts whose state was uncertain or incomplete (see pp. 86f. above). This observation may be of significance in understanding the origin of the Western text of Acts.

Lucanism: conclusion

The 'Lucanism' of the Western text of Acts may be examined either positively or negatively. Postively, one may look for indications that the language and theology of the Western text accords with that of Luke. Here, the work of Boismard and Lamouille in particular has revealed a convincingly Lucan colouring in the language of the Western text (see pp. 58–63 above). Negatively, one may look for signs that there is a gap between the language and outlook of Luke and those of the Western text. Our investigation of the language of the Western text has suggested that, while there are words and phrases found in the Western text of Acts and not in Luke's undisputed writings, the incidence of these is not so high as to preclude common authorship (p. 63 above).

Our study of three test-cases, in which there might be significant divergence between the Western text and the thought of Luke, has suggested that there is a good case for regarding the Western readings as Lucan. The Golden Rule in the Apostolic Decree, quite consistent with the Lucan presentation of the Decree, may have entered the text from a gloss. The non-Western text, by contrast, appears to have undergone editing, either to eliminate obscurity (11.2) or to express the caution typical of the second-century church (8.37, πνικτόν in 15.29). The following chapter considers the possibility that other Western readings may have begun as glosses or marginal annotations, and may also share a Lucan character. This investigation may give some indication of the processes from which our major text-forms of Acts have arisen.

4

MARGINAL ANNOTATION AND THE ORIGIN OF SOME WESTERN READINGS IN ACTS

Introduction

It has long been recognised that some Western readings in Acts appear to have entered the text from marginal readings or glosses. Such annotations, it has been argued, are the explanation for readings which are inconsistent with their context, either grammatically or in content, or which are overloaded and redundant in form.

This approach to the Western readings in Acts has been largely neglected since the generation of Clark and Streeter. Although it is occasionally referred to in recent treatments of the subject,[1] it deserves fuller consideration than it has received for some time. This chapter will first examine the variety of theses which have been proposed to explain some Western readings as originating in marginal notes. We shall then draw attention to some Western readings in Acts which appear to show evidence for the incorporation of marginal or interlined notes. It will then be possible to assess the significance of this feature of the Western textual tradition in Acts.

Scrivener suggested that Acts 8.37 made its way into the text from a marginal note. The credal statement was, he thought, first placed in the margin, and then worked into the text, being given a narrative framework. He noted that Irenaeus (*Adv.Omn.Haer.* 3.12.8) cited only the confession itself, showing both how early the words had entered the text, and what the original form had been.[2]

Blass made more comprehensive use of the notion of marginal annotation as the explanation of Western readings in Acts. In particular, he postulated marginal notes as the explanation of two phenomena: phrases which seem out of place, and expressions which are overloaded.

Acts 18.19D provides an example of displacement:

N–A²⁶
κατήντησαν δὲ εἰς Ἔφεσον
κἀκείνους κατέλιπεν αὐτοῦ,
αὐτὸς δὲ εἰσελθὼν εἰς
τὴν συναγωγὴν διελέξατο
τοῖς Ἰουδαίοις.

Codex D
κατηντήσας δὲ εἰς Ἔφεσον
καὶ τῷ ἐπιόντι σαββάτῳ
ἐκείνους κατέλιπεν ἐκεῖ
αὐτὸς δὲ εἰσελθὼν εἰς
τὴν συναγωγὴν διελέγετο
τοῖς Ἰουδαίοις.

Blass noticed that the phrase τῷ ἐπιόντι σαββάτῳ scarcely seems appropriate to its present position, but would be quite apt if it were attached to the information about Paul's synagogue visit. So he conjectured that at an earlier stage, the Western text had read: καὶ ἐκείνους κατέλιπεν ἐκεῖ αὐτὸς δέ

κατήντησαν δὲ εἰς Ἔφεσον τῷ ἐπιόντι σαββάτῳ εἰσελθὼν εἰς . . .

There was, therefore, an original version of the text which did not mention Paul's leaving Prisca and Aquila at this point.[3]

The overloaded nature of 15.5D also shows, Blass maintained, that two alternative versions have been run together, one properly belonging to the Western text and one to the non-Western.[4] Other points at which marginal annotation may account for Western readings, Blass suggested, were 1.9 and 20.2.[5]

Blass explained these phenomena by his theory of a double edition of Acts. The non-Western form of text (α) was taken from the final form of the work, as it was presented to Theophilus. The Western form (β) represents an earlier stage of the work, which may have been drawn from the author's working copy. Such a working copy might contain the author's marginal annotations, as Galen states was customary,[6] and they would show how the author intended to alter the text for the final form. If the author's working copy were transcribed by someone else, the scribe could have misunderstood these notes, and produced the sort of confused text found at 1.9, 15.5, 18.19, and 20.2.[7] Blass concluded: 'Thus Luke's autograph could have had recension β in the text, with the second in the margins.'[8]

That D was descended from a text with marginal annotations was one of the few points at which Weiss, Blass's most thorough critic, was willing to agree with him: 'That the ancestor of D had several interlined readings seems to me also to be beyond question.'[9] Weiss, indeed, pointed out several additional examples. There were cases, for instance, in which an interlined καί, τε, or δέ had been superfluously included, when it had been intended to replace a conjunction already present (2.3, 4.4, 5.22, 6.15, 7.39,54).[10] Other instances of the incorporation of marginal notes betray themselves because the copyist has written down two versions of a phrase, the text and the note, when in fact the latter should have taken the place of the former (1.5,17, 2.43,47, 7.26, 10.40, 13.29, 14.10, 16.19, 20.7,34, 21.21).[11] There is even evidence for such redundancy due to annotation within the Western text itself, at 14.2 and 18.20.[12]

Weiss, though, interpreted the evidence in a way quite different from Blass. Weiss postulated that the *Vorlage* of D had had a more pure form of Western text from that which D now exhibits. A copyist had annotated D with non-Western readings in places, and these had then been incorporated, contaminating and disturbing the text. Weiss argued that there are a few places at which this process may be detected with some certainty, and he cited 3.11,13, 16.4, 17.1, and 18.8.[13] Weiss's teatment of 3.13 illustrates his case:

N–A[26]	Codex D
κατὰ πρόσωπον Πιλάτου	κατὰ πρόσωπον Πιλάτου
κρίναντος ἐκείνου	τοῦ κρίναντος ἐκείνου
ἀπολύειν.	ἀπολύειν αὐτὸν θέλοντος.

Weiss suggested that the text of D had gone through three stages:

(1) an original Western form: κατὰ πρόσωπον Πιλάτου τοῦ ἀπολύειν αὐτὸν θέλοντος.

(2) collation with a non-Western witness led to the annotation
    κρίναντος ἐκείνου
    κατὰ πρόσωπον Πιλάτου τοῦ ἀπολύειν αὐτὸν θέλοντος.

(3) conflation of the two phrases created the present text of D by thoughtless insertion of κρίναντος ἐκείνου between τοῦ and ἀπολύειν.

In this way, Weiss was able to accept Blass's observation about evidence for the incorporation of marginal notes into the Western textual tradition, but was able also to dispute Blass's conclusion. Certainly, Weiss argued, there is evidence of annotation in the Western text, and in D in particular, but this has nothing to do with the work of the author; it is rather due to the conflation of two text-types by copyists.

Weiss's argument was thus an important and early recognition that the readings of D are not necessarily reliable indications of the primitive form of the Western text. His contention that some of the strikingly redundant or disordered readings of D may be due to conflation with the non-Western text has been taken up by several subsequent critics. Boismard and Lamouille, in particular, identify conflation of TA with TO as the cause of some of D's major defects.[14]

Rendel Harris also found evidence of marginal annotation in the text of D. He found a misplaced gloss in Acts 6.15. He maintained that D has incorporated the words ἑστῶτος ἐν μέσῳ αὐτῶν at the wrong place. They do not belong to the description of Stephen in 6.15 at all, but to that of the high priest in the following verse, 7.1. The Bezan Latin has the more original form of the gloss: *stans in medio eorum*. The nominative participle in the Latin shows that the phrase does not belong with what precedes (*et viderunt faciem eius quasi faciem angeli*), but with the succeeding phrase: *ait autem pontifex Stephano*. Harris argued that the intention of the gloss was to conform the scene more nearly to that of the trial of Jesus (cf. Mk. 14.60, καὶ ἀναστὰς ὁ ἀρχιερεὺς εἰς μέσον ἐπηρώτησεν τὸν Ἰησοῦν ...).[15]

Other passages which Harris thought were misplaced glosses were 15.29 (φερόμενοι ἐν τῷ ἁγίῳ πνεύματι belongs in the following verse, describing the envoys' journey)[16], 5.38 (μὴ μιάναντες τὰς χεῖρας may have been misplaced),[17] and 17.28 (τὸ καθ᾿ ἡμέραν was a misunderstood marginal correction of τῶν καθ᾿ ὑμᾶς in the next line; the annotator wished to alter it to τῶν καθ᾿ ἡμᾶς, but his note was misunderstood, and a copyist incorporated it as an additional phrase τὸ καθ᾿ ἡμέραν).[18]

Harris's proposals concerning 6.15 and 15.29 were severely criticised by Corssen.[19] His most cogent criticism, however, was directed against Harris's suggestion that the readings may have originated in Latin. Harris's proposal concerning 17.28 has attracted further consideration,[20] even if it has failed to win acceptance.

In 1900, A. Pott published a study of the Western text of Acts arising from his work on the minuscule 383 (which he called O).[21] Pott's main contention concerned the 'we-narrative': he proposed that a version of the narrative continued to circulate independently of Acts, and that from one version of it derive some of the readings of the Harclean Syriac, while from another and more corrupt version derive some of the readings of D and its allies. Pott's intricate argument generally failed to convince his readers.[22] One incidental observation of his work, though, was that Codex D showed evidence of the incorporation of marginal notes. He found examples at 14.20 (p. 7), 16.7 (p. 9), 17.7f. (pp. 33f.), 18.8 (p. 13), 20.4 (p. 15), and 21.36 (p. 15). Like Weiss, Pott argued that these annotations were 'corrections' of the underlying Western base of D by material drawn from the non-Western text. A. V. Valentine-Richards reviewed Pott's work carefully and concluded that the instances which Pott cited as examples of annotation could better be explained as cases of simple conflation.[23]

It should be noted that W. M. Ramsay held that the non-Western text of Acts had been contaminated by the incorporation of later glosses.[24] The Western text he believed to be a conscious second-century revision.[25]

B. H. Streeter suggested in his review of Clark's *Acts* that several witnesses to the Western text of Acts may have acquired their distinctive readings through the incorporation of marginal notes added to one of their ancestors. He drew attention in particular to the closely related minuscules 383 and 614,[26] which have a basically Byzantine type of text, but which exhibit Western readings in places. They may be descended from an ancestor arranged rather as the Harclean Syriac is, with marginal variant readings.[27] Streeter discussed a particular instance where marginal readings may have been brought into the text of 19.1.[28]

H. W. and C. F. D. Moule published two brief studies of certain confused passages in Acts.[29] The conventional explanation for these passages is that there was an originally coherent text, which has become confused in the course of transmission. H. W. and C. F. D. Moule, however, made the suggestion that the original text of Acts may itself have been confused at these points; that these were passages left by the author in note form, with alternative drafts lying side by side, and that the first copyists combined drafts which ought to have been taken as alternatives, thus, as H. W. Moule put it, sowing 'the seed of confusion for all time'.[30] The Moules' thesis is another type of theory which ascribes some features of the text of Acts to misunderstood annotation; in this case by the author himself. Although their studies were not concerned with the Western text in particular, their suggestion that Acts has been from the start in an uncertain textual state has profound potential implications for the study of the textual problem of Acts. This point will be pursued further later in this study.

Some attention, then, has been given to the possibility that the Western textual tradition in Acts owes some of its characteristics to marginal annotation, but the possibility has never been the subject of sustained enquiry.

That there are confused and conflated passages in Western witnesses, and in D particularly, is widely recognised. The uncertain questions are how this confusion has come about, and at what stage in the development of the tradition it took place. It has been generally supposed that the cause of confusion and conflation in D and its allies is the interpolation of non-Western material into the Western base of D *et al.*[31] On this view, there was once a more original and clearer version of the Western text in passages in which D is overloaded, repetitive, or confused. This more original version is frequently to be found in the Fleury palimpsest (it[55]), or in the readings of the Harclean Syriac margin. The contamination of 'Texte occidental' (TO) by 'Texte alexandrin' (TA) is one of the main types of degeneration which Boismard and Lamouille have detected in D's readings, and has frequently, they argue, led to incoherent readings representing a fusion of texts.[32]

But a different view is possible of these double readings in the Western tradition. It may be that D and other witnesses which give confused and redundant readings represent a more original version of the text, and those witnesses which give clearer readings may have been revised.

These opposing views can only be judged by consideration of individual variants. There is no *a priori* method of determining in which direction the Western textual tradition has developed. Of each reading it must be asked whether, when there is apparent evidence of conflation in D or in other witnesses, the conflated reading may not be the more original, and the clearer reading a development from it. And if the trail of Western textual history leads back to a text marked in its earliest stages by redundancy and misplacement of material, it must then be asked whether the Western tradition itself may not owe its origin to the incorporation of marginal annotations.

The studies which follow are of examples of variants in Acts which deserve attention because of their overloaded or confused character. If they show evidence of annotation, then it must be borne in mind that they are not likely to represent the sum total of all annotated material in the Western tradition. To establish the existence of annotation as a source of Western readings, it is enough for only some to betray their origins: others may have been incorporated in such a way as to be no longer recognisable.

Texts

(1) Acts 1.5

N–A[26]

ὅτι Ἰωάννης μέν ἐβάπτισεν
ὕδατι, ὑμεῖς δὲ ἐν πνεύματι
βαπτισθήσεσθε ἁγίῳ

οὐ μετὰ πολλὰς ταύτας
ἡμέρας.

Codex D

ὅτι Ἰωάνης μέν ἐβάπτισεν
ὕδατι, ὑμεῖς δὲ ἐν πνεύματι
ἁγίῳ βαπτισθήσεσθαι
καὶ ὃ μέλλεται λαμβάνειν
οὐ μετὰ πολλὰς ταύτας
ἡμέρας ἕως τῆς πεντηκοστῆς.

ἐν πνεύματι βαπτισθήσεσθε ἁγίῳ: ℵ* B 81. 915.

ἐν πνεύματι ἁγίῳ βαπτισθήσεσθε: D it[5]

βαπτισθήσεσθε ἐν πνεύματι ἁγίῳ: p[74] ℵ[c] A C E Ψ Maj. vg; CyrJ
(?Ps-)Did Or

καὶ ὃ μέλλεται λαμβάνειν: D* it[5.51.56.67.] vg[cav.lux.MM.tol.]; Ambstr
Aug (?Ps-)Aug[cath] Ephr Hil Max Ps-Vig.

ἕως τῆς πεντηκοστῆς: D*[33] it[5] sah cop[G67]; Aug Ephr.

There are three units of variation in the text of Acts 1.5. The first is the difference in the order of the words ἐν πνεύματι βαπτισθήσεσθε ἁγίῳ. The variation here is probably due, as Metzger suggests, to two different attempts to modify the chiastic structure of the text given by ℵ* B 81.[34]

The second and third variants are harder to explain. The second is the addition καὶ ὃ μέλλεται λαμβάνειν which is widely attested in the Western tradition. Ropes (*Beg.* III, p. 2) was probably correct to regard D's καὶ ὃ as an error for ὃ καί. As Weiss observed, it is a peculiar addition, because it seems to be repeating in other words what has already been expressed.[35] This additional Western material appears to be an exegetical comment on βαπτισθήσεσθε which has been brought into the text.

Equally interesting is the third variant, the addition of the words ἕως τῆς πεντηκοστῆς in a number of Western witnesses at the close of v. 5. Several commentators have taken this to be a later addition which can be explained either as the result of an interpolator's wish to be more specific about the time of the Spirit's coming,[36] or as part of the Western text's general concern with the Spirit.[37]

Against these views must be set three difficulties which Zahn[38] raised:

(1) If this additional material is intended to refer to the coming of the Spirit at Pentecost, then it should say '*at* Pentecost' rather than '*until* Pentecost'.

(2) Luke is here ostensibly referring to the teaching of Jesus before the crucifixion, and it would be inept to make Jesus, before the passion, already set Pentecost as the time of the Spirit's coming.[39]

(3) Acts 2.1 suggests by its phrasing ('And when the day of Pentecost had fully come ... ') that Pentecost is already known to the reader as a significant point, but without the Western reading at 1.5, Pentecost is unknown to the reader until he comes across it at 2.1.

Zahn's conclusion was that in the Western reading 1.5 is to be taken as a parenthesis, and that ἕως τῆς πεντηκοστῆς refers back to v. 4: 'Do not depart from Jerusalem, but await the promise of the Father which you heard from me (because John indeed baptised with water, but you shall be baptised with the Holy Spirit after these few days) until Pentecost.' Since Zahn followed Blass's view of the textual history of Acts, he proposed that the Western form, with v. 5 in parentheses, was the original version, but that when Luke prepared the second version of the text, he struck out ἕως τῆς πεντηκοστῆς, so that Jesus' speech was made to conclude with the promise of the Spirit. The elimination of ἕως τῆς πεντηκοστῆς was part of the author's work of abbreviating and tidying the text for the second edition.

Ropes also regarded ἕως τῆς πεντηκοστῆς as referring back to v. 4 (although he did not think that it was Lucan[40]), but Metzger has criticised Ropes's interpretation of the reading as 'over subtle'.[41]

The phrase ἕως τῆς πεντηκοστῆς may be another exegetical phrase, like ὃ μέλλετε λαμβάνειν earlier in the verse. In this case, it would be an attempt to interpret ταύτας ἡμέρας. A reader might ask: what are 'these days'? The exegetical gloss would provide the answer: 'the days until Pentecost'. The awkwardness of the two notices of time coming together might suggest that it was not intended to be incorporated quite as bluntly as it has been.

On the other hand, Ropes and Zahn may have been correct to connect ἕως τῆς πεντηκοστῆς with v. 4. 'Do not depart from Jerusalem until Pentecost, but await the promise of the Father' would be a perfectly comprehensible statement. And yet, as Metzger states, as the text stands it is not easy for the reader to

make the connection between 'Do not depart from Jerusalem . . . '
in v. 4 and ' . . . until Pentecost' in v. 5. However, if ἕως τῆς
πεντηκοστῆς were a marginal note intended for v. 4, but wrongly
inserted in v. 5, then the observations of Zahn and of Metzger could
be accepted. It may indeed belong with v. 4, but in its present
position the connection with v. 4 is not very clear.

Of these two interpretations, the second is probably to be
preferred. The adjectival use of ἕως which the first interpretation
presupposes ('the days until Pentecost') is possible (see Matt. 1.17:
αἱ γενεαὶ . . . ἕως Δαυίδ), but is less likely than the connection
with the command not to depart from Jerusalem.

If ἕως τῆς πεντηκοστῆς were originally a marginal note,
whether intended for v. 4 or for v. 5, its present position could be
understood if it is supposed that a copyist who found 'until
Pentecost' in the margin of his exemplar thought that the correct
place to put it was with the reference to the coming of the Holy
Spirit, and after the other notice of time, that is, at the end of v. 5.

The motive for the addition of the words ἕως τῆς πεντηκοστῆς
is almost certainly to be found in 2.1. The addition to 1.5 places a
marker in the text to indicate that Pentecost will be a significant
terminus. It is possible that a later annotator noticed that Pentecost
had not been mentioned before 2.1, but the addition ἕως τῆς
πεντηκοστῆς is the sort of alteration which an author might make
in revising the text of his work.

    (2)   Acts 3.11

N–A[26]	Codex D
κρατοῦντος δὲ αὐτοῦ τὸν	ἐκπορευομένου δὲ τοῦ Πέτρου
Πέτρον καὶ τὸν Ἰωάννην	καὶ Ἰωάνου
	συνεξεπορεύετο κρατῶν
	αὐτούς
συνέδραμεν πᾶς	ὁ λαὸς οἱ δὲ θαμβηθέντες
	ἔστησαν
πρὸς αὐτοὺς ἐπὶ τῇ στοᾷ	ἐν τῇ στοᾷ
τῇ καλουμένῃ Σολομῶντος	ἡ καλουμένη Σολομῶνος
ἔκθαμβοι	ἔκθαμβοι

ἐκπορευομένου . . . αὐτούς: D it[5.55] (it[55] then continues: *et concur-
rit omnis populus ad eos*) cop[G67] (But when Peter and John came,
he went with them, while he clung to them).

οἱ δὲ θαμβηθέντες ... ἔκθαμβοι: D it⁵ cop^G67 (Then all the people gathered to them. They stood astonished in the portico called Solomon's).

ἐπὶ τῇ στοᾷ: Maj.

ἐν τῇ στοᾷ: D 104. 1838.

om. τῇ καλουμένῃ: 1838 eth.

The Western variants at Acts 3.11 pose problems of content and of construction. The problems of content have attracted more attention than those of construction, but both are of interest.

The interest in the content of the readings in this verse concentrates on the topography of the Temple, as each reading portrays it. There is general agreement that Luke's 'Beautiful Gate' is the 'Corinthian Gate' of Josephus[42] and the 'Nicanor Gate' of the Mishnah.[43] The 'Beautiful Gate' would therefore have been one of the entrances to the Temple proper, rather than one of the external gates of the Temple area, and was most likely to have been the gate on the Eastern side which separated the court of the women from the court of the Gentiles.[44] In all probability, Solomon's Portico ran along the eastern side of the Temple area.[45] In Acts 3.8, Peter, John, and the lame man went into the Temple, presumably through the Beautiful Gate. So, in order for them to reach Solomon's Portico in 3.11, they would need to have come out of the Temple again. The Western reading, in all three of its witnesses, supplies the information lacking in the non-Western text, that Peter, John, and the lame man came out of the Temple before they reached Solomon's Portico (ἐκπορευομένου ... συνεξεπορεύετο). Because of this, it is generally recognised that the Western reading shows evidence of accurate knowledge of the Temple, a recognition shared even by critics who regard the Western text generally as a late development.[46]

Some commentators conclude that Luke thought of the Portico as being within the Temple proper, and that the author of the Western reading was better informed than Luke on this point.[47] Others, however, have maintained that the Western reading does no more than make explicit what is already implied in the other reading, and that it is not certain that Luke envisaged the Portico within the Temple.[48] The second view is more convincing: Luke, who has brought the crowd together in v. 9 within the Temple, brings them together again in v. 11, and by doing so suggests that he envisaged a change of scene. There is not a narrative contradiction between the two readings in v. 11, but the Western reading is an accurate clarification of what is implied in the alternative text.

Less frequently noticed is the construction of the Western reading. Metzger alludes to one point: that the solecism of D (ἐν τῇ στοᾷ ἡ καλουμένη κτλ) shows that the additional material cannot be Lucan.[49] But not every grammatical error in D – and there are many of them – is original to the Western text. The omission of *tau* is probably the careless blunder of a copyist.[50]

The real problems of the reading of D at 3.11 are, in the first place, the rapid and unclear changes of subject (Peter and John – the lame man – the crowd), and in the second, the redundancy of the final word ἔκθαμβοι.

It must first be asked whether the rapid changes of subject found in D here are part of the earliest Western text at all, since both it[55] and cop[G67] have easier readings. But it is likely that the harder reading of D can better explain the origin of the other two texts than *vice versa*. The Latin witness seems to have resolved the difficulties by expanding συνεξεπορεύετο to *simul et ipse prodibat* – thus clarifying the alteration in subject[51] – and then by introducing the non-Western material in order to make clear that the crowd ran together in the Portico. The Coptic MS also seems to have a mixed text. Its underlying base seems to have been a text like that of D, but it also has the clause συνέδραμεν πᾶς ὁ λαὸς πρὸς αὐτούς. The clause is introduced by 'then', but there is no conjunction connecting the clause with what follows, suggesting that it has been inserted from the non-Western text in order to account for the otherwise unidentified people who appear immediately afterwards ('*They* stood astonished etc.'). Such treatment of the text is characteristic of cop[G67] elsewhere also.[52]

In the reading of D, it is not clear who was standing in the Portico, or how they came to be there. Weiss thought that the author of the D reading suppressed the phrase συνέδραμεν ... αὐτούς because he judged that it was unnecessary after v. 9 (καὶ εἶδεν πᾶς ὁ λαὸς αὐτόν).[53] But the Western reading narrates a change of scene between v. 9 and v. 11, so it ought to have been necessary to have brought the crowd together in the new setting, rather than saying that 'they' (the same people who had been inside the Temple, or another group?) 'stood' (were they there already, or had they gathered there from somewhere else?) in the Portico called Solomon's. Oddly, then, the Western text describes the apostles and the lame man *in motion* (ἐκπορευομένου ... συνεξεπορεύετο), but describes the crowd *statically* (ἔστησαν), while the non-Western describes the crowd's movement (συνέδραμεν), but not that of the central figures. The two versions give the impression, not of alternatives, but of parts of a whole which have been poorly put together.[54]

The redundancy of D's passage θαμβηθέντες ... ἔκθαμβοι has been ascribed to the contamination of the text of D by the introduction of the word ἔκθαμβοι from the other text.[55] That is one explanation, and certainly, cop[G67] lacks anything corresponding to D's ἔκθαμβοι. It may be that there was an originally coherent Western reading, which D has spoiled, but there is an alternative. It is possible that cop[G67] represents a text which has been tidied up. Why, after all, should a scribe, supplementing his Western base from the non-Western text, borrow the word ἔκθαμβοι while overlooking the far more significant and useful συνέδραμεν πᾶς ὁ λαός?

It is perhaps more likely that the D text is the more original Western reading here. It is also likely that it is not a careful revision of the alternative text, but the result of incorporating new material into the text without proper thought for the consequences. The new material refers to the apostles, the lame man, and the crowd, and has been used as an alternative to the passage κρατοῦντος ... αὐτούς, which also contains the same elements. However, having reached ἐπὶ/ἐν τῇ στοᾷ, the Western reading reverts to the common text. The now redundant ἔκθαμβοι would, then, not be an intrusion into the Western reading, but evidence that the additional material ἐκπορευομένου ... ἔστησαν had been joined to the more usual text in an inconsistent manner.

The simplest way to account for the peculiarities of the Western version of Acts 3.11 would be to suppose that marginal or interlined notes have been incorporated into the text, without being fully assimilated. Such marginal notes might have looked like this (with the marginal notes underlined):

	ἐκπορευομένου τοῦ Πέτρου καὶ Ἰωάννου
<u>συνεξεπορεύετο</u>	κρατοῦντος δὲ αὐτοῦ τὸν Πέτρον
<u>κρατῶν αὐτούς.</u>	καὶ τὸν Ἰωάννην συνέδραμεν πᾶς
<u>οἱ δὲ θαμβηθέντες</u>	ὁ λαὸς πρὸς αὐτοὺς ἐπὶ τῇ στοᾷ
<u>ἔστησαν</u>	τῇ καλουμένῃ Σολομῶνος ἔκθαμβοι.

The marginal material was not intended to replace συνέδραμεν πᾶς ὁ λαός, but to supplement it, otherwise the crowd would not have been brought together in the new scene outside the Temple. Nor should the material be taken as a single block. Ἐκπορευομένου δὲ τοῦ Πέτρου καὶ Ἰωάννου established that Peter and John had left the Temple before the scene in vv. 11ff. had begun. The phrase συνεξεπορεύετο κρατῶν αὐτούς clearly had to follow the reference to Peter and John's leaving the Temple, so that the healed man was also brought into the new scene. Then a reference to the crowd was necessary (συνέδραμεν πᾶς ὁ λαός) before the phrase οἱ δὲ θαμβηθέντες ἔστησαν could make sense, and that phrase will then have been a substitute for ἔκθαμβοι. The Western text of Acts 3.11 is awkward, in other words, because it has been made up of separate marginal notes, which have been run together. The copyist who incorporated συνεξεπορεύετο ... ἔστησαν thought that he had an alternative to συνέδραμεν πᾶς ὁ λαός, when he should have realised that he had an introduction to it (συνεξεπορεύετο κρατῶν αὐτούς) and a sequel for it (οἱ δὲ θαμβηθέντες ἔστησαν).

The intention of the annotator, then, seems to have been to produce a text like this: ἐκπορευομένου δὲ τοῦ Πέτρου καὶ τοῦ Ἰωάννου συνεξεπορεύετο κρατῶν αὐτοὺς [καὶ] συνέδραμεν πᾶς ὁ λαὸς πρὸς αὐτοὺς ἐπὶ τῇ στοᾷ τῇ καλουμένῃ Σολομῶντος, οἱ δὲ θαμβηθέντες ἔστησαν.

The linguistic character of the additional material is indecisive. Among the eight words of the extra material, as set out above, there are two non-Lucan terms, συνεκπορεύεσθαι and θαμβεῖσθαι. However, since ἐκπορεύεσθαι has been used already, συν-εκπορεύεσθαι suggests itself as an easily formed compound, and an apt word to describe the man's movements. In addition to which, the absolute use of ἐκπορεύεσθαι is exclusively Lucan in the New Testament.[56]

The origin of the Western text of Acts 3.11, then, may well lie with marginal notes upon the text, made by a reader who not only had paid careful attention to the narrative, but who also appears to have known something of the topography of the Temple. The notes have been incorporated, though, by an inept hand, giving rise to the cumbersome text given by D, which later scribes and commentators have rightly recognised stands in need of improvement.

(3)   Acts 3.13

N–A[26]	Codex D
κατὰ πρόσωπον Πιλάτου	κατὰ πρόσωπον Πειλάτου
κρίναντος ἐκείνου	τοῦ κρίναντος ἐκείνου
ἀπολύειν.	ἀπολύειν αὐτὸν θέλοντος.

τοῦ κρίναντος . . . θέλοντος: D it⁵ (om τοῦ + θέλοντος D^corr)
illo volente eum dimittere: it⁵⁵
when he wished to release him: cop^G67
when he wished to deliver him from you alive: eth
cum remittere eum vellet: Ir^lat
volentis eum dimittere: Jer
who wished to release him:.Eph

As has already been noted (p. 109), Weiss proposed a way of understanding the textual development of this passage. His thesis was that the text of D arose through the incorporation of the non-Western κρίναντος ἐκείνου into the Western textual base on which D depends. It was one of the five passages at which Weiss thought it was reasonably certain that the text of D had been contaminated by marginal notes drawn from the non-Western text.

Other commentators have agreed that the text of D here has been created by the incorporation of material which did not initially belong to the text, however the incorporation may have come about. Blass noted the 'contamination' of D.[57] Ropes and Lake and Cadbury were also of the opinion that two texts had been combined to create the present text of D.[58] Boismard and Lamouille, too, judge D to have a 'double reading' here, constructed from TA and TO.[59] There can be no question that D's reading is unsatisfactory and overloaded. But it may be asked whether D has become overloaded by conflation of two originally clearer texts, or whether the other Western witnesses are in fact secondary developments from a text like that of D.

It is apparent that there are two elements in the versions of this passage, one of which emphasises the *decision* of Pilate to release Jesus (Majority text), and the other of which emphasises his *desire* to do so (it⁵⁵, cop^G67, eth, Ir, Eph, Jer).[60] The peculiarity of D is to combine the two.[61] Which is likely to be the earlier form of the Western reading?

Weiss reconstructed the uncontaminated Western reading as τοῦ ἀπολύειν αὐτὸν θέλοντος. Boismard and Lamouille based their reconstructed TO here on cop^G67 and Ephr: θέλοντος ἀπολύειν αὐτόν. On their view in D it^{5.55} and eth, the pronoun ἐκείνου has been added under the influence of the Majority text. D has also added τοῦ in order to create an apposition: Πιλάτου ... τοῦ κρίναντος, and it has repositioned θέλοντος at the end of the sentence (although it is accompanied in this by Ir^{lat}).[62]

The great merit of Weiss's proposal was its simplicity: the words κρίναντος ἐκείνου had simply been borrowed from the non-Western text and inserted into D's Western base. But Weiss's suggestion does not account for the other forms of text in the Western tradition. Boismard and Lamouille are able to account for these other forms, but their argument is based on the faithfulness of Ephraem, the Latin version of Irenaeus, and cop^G67. Witnesses such as these are perhaps least helpful when the point at issue is one of exact wording and sentence order. Each of these witnesses, and the Ethiopic and it^{55} also, evidently had something corresponding to the Western material here. But given the limitations of Latin, Syriac, Coptic, and Ethiopic in representing Greek, and bearing in mind also the opportunities for licence in translation, and for inexact citation, it is impossible to be certain about the precise state of the Greek text from which these witnesses are derived. It must also be asked, if Boismard and Lamouille are correct about the textual history of Acts 3.13, what could the motive have been for the progressive transformation of the innocuous and coherent TO into the present state of D? It is possible to see how each step might have happened, but less clear why it should have done.

The history of the text might be better understood if the simpler Western readings were regarded as developments from an initial reading like that of D, rather than as precursors of it. Weiss's point that the redundancy in the text of D could be due to marginal annotation was well made, and could stand in a revised version of the history of the text. We might propose the following stages in the text's development:

τοῦ αὐτὸν θέλοντος

(1) κατὰ πρόσωπον Πιλάτου κρίναντος ἐκεινου ἀπολύειν

The underlined words represent postulated interlined notes, intended to guide a revision of the text. The point of the annotation was to contrast Pilate, who wished to release Jesus, with Peter's hearers, who wished to have him killed. The corrected version would have been: κατὰ πρόσωπον Πιλάτου τοῦ ἀπολύειν αὐτὸν θέλοντος. But the transcriber wanted to retain both text and annotation, and the text he in turn produced was:

(2) κατὰ πρόσωπον Πιλάτου τοῦ κρίναντος ἐκείνου ἀπολύειν αὐτὸν θέλοντος (D* it⁵).

Subsequent copyists recognised the awkwardness of the expression, and improved it, producing the secondary Western forms noted in the apparatus above, including: κατὰ πρόσωπον Πιλάτου κρίναντος ἐκεινου ἀπολύειν αὐτὸν Dᶜᵒʳʳ.

In this way, the range of textual evidence can be accounted for. The strangely divergent forms of this reading are not stages on the way to the eventual production of D's reading, but represent a variety of attempts to deal with a text which, in its earlier form, had resembled D. On Boismard and Lamouille's view, the text of Irenaeus (if correctly reconstructed) is rather odd; it has not followed D and it⁵⁵ in incorporating extraneous material from TA, and yet it has evolved D's word order, putting θέλοντος at the end of the sentence. If Irenaeus' text and it⁵⁵ are precursors of the reading of D, then this is an anomaly. But if they are independent corrections of a text like that of D, these agreements and divergences may be easily understood.

The motive for the annotation behind the Western readings appears to have been to emphasise Pilate's willingness to release Jesus. This emphasis is typical of Luke among the Synoptists. While Matthew emphasises Pilate's detachment ('Whom do *you* wish that I release for you?', Matt. 27.17,21, and see also 27.24f.), and Mark Pilate's malleability (Mk. 15.15), in Luke the stress falls on Pilate's desire to acquit Jesus (Lk. 23.4–6,13–16,20,22 and note particularly 23.20: θέλων ἀπολῦσαι τὸν Ἰησοῦν).[63] It would be quite in accord with Luke's presentation of Pilate to portray his action as springing from personal disposition, although it is also to be noted that Luke is the only Synoptist to narrate that Pilate had *decided* to release Jesus (on two occasions, Lk. 23.16,22). Both the usually accepted text of Acts 3.13, therefore (with κρίναντος), and the postulated annotation (with θέλοντος), contain characteristically Lucan emphases.

(4) Acts 6.1

N–A²⁶	Codex D
Ἐν δὲ ταῖς ἡμέραις ταύταις	Ἐν δὲ ταύταις ταῖς ἡμέραις
πληθυνόντων τῶν μαθητῶν	πληθυνόντων τῶν μαθητῶν

N–A[26]	Codex D
ἐγένετο γογγυσμὸς τῶν	ἐγένετο γογγυσμὸς τῶν
Ἑλληνιστῶν	Ἑλληνιστῶν
πρὸς τοὺς Ἑβραίους	πρὸς τοὺς Ἑβραίους
ὅτι παρεθεωροῦντο	ὅτι παρεθεωροῦντο
ἐν τῇ διακονίᾳ τῇ καθημερινῇ	ἐν τῇ διακονίᾳ καθημερινῇ
αἱ χῆραι αὐτῶν.	αἱ χῆραι αὐτῶν
	ἐν τῇ διακονίᾳ
	τῶν Ἑβραίων.

ἐν τῇ διακονίᾳ τῶν Ἑβραίων: D* it[5]

quod in cottidiano ministerio viduae Graecorum a ministris
Hebraecorum discupierentur: it[55]

eo quod despicerentur in ministerio quotidiano vidue eorum a
ministris hebreorum: vg[MM]

because daily the ministers of the Hebrews were overlooking the
widows of the Hellenists in the alms: cop[G67]

(On the significance of D*, see n. 33.)

The common element of the Western readings at Acts 6.1 is the
notion that the daily alms were in the hands of the 'Hebrews'. It is
less clear whether the Western text originally spoke of the 'ministers of the Hebrews' (it[55], vg[MM], cop[G67]), or of the 'ministry of the
Hebrews' (D).

The reading 'ministers of the Hebrews' has in its favour that it
occurs in three apparently independent witnesses (note the differences between it[55] and vg[MM]), while 'ministry of the Hebrews' is
only in D. It is possible to see how the reading of D could have
given rise to the alternative reading; copyists may have noticed the
repetition ἐν τῇ διακονίᾳ ... ἐν τῇ διακονίᾳ, and may also, as
Zahn suggested, have assumed that διακονία was here a way of
describing the work of deacons in their own day.[64] ἐν τῇ διακονίᾳ is
the more difficult reading. However, to accept the reading of D as
the more primitive means also assuming that the same alteration
('ministry' to 'ministers') has been made independently by all the
other witnesses. It is not possible to be certain about the original
reading in these circumstances. The balance of probability here
suggests that the reading of D is a development from the reading of
the other witnesses, although as the harder reading it cannot be
entirely dismissed.

The purpose of the Western material in Acts 6.1 is bound up with the larger problems to do with 'Hebrews', 'Hellenists', and the appointment of the Seven. Epp has argued that the D-text here is anti-Judaic:

> [The reading] specifies that it is the 'Hebrews' (i.e. Judaizing Jews) who were at fault in the dispute between these 'Hebrews' and the 'Hellenists' (i.e. Graecizing Jews) in the church.[65]

Epp's comment may be a valid explanation of the purpose of the additional material, but it does not address the problem of the surprising *form* which the material has taken. The primitive form of the reading appears to be that shared by D and vg^{MM}, which agree exactly in construction, and differ only in the variant 'ministers'/ 'ministry'. The other two witnesses seem to offer paraphrastic developments of this text. If the Western text is indeed a revision of Acts, why has the reference to the Hebrews been added in a sort of appendix to the passage, rather than being integrated into it? Why not some such text as: παρεθεωροῦντο αἱ χῆραι αὐτῶν ὑπὸ τῶν διακόνων τῶν Ἑβραίων ἐν τῇ διακονίᾳ καθημερινῇ? – the sort of text, in other words, towards which it[55] and cop^{G67} appear to be moving?

The answer appears to be that the phrase ὑπὸ τῶν διακόνων τῶν Ἑβραίων/ ἐν τῇ διακονίᾳ τῶν Ἑβραίων is a gloss, incorporated in the simplest way, by the expedient of putting it at the end of the passage to which it belongs. It glosses the words ἐν τῇ διακονίᾳ καθημερινῇ, and was added by an annotator who believed that the 'daily alms' were distributed by 'the servants of the Hebrews' (or, following D, that the 'daily alms' were 'the alms of the Hebrews').

The distinctive feature of the Western reading at Acts 6.1 is, then, that it makes the 'Hebrews' responsible for the daily alms. In doing this, how well does it represent Luke's portrayal of the situation?

It is often supposed that the Twelve were in charge of the distribution of alms mentioned in 6.1, because of their reply in 6.2, 'It is not right for us to leave the word of God to serve tables', and because of Luke's note in 4.34f. that 'There was not a needy person among them, for as many as were possessors of lands or houses sold them, and brought the proceeds of what was sold, and laid it at the apostles' feet, and distribution was made to each as any had need.' But to understand Luke's meaning in this way creates difficulties in 6.1f. It would mean that the Twelve, because of the growth in the numbers of the disciples, decided to 'overlook' the Hellenists' widows in their charitable disbursements. The Hellenists then began to grumble against the 'Hebrews', rather than against the Twelve. The Twelve then defended their action by saying that it was not right for them to abandon the word of God to serve tables.[66] But if they were not willing to serve tables, then who would look after the non-Hellenist widows? And if they could look after some of the widows, but not all, why had the Twelve begun to discriminate against the Hellenists? The words of the Twelve in 6.1f. look more like the refusal to undertake a new responsibility, rather than abandonment of a responsibility already undertaken.[67]

Luke's meaning becomes clearer if the 'daily alms' of 6.1 are separated from the previous notices of gifts to the needy in Acts. There has been nothing previously in Acts to suggest that a daily distribution took place in the Christian community at Jerusalem.[68] The διαμερισμός of 2.45 and the διάδοσις of 4.35 were for anyone in need, and yet at 6.1 the Hellenists complain quite specifically that their widows were being overlooked. The inference is that the διακονία καθημερινή was different from the Christian διαμερισμός and διάδοσις. Luke gives no reason to suppose that the 'daily alms' of 6.1 were the responsibility of the Christian community at all. It would make better sense to suppose that these alms were given by the 'Hebrews', hence the Hellenists' complaint against *them* rather than the Twelve, and that they were intended for widows, unlike the provision which Luke has twice described as being for anyone in need (2.45, 4.35).

The Western text has therefore correctly interpreted Luke's meaning at 6.1. It may have inferred that the 'daily alms' were the responsibility of the 'Hebrews' from the mention of 'Hebrews' earlier in the verse,[69] but it at least has not followed the false trail laid by 2.45 and 4.35, and supposed that the 'daily alms' were the responsibility of the apostles.

One cannot leave Acts 6.1, though, without asking to whom Luke was referring when he wrote of 'Hebrews'. The widely accepted interpretation is that 'Hebrews' and 'Hellenists' were parties within the church, and that we here have to do with a significant division within the primitive church, a division which Luke portrays in a less serious light than the reality warranted.

Without doubt, the story of Acts 6.1ff. has to do with the rise of an identifiable 'Hellenist' group within the church. 'Hellenists', though, were not all Christians (9.29), nor, we may suspect, were

'Hebrews'. In other contexts (but not in Luke, who uses the word only here) 'Hebrew' is used as an affirmation of loyalty to Judaism; it is likely to have the same connotation here, in which case the 'Hebrews' of Acts 6.1 would be those Jews, within the Christian movement and beyond it, who were marked by faithfulness to the traditions of Judaism.[70]

The 'daily alms' given by the 'Hebrews' to the widows would thus be a charitable institution of the majority community in Jerusalem. The overlooking of the Hellenist widows may be taken as a sign that in the view of traditional Jews in Jerusalem, the Hellenist Christians were no longer within the pale of Judaism. This division between a wing of the Jerusalem church acceptable to traditional Judaism and one unacceptable to it seems mirrored elsewhere also.[71] If this interpretation of 'Hebrews' in Acts 6.1 is correct, then the clash of Hebrews and Hellenists in that verse was not so much a matter of party division within the church, as of the status of Christian Hellenists within Judaism. Seen in that light, the appointment of the Seven becomes, not merely an isolated incident in which the danger of a division within the church was, in Luke's view, averted, but the first intimation of trouble for the Hellenists from the conservative forces in Jerusalem.

If the 'Hebrews' of Acts 6.1 are conservative Jews, then 6.1–6 does more than introduce the figure of Stephen; it represents the beginning of the persecution of the Hellenists (of which the repercussions will occupy 6.8–8.4), and it enables Luke to show, in the story of the appointment of the Seven by the Twelve, that the church stood united in the face of external pressures which might have divided those zealous for the Law (21.20) from those who called no one common or unclean (10.28).

When the Western text places 'the daily alms' in the hands of the Hebrews, it seems to show an understanding of Luke's portrayal of this initial move in the Hellenist crisis.

(5)   Acts 14.2

N–A[26]	Codex D
οἱ δὲ ἀπειθήσαντες Ἰουδαῖοι	οἱ δὲ ἀρχισυνάγωγοι τῶν Ἰουδαίων καὶ οἱ ἄρχοντες τῆς συναγωγῆς

N–A[26]	Codex D
ἐπήγειραν	ἐπήγαγον αὐτοῖς διωγμὸν
	κατὰ τῶν δικαίων
καὶ ἐκάκωσαν τὰς ψυχὰς	καὶ ἐκάκωσαν τὰς ψυχὰς
τῶν ἐθνῶν	τῶν ἐθνῶν
κατὰ τῶν ἀδελφῶν.	κατὰ τῶν ἀδελφῶν
	ὁ δὲ κύριος ἔδωκεν
	ταχὺ εἰρήνην.

ἐπήγειραν + διωγμόν: E 383. 614. 1108. 1518. 1611. 1799. 2138. 2147. 2412. it[50.51.54.58.61.62.63.] syr[h].

οἱ δὲ ἀρχισυνάγωγοι . . . τῶν δικαίων: D it[5] (it[5] gives *incitaverunt* in place of ἐπήγαγον and om. αὐτοῖς)
syr[hmg] (om. τῶν Ἰουδαίων, τῆς συναγωγῆς, αὐτοῖς, κατὰ τῶν δικαίων)
Ephr ('The elders indeed having risen up persecuted the just men').

ὁ δὲ κύριος . . . εἰρήνην: D E (ὁ δὲ θεὸς εἰρήνην ἐποίησεν) it[5.50(as E).51.54.58.59.(61).63.]

vg[654.1186.1189.1199.1213.1258.1259.1260.1266.1277.1282.gk629.]

syr[hmg] cop[G67] nedl[2] prov ger[tepl];
Cass Bede (as E)

Acts 14.2 contains the first in a series of variants which occur in the narrative of the ministry of Paul and Barnabas in Lycaonia, and which mark 14.1–10 in particular.

The Western readings in 14.2 have attracted considerable attention. It has been argued that they represent attempts to explain more fully the course of events at Iconium.[72] It can be maintained that this attempt rests on a misunderstanding of the Majority text. So Haenchen has argued that the aorists of 14.2 are ingressive: the unpersuaded Jews *began* to stir up trouble for Paul and Barnabas, but the result of their action will not be clear until v. 5. The Western reviser, though, mistook Luke's meaning. He supposed that v. 2 meant that the persecution of Paul and Barnabas had already begun, and attempted to make this interpretation explicit in his alterations to the text. However, finding in v. 3 that Paul and Barnabas' work continued 'for a substantial time', the reviser was obliged to insert the clause 'But the Lord quickly gave peace' in order to explain how this continuation was possible.[73]

As Haenchen recognised, though, there are peculiarities of construction in the Western reading at Acts 14.2: 'here αὐτοῖς and κατὰ τῶν δικαίων (formed on κατὰ τῶν ἀδελφῶν in the B text) are competitive readings (as for that matter may be ἀρχισυνάγωγοι and ἄρχοντες κτλ)'.[74] The puzzling nature of these variants was succinctly put by Conzelmann: 'The W-Recension has revised the whole passage, but produced nonsense.'[75] Why should 'competitive readings' occur in D, readings which in this case can hardly be ascribed to conflation of Western and non-Western texts, since both the competitive readings are purely Western? And how has it happened that a recension of the text has produced nonsense? An error of transcription might produce a nonsensical reading, but it is more difficult to see why a reviser should do so.

A striking feature of D's text is its redundancy.[76] The words τῶν Ἰουδαίων are hardly needed after ἀρχισυνάγωγοι. The ἀρχισυνάγωγοι are presumably synonymous with the ἄρχοντες τῆς συναγωγῆς.[77] The word αὐτοῖς is hard to explain. These difficulties disappear in the text of the Harclean Syriac margin. Probably the relatively straightforward text of syr[hmg] is a simplification of a reading originally like that of D. We should take it, then, that D represents the earlier form of the Western reading in 14.2, but how may we account for its peculiarities?

The first peculiar feature is the redundancy of the opening phrases, in which the Jewish leaders are described as both ἀρχισυνάγωγοι τῶν Ἰουδαίων and ἄρχοντες τῆς συναγωγῆς. J.-B. Frey held that the author of the D-reading recognised a fact which is clear from Jewish inscriptions, that the office of ἄρχων and that of ἀρχισυνάγωγος were distinct positions in the Jewish communities of the Diaspora, and that:

> The author of these additions [in Acts 14.2] had a precise knowledge of the circumstances and here distinguishes clearly the synagogue leaders from the archons. [78]

Certainly, the inscriptional evidence suggests that the office of ἄρχων was a distinct one, and that some members of their communities held the posts both of ἄρχων and of ἀρχισυνάγωγος.[79] However, the distinctive feature of D's readings is that it identifies the instigators of the trouble at Iconium as ἄρχοντες τῆς συναγωγῆς. There is no clear parallel to this in the inscriptions, where ἄρχων may refer to a political office distinct from the religious position of ἀρχισυνάγωγης.[80] In D, it would appear that two phrases which ought to be alternatives have been combined (Haenchen's 'competitive readings'). The most convincing explanation for this phenomenon was that offered by Weiss. In Weiss's reconstruction of the text's history, the first Western version was οἱ ἀρχισυνάγωγοι τῶν Ἰουδαίων, with Ἰουδαίων appearing as a trace of the Ἰουδαῖοι of the earlier, non-Western text.[81] Later, a glossator wrote the words ἄρχοντες τῆς συναγωγῆς above οἱ ἀρχισυνάγωγοι τῶν Ἰουδαίων, words which 'a thoughtless copyist' then combined with the text, joining the two phrases with a καί.[82] But Weiss's reconstruction can be taken further: both οἱ ἀρχισυνάγωγοι and οἱ ἄρχοντες τῆς συναγωγῆς could have been interlined notes, expressing alternative drafts of a proposed rewriting of οἱ ἀπειθήσαντες Ἰουδαῖοι, notes which have been needlessly combined, and added to the text.

The presence of αὐτοῖς in D is paralleled in the same witness at 14.27 and 15.2.[83] In all three instances, the influence of Semitic usage has been suspected. In 14.2 it has been suggested that αὐτοῖς represents a Semitic proleptic pronoun, giving the sense: 'the Jewish leaders stirred up[84] against them (i.e. the apostles) a persecution against the righteous'.[85] Wilcox objected to this suggestion, since the form does not accurately reflect that of the proleptic pronoun construction, and argued instead for reading αὐτοῖς as an 'ethic dative', giving the sense: 'the Jewish leaders stirred them up a persecution against the righteous'. 'The expression may then', Wilcox continued, 'reflect a Semitic element underlying the Bezan text, and at this point unrevised.'[86]

The word αὐτοῖς is, however, only redundant because of the occurrence of κατὰ τῶν δικαίων after διωγμόν. But κατὰ τῶν δικαίων is curiously echoed by κατὰ τῶν ἀδελφῶν shortly afterwards (see Haenchen's comment, above). If κατὰ τῶν δικαίων were a misplaced gloss on κατὰ τῶν ἀδελφῶν, then the phrase ἐπήγειραν αὐτοῖς διωγμόν would no longer be marked by redundancy, and would not need explanation from Semitic parallels. The glossing of κατὰ τῶν ἀδελφῶν by κατὰ τῶν δικαίων would be similar to the evident glossing of ἀρχισυνάγωγοι by ἄρχοντες τῆς συναγωγῆς earlier in the verse.[87]

Finally, there is the Western observation at the end of this verse: ὁ δὲ κύριος ἔδωκεν ταχὺ εἰρήνην. This passage commended itself to numerous scribes who occasionally added scraps of Western material to their non-Western textual bases,[88] and so it has gained rather wide currency. Its usefulness is clear: if one reads v. 2 to mean that opposition to Paul and Barnabas was already gathering strength, then the additional material explains how they were able to continue their work untroubled, as v. 3 suggests that they did.

Clark noted that without this material 'the sense halts'.[89] Even if Haenchen's interpretation of the aorists of v. 2 as ingressive is correct (see above), Clark made a valid point. The problem, though, is to explain why this necessary piece of information should have been omitted, if it were original. On Clark's earlier view that the shorter, majority text of Acts was produced by *accidental* omission,[90] the omission here could be ascribed to accident. But on his later view that the greater part of the excess Western material had been removed *deliberately* by an abbreviator, some other explanation is needed. Although Clark discussed this passage at two points,[91] he did not offer such an explanation. It should probably be accepted that the words ὁ δὲ κύριος ἔδωκεν ταχὺ εἰρήνην are a comment which aimed to ease the transition between vv. 2 and 3. The laconic brevity of the expression may suggest a gloss or note. The various elements of the Western textual tradition of Acts 14.2, therefore, may owe their origin to notes upon the text. The text, with its annotations, would have been:

<u>ἀρχισυνάγωγοι ἄρχοντες τῆς συναγωγῆς</u>
οἱ δὲ ἀπειθήσαντες Ἰουδαῖοι ἐπήγειραν
<u>αὐτοῖς διωγμόν</u>
καὶ ἐκάκωσαν τὰς ψυχὰς τῶν ἐθνῶν
<u>κατὰ τῶν</u>
<u>δικαίων</u>   κατὰ τῶν ἀδελφῶν
<u>ὁ δὲ κύριος ἔδωκεν ταχὺ εἰρήνην</u>
ἱκανὸν μὲν οὖν χρόνον . . .

The additional material is too fragmentary to give much linguistic evidence about its origin. The word ταχύς is not particularly characteristic of Luke. It is probably to be read at Lk. 15.22, but elsewhere Luke prefers ταχέως (Lk. 14.21, 16.6), or ἐν τάχει (Acts 12.7, 22.18). The expression οἱ δίκαιοι for οἱ ἀδελφοί would be remarkable for Luke, but would be equally remarkable for any early Christian writer.[92] On the other hand, as Boismard and Lamouille note, ἐπεγείρειν and διδόναι εἰρήνην are found only in Luke in the New Testament.[93]

It has from time to time been pointed out that the early part of Acts 14 is far from perfect in composition, and in particular that the transition from 14.2 to 14.3 is awkward. An earlier school of

criticism understood this as evidence of redaction which has thrown
the text into confusion.[94] Quite possibly, though, Lake and
Cadbury were justified in suggesting that Acts 14.2–7 'is one of the
passages which has escaped final revision'.[95] The problem has
arisen, in other words, not from the degeneration of a previously
polished text, but from the fact that the text had not received its
final revision by the author. Not only the awkwardness of the
narrative, but also the description, unique for Luke, of Paul and
Barnabas as 'apostles' (14.4,14) may support the notion that Luke
had not yet reduced this section to order.

It has frequently been supposed that the Western passage ὁ δὲ
κύριος ἔδωκεν ταχὺ εἰρήνην was an early reader's attempt to
resolve the difficulty in the transition between vv. 2 and 3.[96] Here it
has been suggested that the Western readings in 14.2 as a whole
stem from the incorporation into the verse of half-understood notes
on the text: clarificatory expansions (αὐτοῖς διωγμόν; ὁ δὲ
κύριος ἔδωκεν ταχὺ εἰρήνην) and tentative alternative drafts
(ἀρχισυνάγωγος/ ἄρχοντες τῆς συναγωγῆς; κατὰ τῶν
δικαίων/ κατὰ τῶν ἀδελφῶν). They may have arisen from the
assiduous work of early readers and copyists. But in a passage in
which the author appears not to have completed his work, there is a
strong suspicion that these readings preserve a record of the
author's own comments on the text.

(6)   Acts 15.1–5

The text

N–A[26]	Codex D
1. καί τινες κατελθόντες	καί τινες κατελθόντες
ἀπὸ τῆς Ἰουδαίας	ἀπὸ τῆς Ἰουδαίας
ἐδίδασκον τοὺς ἀδελφοὺς	ἐδίδασκον τοὺς ἀδελφοὺς
ὅτι, ἐὰν μὴ περιτμηθῆτε	ὅτι, ἐὰν μὴ περιτμηθῆτε
τῷ ἔθει τῷ Μωϋσέως	καὶ τῷ ἔθει Μωσέως
	περιπατῆτε
οὐ δύνασθε σωθῆναι.	οὐ δύνασθε σωθῆναι.
2. γενομένης δὲ στάσεως	γενομένης δὲ ἐκτάσεως
καὶ ζητήσεως οὐκ ὀλίγης	καὶ ζητήσεως οὐκ ὀλίγης
τῷ Παύλῳ καὶ τῷ Βαρναβᾷ	τῷ Παύλῳ καὶ Βαρνάβᾳ
πρὸς αὐτοὺς	σὺν αὐτοῖς,
	ἔλεγεν γὰρ ὁ Παῦλος

N–A[26]

Codex D

μένειν οὕτως καθὼς
ἐπίστευσαν διϊσχυριζόμενος.
οἱ δὲ ἐληλυθότες
ἀπὸ Ἰερουσαλὴμ

ἔταξαν ἀναβαίνειν	παρήγγειλαν αὐτοῖς
Παῦλον καὶ Βαρναβᾶν	τῷ Παύλῳ καὶ Βαρνάβᾳ
καί τινας ἄλλους ἐξ αὐτῶν	καί τισιν ἄλλοις ἀναβαίνειν
πρὸς τοὺς ἀποστόλους	πρὸς τοὺς ἀποστόλους
καὶ πρεσβυτέρους	καὶ πρεσβυτέρους
εἰς Ἰερουσαλὴμ	εἰς Ἰερουσαλὴμ
	ὅπως κριθῶσιν ἐπ᾽ αὐτοῖς
περὶ τοῦ ζητήματος τούτου.	περὶ τοῦ ζητήματος τούτου.

3.
οἱ μὲν οὖν προπεμφθέντες	οἱ μὲν οὖν προπεμφθέντες
ὑπὸ τῆς ἐκκλησίας διήρχοντο	ὑπὸ τῆς ἐκκλησίας διήρχοντο
τήν τε Φοινίκην	τήν τε Φοινίκην
καὶ Σαμάρειαν	καὶ τὴν Σαμαρίαν
ἐκδιηγούμενοι τὴν	ἐκδιηγούμενοι τὴν
ἐπιστροφὴν τῶν ἐθνῶν	ἐπιστροφὴν τῶν ἐθνῶν
καὶ ἐποίουν χαρὰν μεγάλην	καὶ ἐποίουν χαρὰν μεγάλην
πᾶσιν τοῖς ἀδελφοῖς	πᾶσιν τοῖς ἀδελφοῖς

4.
παραγενόμενοι δὲ εἰς	παραγενόμενοι δὲ εἰς
Ἰερουσαλὴμ	Ἰερουσαλὴμ
παρεδέχθησαν	παρεδόθησαν μεγ[άλ]ως
ἀπὸ τῆς ἐκκλησίας	ὑπὸ τῆς ἐκκλησίας
καὶ τῶν ἀποστόλων	καὶ τῶν ἀποστόλων
καὶ τῶν πρεσβυτέρων,	καὶ τῶν πρεσβυτέρων
ἀνήγγειλάν τε ὅσα ὁ θεὸς	ἀπηγγείλαντες ὅσα ἐποίησεν
ἐποίησεν μετ᾽ αὐτῶν.	ὁ θεὸς μετ᾽ αὐτῶν.

5.
	οἱ δὲ παραγγείλαντες αὐτοῖς
	ἀναβαίνειν πρὸς τοὺς
	πρεσβυτέρους
ἐξανέστησαν δέ τινες	ἐξανέστησαν λέγοντές τινες
τῶν ἀπὸ τῆς αἱρέσεως	ἀπὸ τῆς ἐρέσεως
τῶν Φαρισαίων	τῶν Φαρισαίων
πεπιστευκότες λέγοντες	πεπιστευκότες
ὅτι δεῖ περιτέμνειν αὐτοὺς	ὅτι δεῖ περιτέμνειν αὐτοὺς
παραγγέλλειν τε	παραγγέλλειν δὲ
τηρεῖν τὸν νόμον Μωϋσέως.	τηρεῖν τὸν νόμον Μωσέως.

---

v. 1 Ἰουδαίας) + τῶν πεπιστευκότων ἀπὸ τῆς αἱρέσεως τῶν
Φαρισαίων: Ψ 383. 467. 614. 1799. 2147. 2412. syr[hmg].

καί + (τῷ ἔθει …): D it⁵ syrʰᵐᵍ sah cop^G67; Ir^lat 97

Μωϋσέως) + and by the other customs with which he was charged: Didasc ConstAp.

περιπατῆτε: D it⁵ syrʰᵐᵍ sah cop^G67; Ir^lat Didasc ConstAp.

v. 2 ἔλεγεν … ἐπίστευσαν: D it⁵

it⁵¹(*manere eos*)

it⁵⁸(*docebant enim P. et B. ut manerent unusquisque sicut credidit*)

it⁶³ vg⁴²²(as it⁵⁸)¹²¹³·¹²⁵⁹*·¹²⁶⁰·¹²⁷⁷.

syrʰᵐᵍ(… as *he* believed …) cop^G67 prov ger^tepl; Ephr.

διϊσχυριζόμενος: D (om.it⁵) syrʰᵐᵍ(robustly) cop^G67; ?Ephr.

οἱ δὲ ἐληλυθότες … καί τισιν ἄλλοις: D it⁵

syrʰᵐᵍ(… ordered *them* P. and B …)

cop^G67(then they who had come decided that …) Ephr^cat.

ὅπως κριθῶσιν ἐπ᾽ αὐτοῖς: (-οῖς D* 383. 1799; -ῶν Dᶜ 614. 2412) after Ἰερουσαλήμ D it⁵; after τούτου 383. 614. 1799. 2412. syrʰ** Ephr.

v. 4 παρεδόθησαν: D* (παρεδέχθησαν D^corr B).

μεγάλως: C D (μεγως D*) 6.257.383.614.1108.1611.1704. 1799.2138.2147.2412. it⁵· syrʰ** sah; Ambr Cass.

v. 5 οἱ δὲ παραγγείλαντες … λέγοντές τινες: D it⁵(+ om. λέγοντες in λέγοντες ὅτι δεῖ)

syrʰᵐᵍ (but those who had ordered them to go up to the elders rose up against the apostles, being those who believed from the sect of the Pharisees).

Introduction

'In the final judgement on the textual question', wrote Lake and Cadbury of Acts 15.1–5, 'if such ever be reached, this passage will certainly play a considerable part.'⁹⁸ Other critics have shared their conviction that this is a passage of particular textual importance. Several scholars have detected a difference in point of view between the two textual traditions here. Ropes, for instance, cited this passage as a major objection to Blass's hypothesis that both traditions had their origins in Luke's work.⁹⁹ The alleged difference in point of view has been detected at several points.

The Western text unambiguously identifies those who troubled the church at Antioch (v. 1) with those who accused Paul and Barnabas at Jerusalem (v. 5: see Ψ 614 etc. in v. 1, and D syrʰᵐᵍ in v. 5). Luke, on the other hand, is said to have distinguished the two groups. Those at Antioch raised only the issue of Gentile circumcision (v. 1, Majority text), while a different group, drawn from the believing Pharisees, raised at Jerusalem the issue of Gentile law-keeping, with circumcision merely the preliminary to it (v. 5). However, in the Western text, the Judaeans make the same demand in v. 1 as the Pharisees in v. 5: Luke's distinction has been lost.[100]

The Western text also allegedly minimises the controversy. In part this has been done by identifying the Judaeans of v. 1 with the Pharisees of v. 5: the 'Judaising' group is thus made to seem smaller and of less account.[101] In part, too, the controversy has been minimised by giving the impression in v. 2 that Paul was willing to go to Jerusalem to 'stand trial' on the issue troubling the Antiochene church.[102] And in part, the minimising has been accomplished by the introduction of μεγάλως in v. 4: the warmth of the welcome given to Paul and his party assures the reader that no serious division can exist between Paul and Jerusalem.[103]

Finally, the Western reading οἱ δὲ ἐληλυθότες ἀπὸ Ἰερουσαλήμ (v. 2) has been taken as evidence that the Western readings rest on a misunderstanding of the alternative text. The subject of ἔταξαν, it has been said, is the 'brothers' at Antioch in v. 1. The Western version is a clarificatory expansion, but the Western paraphrast has assumed that the subject of ἔταξαν is the 'certain men' of v. 1.[104] It was this aspect of the difference between the two texts which most strongly impressed Ropes (see n. 99 above).

These readings are, therefore, particularly important for the study of the text of Acts. A number of scholars have appealed to them as evidence for the non-Lucan origin of the Western readings in Acts, mainly on the basis of their content. These readings, however, also display peculiariies of form, which deserve attention quite as much as do their distinctive contents. The main variants in the passage will here be dealt with individually.

Verses 1 and 5

The variants describing Paul's opponents in vv. 1 and 5 should be taken together. What seems to be one branch of the Western tradition (Ψ 383. 614. etc. syr[hmg]) introduces a description of the Judaeans into v. 1: they were 'some of those who had believed from the party of the Pharisees'. A very similar phrase occurs in the Majority text as a description of Paul's Jerusalem opponents in v. 5. In v. 5 the two major witnesses to the Western text in these verses

(D and syr[hmg]) give two descriptions of the people who spoke at Jerusalem in favour of circumcising the Gentiles: they were 'those who ordered them (the group from Antioch) to come up to the elders' and they were 'some of those from the party of the Pharisees who had believed'. The first question to be decided is what has happened to the Western textual tradition to bring about these variants in vv. 1 and 5.

To begin with v. 5, it seems clear that the overloaded state of the text in D and syr[hmg] is the result of interpolation. There are two descriptions of the speakers, and the text would make sense with either description, but hardly with both.

Ropes offered a reconstruction of the development of the Western text of vv. 1 and 5.[105] In its original state, the Western text drew the words τῶν πεπιστευκότων . . . Φαρισαίων to v. 1 from v. 5, and then omitted the words τινες τῶν ἀπὸ . . . πεπιστευκότες from v. 5. The text of Ephraem and of the *Apostolic Constitutions*, Ropes argued, does not seem to have mentioned 'Pharisees' in v. 5, and so was based on the original Western text. At a later stage, a scribe interpolated the words τινες ἀπὸ . . . πεπιστευκότες into v. 5 from the Majority text, giving the reading found in syr[hmg]. The roughness of the text has been slightly alleviated in syr[hmg], but from the way that the interpolated material in v. 5, as found in D, separates λέγοντες from ὅτι, it is clear what has taken place.[106] Later still, a copyist removed τῶν πεπιστευκότων . . . Φαρισαίων from v. 1, since it now appeared in v. 5, thus producing the text of D.

Ropes's suggestion is open to two objections. There is in the first place no substantial evidence for his postulated original Western text. Neither Ephraem nor the *Apostolic Constitutions* give a complete text, and it would be unwise to build too much on their omissions. It cannot be argued with any certainty that they witness to a text without τινες ἀπὸ . . . Φαρισαίων in v. 5. In the second place, the conflation which Ropes suggested is very awkward.[107] It is hard to see why the conflation should have been made so poorly, when it could have been made so much more neatly. Conflation has evidently taken place, but Ropes gives no explanation of why it should have taken this particular form.

It could more convincingly be argued that the Western text of v. 5 has become overloaded by the incorporation of the specifically Western material into a text which did not originally have it. The block of material οἱ δὲ παρηγγείλαντες . . . λέγοντες seems to be an alternative to ἐξανέστησαν δὲ ... λέγοντες, but it has been added to the latter phrase, rather than being substituted for it. The only alteration made to accommodate the new material has been the removal of the now-redundant λέγοντες after πεπιστευκότες. The creation of the Western text of v. 5 would be comprehensible if the material οἱ δὲ παρηγγείλαντες ... λέγοντες stood first as a marginal note to v. 5, which has been added to the verse, instead of taking the place of ἐξανέστησαν δὲ ... λέγοντες, as it was apparently intended to do.

In v. 1 the phrase τῶν πεπιστευκότων ... Φαρισαίων could be original to the Western text, and could have been excised from D at a later stage, as Ropes supposed. Certainly, D omits material from the common tradition on occasion (see, for example, 2.18f., 31, 3.8, 11.26, 17.18, 34, 19.27, 40, 20.16). It may also omit material which was originally present in the Western tradition.[108] But omission is the exception in D: when it occurs it requires explanation,[109] and no very convincing explanation is to hand to account for D's omission of this phrase in 15.1 if it were originally part of the Western text. Ropes argued that it was the result of D's adding the phrase about the Pharisees to v. 5; the description of Paul's opponents was no longer needed at v. 1. But a copyist would be more likely to delete the second, and more clumsy, reference to the Pharisees when he came across it in v. 5, rather than the first and more elegant one in v. 1. The balance of probability indicates that the phrase τῶν πεπιστευκότων ... Φαρισαίων in v. 1 is a secondary development in the textual tradition,[110] but no complete certainty is possible.

The Western version of Acts 15.5 clearly identifies the men who caused the controversy at Antioch with those who raised the issue of Gentile law-keeping at Jerusalem. Does this show a clear departure from Luke's portrayal of the controversy?

The evidence that Luke differentiated between the group which arrived at Antioch from Judaea and those who spoke in favour of circumcision at Jerusalem is not as strong as is sometimes supposed. The Apostolic Letter (15.23–9) explicitly states that it was τινὲς ἐξ ἡμῶν ἐξελθόντες[111] who had troubled the Antiochenes (15.24). The implication is evident that the group which had gone to Antioch was represented among the 'we' of the Jerusalem Council. The statement of 15.24 does not rule out the possibility that the τινές of 15.1 and 15.24 were thought by Luke to have been present at the Council. The least that can be said is that the Western version of 15.5, according to which the very people who had gone to Antioch were present at the Council, is not inconsistent with the τινὲς ἐξ ἡμῶν of 15.24.

v. 1 καὶ ... περιπατῆτε

The expression in the non-Western text ἐὰν μὴ περιτμηθῆτε τῷ ἔθει τῷ Μωϋσέως is unusual, and several scholars have remarked upon it.[112] A particularly odd aspect of the phrase 'to be circumcised according to the custom of Moses' is that circumcision, as Luke was aware (Acts 7.8), was instituted by Abraham, according to the Pentateuch, and not by Moses. Elsewhere, Luke seems to draw a distinction between circumcision (which he nowhere else associates with Moses) and the customs received from Moses (see Lk. 2.21f., Acts 15.5, 21.21). The Western reading 'unless you are circumcised and walk according to the custom of Moses' accords well with Lucan usage. Cerfaux was willing to accept it.[113]

An objection to the Western reading would be that it simply alters the demands of the Judaeans in Antioch to bring them into line with those of Paul's opponents in Jerusalem, because of the reviser's conviction that they were the same people.[114] But v. 1 has not been mechanically conformed to v. 5 (the construction and vocabulary of the two passages remains different), and comparison with 21.21 shows that the Western reading well represents Luke's characteristic way of portraying the demands of Judaistic Christians. If, as has been argued above (pp. 136f.), Luke did not radically distinguish the Judaisers at Antioch from those at Jerusalem, then the Western version of their demands at 15.1 has been cast in a convincingly Lucan form.

v. 2 ἔλεγεν γὰρ ... παρήγγειλαν αὐτοῖς

This long additional section in the Western text of 15.2 consists of two parts, with slightly different MS evidence for each. The first part describes what Paul was saying to cause his dispute with the Judaeans (ἔλεγεν γὰρ ... διϊσχυριζόμενος). The second part identifies the Judaeans specifically as having come from Jerusalem, and states that it was they who ordered Paul and Barnabas and some others to go to Jerusalem. The second element is missing in the Latin witnesses except the Latin column of D (it⁵), which is dependent on the Greek of D here. Ropes was probably right to maintain that the Western readings originally contained both elements.[115] The Latin witnesses seem to have omitted the second element of the reading, quite possibly because the thought of Paul being ordered to Jerusalem by the Judaisers was offensive.

The first element (ἔλεγεν γὰρ ... διϊσχυριζόμενος) is evidently an explanatory note. The imperfect tense may imply that it is attempting to tell the reader what Paul habitually said about Gentile converts, rather than to report what Paul said in the dispute at Antioch. Until this point, after all, the reader has not been told that Paul did not circumcise his Gentile converts.

The description of Paul's policy towards Gentile converts is reminiscent of his own words in 1 Cor. 7. Ropes took it that 1 Cor. 7.8,20,24,40 was the source of this reading.[116] The parallels with 1 Cor., though, are not clear enough to establish literary dependence. This note on the text of Acts has been composed by someone who knew what Paul's policy was with uncircumcised converts, and that knowledge could have been acquired without having read 1 Corinthians.[117]

The language of this first element in the reading has two significant Lucan features. The phrase οὕτως καθώς is used by Luke alone in the New Testament (Lk. 24.24 – where D has οὕτως ὡς, but cf. Phil. 3.17, ουτω ... καθώς), and the same is true also of διϊσχυριζόμενος (Lk. 22.59 and Acts 12.15).

The second element of the Western reading in 15.2 has been taken by some commentators as decisive evidence against Lucan authorship of the reading: Luke portrays the brothers at Antioch as ordering Paul's party to go to Jerusalem, while the Western text wrongly interprets the subject of ἔταξαν as the 'certain men' of v. 1.[118]

Others, though, have argued that the Western interpretation of ἔταξαν is correct.[119] It makes better sense grammatically, and it would be difficult to accept an interpretation of 15.1f. according to which the brothers at Antioch ordered Paul and Barnabas to go to Jerusalem. Luke's ecclesiology is not congregationalist. In Luke's view, decisions are made by the church's leaders, and battles fought by them on the congregations' behalf. Paul's farewell speech to the Ephesian elders (20.18–35) well sets out Luke's view. Like the 'grievous wolves' of 20.29, the 'certain men' of 15.1 are a threat to the brothers' faith. As a guardian of the flock (20.28), Paul stands in 15.2 to do battle for the brothers. This is a struggle which goes on over the heads of the congregation: Luke's chosen image of a flock is significant. It is through the leadership of apostles, prophets, and elders that the church is guided by the Holy Spirit (Acts 1.23–6, 6.2, 9.27f., 10.9–48, 11.27–30, 13.1–3, 15.6,22, 21.18–25). The task of guiding a congregation is passed to recognised leaders, themselves appointed by a previous generation of leaders (14.23, 20.28–30). Indeed, the whole perspective of Acts, in which a few major figures are the focus of attention, while the life of the congregations is dealt with in a summary fashion, is another indication of Luke's outlook.[120]

Because of Luke's concept of the proper relation of a congregation to the leading figures within it, it would be most irregular, in his view, for 'the brethren' at Antioch, or elsewhere, to give orders to Paul. The Western text is probably correct to suppose that in this narrative, it was the 'certain men' from Judaea who ordered Paul and Barnabas to Jerusalem. Acts 15.24 indicates that the 'certain men' were members of the group of 'apostles and elders'. Their acting with authority at Antioch would be consistent with his understanding of the relationship of Antioch to Jerusalem (cf. 11.22) even if – and this is the point of the remark in 15.24 – they had not formally been sent by the entire body of apostles and elders.[121]

Two points in the construction of the Western reading at Acts 15.2 deserve attention. The first is the point made by Ropes, that in none of the versions is the Western material 'introduced after the genitive absolute with complete grammatical success'.[122] The second point was also made by Ropes, that 'αυτοις . . . cannot easily be explained'.[123]

Wilcox found two possible explanations for the αὐτοῖς of 15.2, either of which might indicate Semitic, and probably Aramaic, influence on the text. It might be an example of the proleptic pronoun, anticipating τῷ Παύλῳ καὶ Βαρνάβᾳ, or it might be an ethic dative: 'Those who had come from Jerusalem instructed them [i.e. for themselves] Paul and Barnabas.'[124] Either explanation is possible, though neither is at all certain, and an explanation is to be preferred which can also account for the lack of connection with the context, Ropes's first point.

Both features of the Western reading can be explained if the material is regarded as originating in a marginal note, or rather, in two marginal notes. The words ἔλεγεν γὰρ . . . διϊσχυριζόμενος can be seen as a note on γενομένης δὲ στάσεως . . . πρὸς αὐτούς, a phrase which is otherwise unexplained, since the reader does not yet know from the text what Paul thought about the circumcision of Gentile converts. The note has been incorporated without its being recognised that the γάρ-clause does not follow smoothly after the genitive absolute. The second note, οἱ δὲ ... αὐτοῖς, is an explanatory gloss on ἔταξαν. It answers the question: who ordered them? The αὐτοῖς is a reference to 'Paul and Barnabas and some others of them', but has been incorporated unnecessarily, creating redundancy (only slightly alleviated by the omission of ἐξ αὐτῶν). The two notes have been run together, but they did not originally belong together. The second element is joined to the first by δέ, but it is an inappropriate conjunction, since there is no real sequence of thought between the two elements: 'For Paul used to say ... but those who had come from Jerusalem ordered them ... '

This reading's poor connection with its context, its lack of inner cohesion, and its redundancy are best accounted for by the supposition that it represents two marginal notes, which have been placed rather clumsily into the text.

v. 2 ὅπως κριθῶσιν ἐπ᾽ αὐτοῖς

The Greek witnesses to this reading give two forms: in one ἐπί takes the dative (D* *et al.*), and in the other the genitive (D^corr c *et al.*). Most commentators suppose that they have the same meaning: 'so that they might be judged before them'.[125] In Luke's usage, though, there is a distinction. In Luke, κρίνεσθαι ἐπί + dative means 'to be judged concerning', with ἐπί introducing the ground of accusation (Acts 4.9 [ἀνακρίνεσθαι], 26.6), while with the genitive it means 'to be judged before', with ἐπί introducing the court of judicature (Acts 24.21, 25.9).[126] The reading with the genitive, therefore, would emphasise Paul's subservience to Jerusalem, while that with the dative ('to be judged concerning them', i.e. the Gentile converts) would virtually amount to an equivalent of περὶ τοῦ ζητήματος τούτου.

The fact that a corrector of D altered the dative to the genitive[127] may suggest that there was a tendency towards the genitive among later copyists, in which case the dative would be more likely to be original. On the other hand, the exemplar of Thomas of Harkel may already have had the genitive ('*before* them' in syr^h**), unless, of course, Thomas failed to appreciate the distinctive use of the genitive.

The evidence for the two readings is finely balanced. If anything, the correction of the reading of D from the dative to the genitive may indicate a trend possibly operative elsewhere to replace the dative. If so, this would suggest that the dative is the more original reading. If this is the case, then not only is the reading Lucan in style, but it gives a less inquisitorial picture of Paul's position before the Jerusalem church than is usually supposed. The parallel with περὶ τοῦ ζητήματος τούτου would also mean that this reading would provide another example of the Western text's incorporating an alternative draft of an expression in the common text.

v. 4 μεγάλως

The line of D on which the word μεγάλως occurs has suffered at the hands of copyists. The original scribe wrote παρεδόθησαν μεγως. A later corrector[128] made interlined corrections to give παρεδέχθησαν μεγάλως, which we may suppose to be what the original reading of D's *Vorlage* was.

The occurrence of μεγάλως in this context is curious. It was evidently present in the Greek text used by Thomas of Harkel. English versions of the reading render μεγάλως 'heartily',[129] but if that is what the word means here, it is a peculiar use, outside the word's normal range. It is not impossible, but μεγάλως is not the word one would expect to describe a warm welcome.

Immediately before the reference to the reception by the church at Jerusalem, there occurs in v. 3 the phrase ἐποίουν χαρὰν μεγάλην, describing the rejoicing of the Phoenician and Samaritan churches on hearing of the conversion of the Gentiles. The fact that μεγάλην has occurred so close to the μεγάλως of 15.4 (Western) makes the latter even more curious. Possibly a copyist, having just written μεγάλην, found that μεγάλως suggested itself as an adverb to heighten the account of the reception in Jerusalem. Or alternatively, μεγάλως may have stood as a marginal note to the end of v. 3, expressing an annotator's intention to alter it from a noun- to a verbal phrase by incorporating an adverb in place of the adjective, giving ἐποίουν χαρῆναι μεγάλως πάντας τοὺς ἀδελφούς. The word μεγάλως could have reached its present position by being misplaced in the process of copying. This alternative explanation cannot be demonstrated to be correct, but certainly the word would be more appropriate to describe the rejoicing of the Phoenicians and Samaritans than it is to describe the welcome of the Jerusalem church.

15.1–5: Conclusion

From this study of the Western variants in Acts 15.1–5 it has emerged that they may have originated, in large part if not entirely, in marginal and interlined notes on the text. They give the appearance of having been placed in the text without being fully integrated into it (ἔλεγεν γὰρ ... αὐτοῖς, v. 2). They seem to incorporate alternative drafts which have been needlessly combined with the existing text (οἱ δὲ ... λέγοντες, v. 5; ?ὅπως ... αὐτοῖς, v. 2). In v. 2, two notes seem to have been run together (ἔλεγεν γὰρ ... διϊσχυριζόμενος, οἱ δὲ ... αὐτοῖς). There may be evidence of misplacement (μεγάλως, vv. 3/4). These features are what might be expected of a text into which marginalia have been incorporated.

Linguistically, the Western material is satisfactorily Lucan. It contains one word found nowhere else in Lucan writings (μεγάλως), but there are several Lucan expressions in it (τῷ ἔθει Μωϋσέως περιπατῆτε, οὕτως καθώς, διϊσχυριζόμενος, κρίνεσθαι ἐπί τινι/τινος). In its concept of the relationship between Paul and the 'certain men', the Western text seems adequately to represent Luke's view. There is not the gap between them which has often been alleged.

The Western readings at Acts 15.1–5, then, appear to have arisen as marginal notes on the text, added by someone largely faithful to Luke's vocabulary and style, and to his presentation of the narrative. The possibility that the Western readings here arose from the author's own annotations must be an open one.

       (7)   Acts 15.34

N–A[26]

—————

Codex D
ἔδοξε δὲ τῷ Σειλέᾳ
ἐπιμεῖναι αὐτούς,
μόνος δὲ ᾿Ιούδας ἐπορεύθη.

—————————————————

ἔδοξε δὲ ... αὐτοῦ: (αὐτούς: C D it[5])
C D 33. 36. 88. 181. 242. 257. 323. 383. 431. 453. 467. 522. 536. 614. 915. 945. 1108. 1175. 1522. 1611. 1739. 1799. 1891. 2147. 2298. 2412. pc.
it[5.6.51.58.61.62.63.67.] vg[BG.cav.tol.1260.1266.1276.1700.gk629.]

syr[h**] sah boh[mss] arm geo nedl ger[tepl] prov eth; Cass Ephr (?Ps-)Oec Theoph.

μόνος δὲ . . . ἐπορεύθη: D it$^{5.6.51.58.61.62.63.67.}$
vg$^{BG.tol.1260.1266.1700.}$ arm^{osc} nedl prov; Cass
add: to Jerusalem: it^{58} arm^{osc}; Cass

Acts 15.34 is a conspicuous Western reading which has been the subject of discussion since the sixteenth century. The first clause of the reading found its way, through Erasmus' edition, into the Textus Receptus, and thus into the versions which relied on that text.[130] The consensus of nineteenth-century criticism, though, saw this passage as part of the dead wood of the Textus Receptus, which had to be cut away to reveal the original text. In 15.33 Silas and Judas were dismissed from Antioch to return to Jerusalem, but in 15.40 Silas was apparently still in Antioch, and available to join Paul after the rift with Barnabas. Several scholars have noted that the addition of 15.34 would ease this inconsistency in the narrative.[131] If the inconsistency was a result of Luke's bringing together blocks of source material, then the Western addition of 15.34 could be seen as part of the process by which that text smooths out the seams between different source blocks in Acts.[132]

Other scholars, while agreeing that 15.34 is secondary, have argued for a theological, rather than a narrative motive. On this view, Silas chose to remain at Antioch as a protest against the terms of the Apostolic Decree. According to the Western text, Silas had brought the Decree from Jerusalem to Antioch, but once there, preferred to remain with Paul in order to dissociate himself from the Judaisers. This understanding of 15.34 sees it derived, not from the notice of 15.40, that Silas was in Antioch, but from that of 15.41, that he accompanied Paul in place of Barnabas.[133]

Among those who have argued for the authenticity of 15.34 are Ramsay (who was not convinced of the general reliability of the Western text: see n. 25 above), Blass, Clark, and Delebecque.

Ramsay's argument was that 15.34 stood originally as it is in the Textus Receptus: 'But it seemed good to Silas to remain.' This original and Lucan text developed in two ways. On the one hand, the Bezan reviser added the clause: 'and Judas went alone'; on the other, some copyists deliberately omitted v. 34, because they supposed that there was a contradiction between v. 33 and v. 34. They mistakenly thought that v. 33 narrated the actual departure of Silas and Judas, whereas it only stated that they were given permission to leave, and v. 34 in its original form added that Silas did not avail himself of the permission.[134]

Blass maintained that the whole of 15.34 was Luke's composition. The vocabulary and style are thoroughly Lucan. The first edition of Luke's work contained the entire verse, Blass argued, but in the second edition, the author removed the second clause as unnecessary. An early copyist inadvertently passed over the words ἔδοξε ... αὐτοῦ, producing the text as it is in the majority of witnesses. This error in copying produced the inconsistency between 15.34 and 15.40, a blemish on the text which in the form of both its first and second editions was quite coherent.[135]

In Clark's opinion, the inconsistency between 15.33 and 15.40 was the result, and indeed the hallmark, of the work of an abbreviator.[136] Delebecque, like Blass, has pointed out the 'Lucanism' of the vocabulary in 15.34, and like Ramsay, has argued that 15.33 narrates only the permission given to Silas and Judas to leave Antioch.[137]

Boismard and Lamouille have reconstructed vv. 33 and 34 TO in such a way that they do not contradict: ποιήσας δὲ χρόνον ὑπέστρεψεν Ἰούδας εἰς Ἱεροσόλυμα. ἔδοξε δὲ τῷ Σιλᾷ ἐπιμεῖναι αὐτοῦ. In order to arrive at this reading, Boismard and Lamouille have deserted all MS witnesses, and rely on the reading of Ephraem.[138] But it is precisely in this type of reading that Patristic evidence is least helpful, and that unimaginative copyists are most reliable. Thoughtful copyists, and to a still greater extent ecclesiastical writers, were able to notice difficulties in the text, and to do something about them. Ephraem's version of 15.30–5 is a paraphrase, and Ephraem has clearly taken the opportunity to clarify the text. He evidently had something corresponding to 15.34, but his Commentary is not at this point to be relied upon to provide an original text lost in all MS witnesses.

The difficulty with the verse is that it looks neither like part of Luke's original text nor like the revision of a later scribe. If it were part of the original text (Blass, Clark, Delebecque) – or if only the first clause were part of the original text (Erasmus, Ramsay) – it would be hard to explain why it should have been removed. Only Ramsay has offered a motive: that it was to remove the perceived contradiction with v. 33. But a scribe faced with this problem should have asked: did Silas and Judas leave, or did they not? The answer given by v. 40 is that Silas, at least, did not. It should then have been v. 33 which was altered, and not v. 34 – in much the way in which Ephraem understood it. No substantial reason can be given for the removal of v. 34, if it were originally in the text.

A very clear reason can be given for the addition of v. 34, and the fact that it exists in two forms might suggest that it was a growing text; first the initial clause was added to harmonise with v. 40, and then the second clause was added to answer the question of whether Judas did as Silas had done.[139] But this solution also faces problems. The linguistic traits of 15.34 may not amount to proof that it is a Lucan composition, but they should be taken into account. More than that, the aim of harmonising v. 33 with v. 40 would appear to have been achieved at the cost of creating an even clearer inconsistency between vv. 33 and 34. In v. 33 the envoys have been dismissed, and v. 34, coming directly afterwards, reads like a flat contradiction. The argument that ἀπελύθησαν means merely that the Antiochenes gave the Jerusalem envoys permission to depart (Ramsay, Delebecque) has little force. Silas and Judas were not waiting for permission to leave, and their dismissal is not portrayed as a release from Antioch, but as a sending *to* those who had first sent them (πρὸς τοὺς ἀποστείλαντας αὐτούς). When ἀπολύειν is used in this context elsewhere in Acts, it quite clearly implies movement, and not merely permission to move (Acts 4.23, 15.30). A scribe with the intelligence to note the contradiction between 15.33 and 15.40 might be expected to have introduced the necessary information in a less clumsy way.

There is therefore an inconsistency between 15.33 and 15.34. It is of a sort more likely to have arisen if v. 34 were originally a self-contained unit which has been inserted into the text than if it were the product of careful rewriting. Acts 15.34, then, is best understood as a marginal note, added here by someone who was aware of Silas' presence at Antioch in v. 40. The note has been incorporated whole, without making the necessary adjustments to v. 33. Such a process of adding new material to the text without proper thought for the grammatical or narrative consequences has been seen to be typical of the Western text elsewhere in Acts, also.

On two final important points it is impossible to reach a firm conclusion. It is not clear in the first place who composed 15.34. The language is convincingly Lucan, but not exclusively so. Lucan authorship is permitted by the linguistic evidence, but not demanded by it. It is the sort of alteration which an author might make in the course of improving a draft of his work, but equally it is the sort of note which any reader might make on his text. In the second place, it is difficult to judge between the longer and shorter forms of the verse. The longer may be an expanded version of the shorter, spelling out its implication, or the shorter may be a secondary form of the longer, pruned of unnecessary detail. In view of the further addition made by it[58], it may be that the shorter version was original, and that it has suffered from a tendency to expand. If this is correct, then 15.34 would be an instance in which D does not exhibit the more original form of Western reading.

(8)   Acts 16.4

N–A[26]	Codex D
ὡς δὲ διεπορεύοντο	διερχόμενοι δὲ
τὰς πόλεις	τὰς πόλεις
	ἐκήρυσσον καὶ
παρεδίδοσαν αὐτοῖς	παρεδίδοσαν αὐτοῖς
	μετὰ πάσης παρρησίας
	τὸν κύριον Ἰησοῦν Χριστὸν
	ἅμα παραδιδόντες καὶ
φυλάσσειν τὰ δόγματα	τὰς ἐντολὰς
τὰ κεκριμένα ὑπὸ τῶν	
ἀποστόλων καὶ πρεσβυτέρων	ἀποστόλων καὶ πρεσβυτέρων
τῶν ἐν Ἱεροσολύμοις.	τῶν ἐν Ἱεροσολύμοις.

διερχόμενοι δέ: D it[5.51](*ergo*) sah.
ἐκήρυσσον καὶ παρεδίδοσαν αὐτοῖς: D it[5] syr[p.] syr[hmg]; Ephr(they preached).
μετὰ πάσης ... Χριστόν: D it[5] syr[hmg].
ἅμα ... ἐντολάς: D it[5]
om. τῶν (before ἀποστόλων): D.

Acts 16.4 relates in summary form the ministry of Paul and Silas in Lycaonia and Pisidia on Paul's 'second missionary journey'. According to the usually accepted text, this ministry consisted of handing on to the churches the stipulations of the Apostolic Decree (15.29). According to D and the Syriac, it consisted of preaching while also handing on the Decree (ἐκήρυσσον ... παραδιδόντες).

The significance of these differences has been variously estimated. Weiss argued that the text of D had been created in order to explain why the church was said in the next verse to have grown in numbers.[140] Fascher suggested that the D-text of Acts 16.4 subordinates the delivery of the Apostolic Decree to the preaching of Jesus by restructuring the sentence so that the main clause deals with preaching, and the Decree appears only in an appended subordinate clause.[141] Epp incorporated Fascher's observation into his own thesis that there is in the Western text an overall tendency to devalue 'the significance both of the "decree" and of the disputation which occasioned it'.[142]

The structure of the readings is also of interest. It has generally been thought that D's reading is a secondary development, by way of contamination from the non-Western text. Ropes saw the key to the problem in the awkwardly placed καὶ παρεδίδοσαν αὐτοῖς:

> και παρεδιδοσαν αυτοις is not found in hcl.mg. and is plainly a case of contamination from the B-text, since it breaks the connexion and is covered by αμα παραδιδον-τες just below.[143]

Boismard and Lamouille reconstruct the primitive TO as διερχ-όμενοι δὲ τὰς πόλεις ἐκήρυσσον μετὰ πάσης παρρησίας τὸν κύριον Ἰησοῦν [?Χριστόν]. They comment:

> TO did not have v. 4b (not known to Ephraem) since it had already expressed the theme in 15.41 – D joins the two texts together, but the borrowed matter from TA is strongly influenced by the text of TO in 15.41; it should be noted that the words παρεδιδοσαν αυτοις are in the wrong position – the primitive TO probably did not have the title χριστον.[144]

Here, as in 15.34, Boismard and Lamouille rely on the witness of Ephraem to the original state of TO, which has been corrupted in D. But Ephraem's reading has several lacunae, and is clearly not a straightforward rendering of an underlying Greek text. Conybeare's Latin translation of Ephraem in Acts 16.4f. is as follows:

> [Dum] transibant civitates et manifestum [faciebant et ap]ostolatu intrepido praedicabant il[li verbum spiritus sanc]ti, et donec ecclesiae confirmaban[tur inter filios] virorum per signa quae facta sunt [cotidie in] illis.[145]

Boismard and Lamouille note that Ephraem agrees with D in omitting τῇ πίστει in 16.5, but they do not draw attention to his singular reading: '(among the sons) of men by the signs which were done'. If Ephraem alone gives the true TO in 16.4, why is his equally idiosyncratic reading in 16.5 passed over in silence? It seems more likely that Ephraem has left out any reference to the

Decree in 16.4 because he was more concerned with the apostolic preaching, and he has added a reference to signs because 16.5 put him in mind of 2.42–7. All reliable Western witnesses, therefore, mention both preaching and handing on the Decree.

Ropes's explanation is also doubtful. While it is true that the text of D reads more smoothly if the words καὶ παρεδίδοσαν αὐτοῖς are removed, D reads so well without them that it is hard to see why a copyist should have disrupted it by incorporating material which, as Ropes pointed out, is otiose in view of the ἅμα παραδιδόντες at a later point.

The origin of the D-text is perhaps better explained as due to the incorporation of marginal notes on a text like that of the non-Western witnesses:

	διερχόμενοι
ἐκήρυσσον	ὡς δὲ διεπορεύοντο τὰς πόλεις
μετὰ πάσης	
παρρησίας	παρεδίδοσαν αὐτοῖς φυλάσσειν
τὸν κύριον Ἰησοῦν	
Χριστὸν ἅμα	τὰ δόγματα τὰ κεκριμένα ὑπὸ τῶν
παραδιδόντες	
καὶ τὰς ἐντολάς	ἀποστόλων καὶ πρεσβυτέρων τῶν ἐν
	Ἱεροσολύμοις.

The interlined διερχόμενοι was intended to replace ὡς δὲ διεπορεύοντο as it does in D it[5.51] sah. The material in the margin was intended to take the place of παρεδίδοσαν ... ὑπό. The version intended by the annotator would have been: διερχόμενοι δὲ τὰς πόλεις ἐκήρυσσον μετὰ πάσης παρρησίας τὸν κύριον Ἰησοῦν Χριστὸν ἅμα παραδιδόντες καὶ τὰς ἐντολὰς τῶν ἀποστόλων καὶ πρεσβυτέρων τῶν ἐν Ἱεροσολύμοις.

The transcriber appears to have been anxious to lose as little text as possible from the main body or from the annotation. Consequently, he has kept the two main verbs, ἐκήρυσσον and παρεδίδοσαν, even though the additional material itself intended to subordinate the 'handing over' of the Decree to the 'preaching' of the Lord Jesus Christ. The incoherent text which resulted from this incorporation has been made easier in the secondary Western versions (syr[p.hmg] Ephr).

The language of the additional material is Lucan in character. The phrase μετὰ παρρησίας is unique to Luke in the New Testament. The substitution of ἐντολαί for δόγματα is in accord

with Lucan usage, since elsewhere Luke uses δόγμα for commands
of the secular power alone (Lk. 2.1, Acts 17.7), but uses ἐντολή for
religious commands (Lk. 1.6, 18.20, 23.56) and for personal
injunctions (Lk. 15.29, Acts 17.15). The title 'the Lord Jesus
Christ' is to be found elswhere in Acts (11.17, 28.31; cf. 15.26). But
against this observation must be set two points. The first is that the
title 'the Lord Jesus Christ' is far more common in the Western text
of Acts than in the usually accepted text.[146] The second is that the
exact phrase 'preaching the Lord Jesus Christ' is not found in any
undisputed Lucan passage. Linguistically, then, the Western
additional material at Acts 16.4 has Lucan traits, but also some
features characteristic of the Western text in Acts.

It has already been noted that the content of the Western reading
amounts, in the view of Fascher and Epp, to a denigration of the
Decree. The attitude displayed by the longer text would thus be at
variance with that of Luke, for whom the Decree is clearly of great
significance. However, the evidence could more convincingly be
taken as pointing the other way. By binding together Paul's
passing on the Decree with his preaching, the longer text seeks to
dispel any suggestion that Paul was uncertain about the Decree.
Handing on the Decree was an integral part of his message, even
beyond the area to which it was addressed (15.23); it was the
διδαχή which complemented the κήρυγμα of the Lord Jesus Christ.
So, far from belittling the status of the Decree, the longer text of
Acts 16.4 appears to enhance it.

A similar conclusion may be drawn from the Western text of Acts
15.41. Here, several Western witnesses add to the statement that
Paul went through Syria and Cilicia strengthening the churches the
observation παραδιδοὺς τὰς ἐντολὰς τῶν πρεσβυτέρων. Tissot
has thought to find here more evidence for Epp's thesis that there is
a denigration of the Decree in the Western text. He has pointed out
that the 'elders' appear in this reading unaccompanied by the
'apostles', from which we are to conclude that in the view of the
Western reviser the Decree was the work of the Judaising elders,
and not of the more authoritative apostles.[147] More likely, though,
the true significance of this reading is that given to it by Lake and
Cadbury: it intends to reinforce the notion that Paul assented to the
Decree and himself laid it upon the congregations he visited on this
journey.[148] By introducing a reference to the Decree in 15.41 the
Western text runs the risk, if anything, of making Paul appear, in
Jacquier's words, 'a simple colporteur of the Apostolic Decree'.[149]

In both 16.4 and 15.41, therefore, the intention of the Western readings is to associate the Apostolic Decree more closely with Paul on this 'second missionary journey'. In the view of the Western text, the Apostolic Decree was a powerful instrument for the strengthening of the life of the churches.[150] There can be little doubt that this was also the view of Luke himself.[151]

The additional Western material in Acts 16.4, then, is best understood as originating in notes on the text which have been incorporated into the text in some witnesses. Codex D exhibits the resultant text in its most primitive form, and the other witnesses in modified forms. In language and theology, the material is at least consistent with Luke's work elsewhere. The annotator and the author may have been the same person.

(9)   Acts 17.1

N–A[26]	Codex D
διοδεύσαντες δὲ τὴν	διοδεύσαντες δὲ τὴν
᾽Αμφίπολιν	᾽Αμφίπολιν
καὶ τὴν ᾽Απολλωνίαν	καὶ κατῆλθον εἰς
	᾽Απολλωνίδα
ἦλθον εἰς Θεσσαλονίκην.	κἀκεῖθεν εἰς
	Θεσσαλονίκην.

διοδεύσαντες] διελθόντες: E it[50]
κατῆλθον εἰς ᾽Απολλωνίδα κἀκεῖθεν: D it[5].

Weiss found in this passage evidence that the text of D had been disturbed by the intrusion of marginal notes.[152] The note arose through correction of an error in copying. He proposed that the text had passed through four stages in order to reach its present state.

The first form of the Western text was:
(1) τὴν ᾽Αμφίπολιν καὶ τὴν ᾽Απολλωνίαν κατῆλθον εἰς Θεσσαλονίκην.
By an error of transcription, the words τὴν ᾽Απολλωνίαν were omitted:
(2) τὴν ᾽Αμφίπολιν καὶ κατῆλθον εἰς Θεσσαλονίκην.
A copyist who noticed the mistake added a note to indicate the material to be added:
καὶ ᾽Απολλωνίαν
(3) τὴν ᾽Αμφίπολιν καὶ κατῆλθον εἰς Θεσσαλονίκην.

A further copyist, however, added the missing material on the wrong side of the verb, and continued the sentence with κἀκεῖθεν, giving the text of D:

(4) τὴν Ἀμφίπολιν καὶ κατῆλθον εἰς Ἀπολλωνίαν κἀκεῖθεν εἰς Θεσσαλονίκην.

Weiss's reconstruction explains the redundant καί of D. One objection to his reconstruction would be that it proposes a development which has strangely left no trace except in D itself. This is particularly striking in the case of stage (1), the supposed original Western reading, although it has to be recalled that the Western witnesses are rather meagre at this point: it[55] and cop[G67] are not extant here, and the variant may have been too trivial to be placed in the Harclean Syriac margin.

A further objection is that there is little apparent reason for a copyist to have misplaced the marginal note. It fitted only with difficulty after the verb, but would fit very neatly before it. Why, then, should it have been misplaced? Weiss's solution is by no means impossible, but a simpler one would be preferable, if one could be found.

Haenchen also noted the redundant καί in D. D, he held, was here a mixed text, and the καί was the remnant of the 'neutral text'.[153] This conflation theory is open to the same objection as Weiss's annotation theory: there is no evidence of any Western reading here other than that of D. The reconstruction of an original and purer Western text can only be conjectural.

The redundant καί certainly suggests a disturbance of the text. A simpler solution would be to suppose that the words κατῆλθον εἰς Ἀπολλωνίδα[154] stood as a marginal note to the text. Instead of being incorporated consistently, they were added in place of τὴν Ἀπολλωνίαν ἦλθον with κἀκεῖθεν appended to make the connection with the rest of the sentence. The word καί was left to introduce the reference to Apollonia, but now had no function.[155]

The point of the alteration seems to have been to place more emphasis upon Apollonia. Lake's first comment on this reading was that it rearranges Paul's journey, dividing the passage from Philippi to Thessalonica into two stages instead of three (Philippi – Apollonia – Thessalonica instead of Philippi – Amphipolis – Apollonia – Thessalonica). It has done this, Lake maintained, by interpreting διοδεύσαντες to mean 'passing through', and elevating Apollonia as the only stopping-place on the journey between the major centres of Philippi and Thessalonica.[156] Lake later revised his opinion of the reading. In *Beg.* IV, he translated the reading: 'Taking the road through Amphipolis, they came down to Apollonia, and from it to Thessalonica.' He drew the conclusion that the reading implies a longer stay than usual in Apollonia.[157] There is, though, little evident reason for the alteration; the Western reading has nothing specific to say about Apollonia, so why should it call attention to the town in this way?

The answer to the problem appears to be geographical. It is usually assumed that Apollonia Mygdonia lay on the *Via Egnatia*, and certainly an Apollonia is mentioned in the *Itineraries*.[158] The exact course of the road at this point is not known, but the nature of the terrain to the south of Lake Bolbe makes it highly likely that the road more or less followed the shoreline. The site of Apollonia Mygdonia, however, is one kilometre south of the road, and eighty metres above it, at a place known in modern times as Polina. It is possible that the road climbed the hill to pass through the town, but this is unlikely, particularly when it is recalled that the *Via Egnatia* to the east of Thessalonica was principally of military importance,[159] and could therefore well have missed a town of purely local significance.

The Apollonia of the *Itineraries* may not, then, be the town of Apollonia Mygdonia itself. This conjecture is borne out by the evidence of the *Itinerarium Burdigalense* (605.1) of AD 333, which places roadside settlements into categories. Apollonia appears as a *mansio*, a mere stopping-place, in contrast to the *civitates* of Philippi, Amphipolis, and Thessalonica. Apollonia Mygdonia does not seem to have declined in status by the fourth century, since it remained a πόλις in the reign of Justinian,[160] and was the seat of a bishop by the eighth century.[161] The *mansio* must, then, have been a separate site. The city of Apollonia Mygdonia stood at some distance from the road, but the traveller on the *Via Egnatia* would pass the *mansio* of Apollonia at some point near the city.

The D-reading at Acts 17.1 may demonstrate knowledge of the topography of Apollonia. The majority reading states that Paul and his companions passed through both Amphipolis and Apollonia. The originator of the D-text seems to have realised that the passage is not concerned with *mansiones* through which Paul passed, but with cities which he visited. He seems to have recognised also that Paul would not have passed through the city of Apollonia Mygdonia if he had kept to the road. Some expression had to be added to make clear that Paul visited the city of Apollonia Mygdonia, and had not merely passed the *mansio* of Apollonia. Hence the annotation κατῆλθον εἰς ᾿Απολλωνίδα/-ίαν, which, it has here been argued, is the likely origin of the D-reading.

If the reading of Acts 17.1D shows an acquaintance with the topography of Apollonia, it may be taken as one of a small group of variants which exhibit an interest in Macedonia.[162]

(10) Acts 17.4

N–A[26]	Codex D
καί τινες ἐξ αὐτῶν	καί τινες ἐξ αὐτῶν
ἐπείσθησαν	ἐπίσθησαν
καὶ προσεκληρώθησαν	καὶ προσεκληρώθησαν
τῷ Παύλῳ καὶ τῷ Σιλᾷ,	τῷ Παύλῳ καὶ τῷ Σιλαίᾳ
	τῇ διδαχῇ
τῶν τε σεβομένων	πολλοί τῶν σεβομένων
῾Ελλήνων πλῆθος πολύ,	καὶ ῾Ελλήνων πλῆθος πολὺ
γυναικῶν τε τῶν πρώτων	καὶ γυναῖκες τῶν πρώτων
οὐκ ὀλίγαι.	οὐκ ὀλίγαι.

---

om. καὶ προσεκληρώθησαν: p[74].
τῇ διδαχῇ πολλοὶ τῶν σεβομένων: D it[5] syr[p](and many of the Greeks who feared God); ?Cass
σεβομένων] + καί: p[74] A D 33. 81. 181. it[5.51] vg boh.
om. ῾Ελλήνων: 323
καὶ γυναῖκες: D it[5.51] vg syr[p] geo eth; Cass.
om. τῶν πρώτων: it[51] ndl[1] eth[mss].

Various attempts have been made to explain the peculiarities of the text of D in Acts 17.4, and in particular, the awkward and apparently unnecessary τῇ διδαχῇ. Blass suggested that τῇ διδαχῇ had become displaced from its proper position after ἐπείσθησαν and reinserted at the wrong point.[163] Clark embodied the suggestion in his reconstruction of the Western text (Z). Because the supposed transposition occurs at the end of two lines of Codex D, it fitted particularly well with his contention that the sense-lines of D are an ancient element of the text.[164] Displacement of words or phrases clearly has taken place in D. It can be observed in Acts at 1.2 (ἀνελήμφθη), 2.14 (πάντες – from the end of one line to the end of the next), 2.45f. (καθ᾿ ἡμέραν), 5.29 (transposition of two lines), 12.7 (αὐτοῦ), 13.15 (ἐν ὑμῖν), and 13.30f. (ἐφ᾽ ἡμέρας πλείονας). In the case of 17.4, though, there is no evidence that τῇ διδαχῇ ever stood at a different point in the text.

This lack of evidence is a major point against Boismard and Lamouille's reconstruction of TO here. They argue that τῇ διδαχῇ ought to follow ἐπείσθησαν, and therefore at some previous stage it must have done so, and the words καὶ προσεκληρώθησαν τῷ Παύλῳ καὶ τῷ Σιλᾷ in D must be an intrusion from the alternative text.[165] Ropes had argued something similar.[166] But evidence for any other Western reading than that of D is completely lacking. It is also hard to see why a copyist with two good texts before him should produce such a poor text as the result of his conflating work.

Weiss suggested that a scribe had added τῇ διδαχῇ as a marginal note, with the intention that it should be incorporated as τῇ διδαχῇ τοῦ Παύλου καί τοῦ Σιλοῦ. Instead, another copyist has added the note 'quite mechanically' after the names.[167]

Weiss's suggestion has the advantage that it does not postulate a completely vanished 'pure' Western text, and does not envisage a copyist ruining two good texts in order to produce a poor one. It is likely that the words τῇ διδαχῇ in Acts 17.4D were once a marginal note, and have been brought into the text by a copyist who did not have the initiative, or did not want to take it, to reorder the expression of the verse to take account of the new material.

It is impossible to say at what point these words entered the text. The most that can be said is that D's text appears to have incorporated a marginal note, added ineptly at an uncertain period, a note which seems to have been intended to guide a rewriting of the passage.

(11)   Acts 18.8

N–A[26]	Codex D
Κρῖσπος δὲ ὁ Ἀρχισυνάγωγος	ὁ δὲ Ἀρχισυνάγωγος Κρίσπος
ἐπίστευσεν τῷ κυρίῳ	ἐπίστευσεν εἰς τὸν κύριον
σὺν ὅλῳ τῷ οἴκῳ αὐτοῦ,	σὺν ὅλῳ τῷ οἴκῳ αὐτοῦ,
καὶ πολλοὶ τῶν Κορινθίων	καὶ πολλοὶ τῶν Κορινθίων
ἀκούοντες ἐπίστευον	ἀκούοντες ἐπίστευον
καὶ ἐβαπτίζοντο.	καὶ ἐβαπτίζοντο πιστεύοντες
	τῷ θεῷ διὰ τοῦ ὀνόματος
	τοῦ κυρίου ἡμῶν Ἰησοῦ
	Χριστοῦ.

εἰς τὸν κύριον: D it⁵·⁵⁵ vg⁴⁹³ syrᵖ·ʰ sah.
πολλοί] πολὺ πλῆθος: it⁵⁵; Ephrᶜᵃᵗ.
ἀκούοντες] + *verbum domini* it⁵⁵
om. ἐπίστευον καί: it⁵⁵
πιστεύοντες τῷ θεῷ: D it⁵·⁵⁵
ἐπίστευον] + τῷ θεῷ [καὶ ἐβαπτίζοντο: syrᵖ arm
διὰ τοῦ ὀνόματος τοῦ κυρίου ἡμῶν Ἰησοῦ Χριστοῦ: D (383.
    614. 2147) it⁵·⁽⁵⁵⁾· syrʰ**
    (om. ἡμῶν: 383. 614. syrʰ**)
    (om. τοῦ κυρίου ἡμῶν: it⁵⁵)
    (placed before καὶ ἐβαπτίζοντο: 614 2147. syrʰ**).

The problem to be addressed in this collection of readings is the overloaded nature of the reading of D. One way of understanding it would be to argue that the Fleury palimpsest (it⁵⁵) contains the original Western reading: ἀκούοντες ἐβαπτίζοντο πιστεύοντες τῷ Θεῷ διὰ τοῦ ὀνόματος Ἰησοῦ Χριστοῦ. The reading of D will then have arisen through the addition of superfluous material from the other text.¹⁶⁸ Weiss suggested that the redundancy in D was brought about by the incorporation of ἐπίστευον καί from an interlined note, without the copyist's noticing the tautology of the new reading.¹⁶⁹

This way of explaining the text, though, fails to give a reason for a copyist to add to his text words which are utterly superfluous. Although it is possible to see *how* the text of D could have arisen from that of it⁵⁵, it is less easy to see *why* it should have done so. It is easier to take the reading of D as the ancestor of the other readings. Their origin could then be explained as attempts to remove the tautology in these ways: (1) by excising ἐπίστευον καί: (it⁵⁵); (2) by excising πιστεύοντες τῷ θεῷ, and (a) leaving διὰ τοῦ ὀνόματος κτλ in place (383), or (b) attaching it to ἐπίστευον (614. 2147. syrʰ**).

How, then, could the tautologous reading of D have arisen in the first place? Weiss may have been correct in suggesting that it arose from the incorporation of an annotation or gloss, but more likely than his suggestion that ἐπίστευον καί was added to the Western text is the probability that the additional material of D (πιστεύοντες τῷ θεῷ διὰ τοῦ ὀνόματος τοῦ κυρίου ἡμῶν Ἰησοῦ Χριστοῦ) was itself an interlined or marginal note. Its intention was to make more explicit the nature of the converts' faith at baptism (an interest shown by the Western text elsewhere in Acts: 2.41, 8.37,

11.17). It was incorporated by a copyist who either did not notice the overloading of the resultant text, or who had such a high regard for the marginalia and the text of his exemplar that he wanted to retain as much as possible of both.

By whom could this annotation have been made? Clearly by someone who appreciated Lucan usage. Epp has carefully studied the material dealing with 'believing in the Lord/ believing in God' in Acts, and has shown that Luke habitually draws a distinction between Jewish converts (like Crispus) who are said to 'believe in the Lord', and Gentiles (like the Corinthians) who are said to 'believe in God'.[170] The Western material here is in conformity with Luke's usage.

(12)   Acts 24.27

N–A[26]	614
ἔλαβεν διάδοχον ὁ Φῆλιξ	ἔλαβε διάδοχον ὁ Φῖλιξ
Πόρκιον Φῆστον	Πόρκιον Φῆστον
	τὸν δὲ Παῦλον εἴασεν ἐν
	τηρήσει διὰ Δρούσιλλαν·
θέλων τε χάριτα καταθέσθαι	θέλων δὲ χάριν καταθέσθαι
τοῖς Ἰουδαίοις	τοῖς Ἰουδαίοις
ὁ Φῆλιξ κατέλιπε	ὁ Φῖλιξ κατέλιπε
τὸν Παῦλον δεδεμένον.	τὸν Παῦλον δεδεμένον.

τὸν δὲ ... Δρούσιλλαν: 614. 2147. 2412 syr[hmg]
om. θέλων ... δεδεμένον: syr[hmg]
χάριν: ℵ[c] E L Ψ 242. 323. 945. 1739. 1891. 2495. al.;
χάριτα: ℵ* A B C 33. 104. 1175. pc.; χάριτας: Maj.
κατέλιπε: Maj.; κατέλειπεν: p[74] A H L 81. 88. 104.
    181.453.1175.2464 pc.

Three minuscules with marked 'Western' tendencies give in Acts 24.27 two reasons for Felix's leaving Paul in prison at the end of his governorship. Not only, as in the Majority text, because he wished to placate 'the Jews', but also 'because of Drusilla' his wife.[171] The Harclean Syriac has the marginal reading ('Paul he left under guard because of Drusilla') against that of its text ('Wishing to please the Jews, Felix left Paul bound').

The Western reading here is almost certainly to be taken with the reading of the Harclean Syriac margin at v. 24, which adds to the

Majority text that Drusilla, being Jewish, 'asked to see Paul, and to hear the word, wishing therefore to satisfy her [Felix sent for Paul]' (syr^hmg with support from Bohemian and Cass).[172]

There appears to be a conscious Western point of view in this episode. According to the Western text, Drusilla played a major part in Felix's relation with Paul. But it was a strange and rather contradictory part. At first Drusilla was eager to see Paul and to hear his message (v. 24, Western), but by the end of Felix's tenure of office, it is presumably her malice towards Paul which prevents him from being freed (v. 27, Western). There is no explanation for this change of mind. Possibly the reader is to suppose that she was angered by Paul's preaching on ἐγκράτεια (v. 25),[173] but the text gives little indication that this was so. It may again be evidence of the Western text's anti-Judaic and anti-feminine tendency.[174] On the other hand, in the Western as in the Majority text, it is Felix, not Drusilla, who prolongs Paul's detention in the hope of financial gain (vv. 25f.). Drusilla's implied attitude in v. 27 Western text is a surprise to the reader, since her previous attitude to Paul had been shown as positive, in contrast to that of her husband.

As an explanation of Paul's continued imprisonment after Felix's departure the Western reading of 24.27 is hard to understand. It is equally inconsistent as a *description* of Paul's continued imprisonment. The τήρησις to which it refers recalls the τηρεῖσθαι of v. 23, and the liberal regime under which Paul was kept by Felix, rather than the δεδεμένος of v. 27, which seems to imply harsher treatment after Felix had left (note also ἄνεσις 24.23, with οἱ δεσμοὶ οὗτοι, 26.29).[175]

The Western additional material now at 24.27, if placed at the start of v. 26, would provide a consistent picture of Drusilla, and a consistent picture of Paul's imprisonment under Felix. It would refer quite naturally to the period of Paul's imprisonment under Felix. Drusilla wished to hear Paul (24.24, Western), so Felix kept Paul in custody, partly in order to gratify her[176] (24.27, Western material), and partly also in the hope of gaining a bribe (ἅμα καὶ ἐλπίζων κτλ 24.26). It would also introduce the rest of v. 26 well: both Felix and Drusilla had their reasons for detaining Paul. The Western additional material at 24.27 is best thought of as having begun in the form of a marginal note. This assumption would explain its laconic brevity: διὰ Δρούσιλλαν reads more like a shorthand note to be explained than a sufficient explanation in itself. The assumption could also explain the misplacement of the material: a copyist who assumed that the 'leaving in custody' here referred to the same state as the 'leaving bound' in v. 27 might think that he should use this material to supplement the narrative at that point.

It is difficult to be precise about the origin of this material. The use of ἐάω in the sense of 'leave behind' is not paralleled elsewhere in the undisputed work of Luke, while there is a clear parallel in the Western reading of Acts 18.21: τὸν δὲ ᾿Ακύλαν εἴασεν ἐν ᾿Εφέσῳ. The phrase ἐν τηρήσει, on the other hand, is used by Luke elsewhere (Acts 5.18: see also Acts 4.3).

The Western material in Acts 24.27, therefore, appears to have the character of a misplaced annotation. Lucan authorship is a possibility, although it cannot be demonstrated beyond doubt.

Conclusion

Development of Western readings

This chapter has been largely concerned with passages in which Western witnesses have a confused text. This confusion is often most noticeable in D, and it has been seen that in many cases D's awkwardness has been ascribed to conflation with non-Western readings. It has here been argued that D frequently offers the most original form of the Western text, and that the developments within the Western tradition are best understood as attempts to alleviate the difficulties of a text like that of D. It must be recalled that D's closest allies are translations, and that, while a copyist working in one language only can reproduce what is in his exemplar, whether he understands it or not, a translator is obliged to think about what a passage means if he is to put it into another language. Some of the tidying-up of the Western text may, therefore, be due to the necessities of translation.

D, of course, has a manuscript history of its own, and does not invariably preserve the earliest form of the Western text. It has been seen, for example, that at 15.34 D may offer a relatively late form of text (see pp. 145f. above) and that at 11.2 D may have lost a preposition under the influence of the accompanying Latin (see pp. 80f. above). D's readings, like those of any other witness, must be examined on their merits.

But D's redundant and confused readings in Acts are unlikely to be merely the product of conflation with the non-Western text.

Quite apart from the general consideration that the hypothesis of conflation envisages the sacrifice of two coherent texts to make one incoherent text, such a hypothesis is also unable to explain specific instances in which the Western confusion owes nothing to the non-Western text. An example of this is 14.2 (see see pp. 126–31 above), where two alternative phrases appear to have been combined, both of them purely Western. A further possible example, 14.10, will be considered below.

The hypothesis which has arisen from the observations of this chapter is that the confusion of the Western readings is often best explained as the result of the incorporation of marginal or interlined notes, containing the characteristically Western material, into an originally non-Western textual base. Several features of the readings betray the origin of these notes: redundancy, inconsistency with context, and the phenomenon of notes being run together when they should have been incorporated separately.

Redundancies

Redundancy may be the mark of plain conflation. But conflation assumes the existence in the first place of two pure texts which have been brought together. It is not always possible to demonstrate the existence of a pure Western text behind the apparently conflate Western readings. What appear at first sight to be relatively pure readings can be shown in some instances to be developments from an earlier text marked by redundancy. Examples of this are 3.11 (pp. 115–19), 3.13 (pp. 120–2), 15.5 (pp. 134–7), 16.4 (pp. 146–50), and 18.8 (pp. 154–6). In these instances, the history of the Western text's development leads back, not to a coherent original Western text, but to a primitive form already characterised by redundancy.

Other readings in which the Western text is marked by redundancy, and which have been considered in this chapter are: 6.1 (pp. 122–6), 14.2 (pp. 126–31), possibly 15.2 (pp. 137–41), and 17.4 (pp. 153f.).

Further examples of redundant readings in the Western text, which are explicable on the hypothesis that they represent marginal notes, may be found elsewhere in Acts. Acts 2.47 has evidently a rather complex textual history, in common with the whole section 2.45–3.1. Part of the development could have been due to the insertion at a primitive stage of the Western tradition of the words ἐν τῇ ἐκκλησίᾳ after ἐπὶ τὸ αὐτό (see D it [5.54.] cop [G67]). These two elements have been transposed for the sake of sense in E Ψ Maj syr. In origin ἐν τῇ ἐκκλησίᾳ appears to have been an explanatory gloss upon ἐπὶ τὸ αὐτό.[177] The two phrases have been combined by a copyist and have become one of the most widely accepted of Western readings in the ancient textual tradition.

In 3.1, Luke adds his own explanation of 'the hour of prayer' – that is, 'the ninth' (τὴν ὥραν τῆς προσευχῆς τὴν ἐνάτην). D goes further and adds τὸ δειλινόν, 'late in the day'. The additional phrase could well be understood as an alternative. Incorporated into the text it is otiose.

In 5.12 the words ἐν τῷ ἱερῷ D (E) (it[5]) sah cop[G67] added before ἐν τῇ στοᾷ Σολομῶν(τ)ος may be evidence of a gloss intended to conform 5.12 to 2.46, which has been added to the text, instead of taking the place of ἐν τῇ στοᾷ Σολομῶν(τ)ος.

Weiss suspected that in 7.26, εἶδεν αὐτοὺς ἀδικοῦντας was interlined in order to make a firmer connection with the words ἱνατί ἀδικεῖτε;. But instead of taking the place of the earlier material, the words have been added to the text as a supplement to it.[178]

At 12.5 the majority of witnesses read: προσευχὴ δὲ ἦν ἐκτενῶς γινομένη ὑπὸ τῆς ἐκκλησίας πρὸς τὸν θεὸν περὶ αὐτοῦ. But D has: πολλὴ δὲ προσευχὴ ἦν ἐν ἐκτενείᾳ περὶ αὐτοῦ ἀπὸ τῆς ἐκκλησίας πρὸς τὸν θεὸν περὶ αὐτοῦ. The repetition περὶ αὐτοῦ . . . περὶ αὐτοῦ suggests that two versions of the sentence have been run together. Since several witnesses (it[54] eth[mss] ndl[1]) have περὶ αὐτοῦ in the first position, but not the second, it may be that they witness to the more primitive text, with D representing a text contaminated by the Majority reading. But equally, D may be the earlier Western reading, and the other witnesses refinements of it. In which case the reading of D could have arisen from the thoughtless incorporation of a marginal note containing an alternative version of the sentence: πολλὴ δὲ προσευχὴ ἦν ἐν ἐκτενείᾳ περὶ αὐτοῦ ἀπὸ τῆς ἐκκλησίας πρὸς τὸν θεόν. The scribe who incorporated the note, having reached the words τὸν θεόν at the end of the material, would have mechanically continued copying after τὸν θεόν in the existing text, producing the redundant reading of D.

The phrase εὐθέως παραχρῆμα is found at 14.10 in D it[5] syr[hmg] cop[G67] (εὐθέως: 1838 eth[mss]; παραχρῆμα: E it[50]). As in 14.2, at a slightly earlier point in the Western version of the narrative, two alternative elements seem to have been added together. Interlined notes provide a likely origin for this type of reading.[179] Similarly, in 20.7, the addition of πρώτῃ to μιᾷ in D (diff. it⁵) may be due to the incorporation of a note which was meant to take the place of the other word.[180]

The Western version of 16.35–40 presents a number of complex problems. One of the most curious verses is 16.38, where N–A²⁶ has: ἀπήγγειλαν δὲ τοῖς στρατηγοῖς οἱ ῥαβδοῦχοι τὰ ῥήματα ταῦτα, and D gives: ἀπήγγειλαν δὲ αὐτοισοι [sic] στρατηγοῖς οἱ ῥαβδοῦχοι τὰ ῥήματα ταῦτα τὰ ῥηθέντα πρὸς τοὺς στρατηγούς. Material corresponding to τὰ ῥηθέντα is found in syrᵖ, but D and it⁵ are alone in giving πρὸς τοὺς στρατηγούς. Boismard and Lamouille's discussion of the reading is coloured by their observation that πρὸς τοὺς στρατηγούς cannot be connected with ἀπήγγειλαν, since the latter is always followed by the dative.[181] Only a little earlier in the narrative, however, we find ἀπήγγειλεν δὲ ... τοὺς λόγους πρὸς τὸν Παῦλον (16.36). It seems quite possible that τὰ ῥηθέντα πρὸς τοὺς στρατηγούς was intended as a substitute for τοῖς στρατηγοῖς οἱ ῥαβδοῦχοι τὰ ῥήματα ταῦτα. The incorporation of what was intended as an alternative has gravely disturbed the text, and given the tautologous reading we find in D. Clumsy handling of a marginal note may again be suspected.

In 22.29 several Western witnesses (614. 1611. 2412. syrʰ** sah: D def.) add the words καὶ παραχρῆμα ἔλυσεν αὐτόν. This means that the phrase ἔλυσεν αὐτόν in v. 30 is now redundant.[182] The same witnesses (except sah) add πέμψας before ἔλυσεν in v. 30. The redundancy of the Western readings in these verses seems well explained as the result of incorporating marginal notes which were intended to guide the rewriting of the narrative. The rewritten passage would have had Paul released by Lysias immediately his Roman citizenship became known (v. 29). The πέμψας of v. 30 may have referred to sending for 'the chief priests and the Sanhedrin'. But instead of leading to a rewriting of the passage, the notes have merely been added to it, and have produced a text marked by redundancy.

The Latin witness it⁵¹ has at 24.5 the redundant reading, *non tantum generi nostro sed fere universo orbe terrarum et omnibus Judeis* in place of *omnibus Iudaeis in universo orbe* (vg). As Blass and Clark noted, this reading appears to combine two phrases, hence the appearance of the Jews twice (*generi nostro ... et omnibus Judeis*).[183] If, as may be suspected, a gloss has been incorporated here, then the original text of the gloss may have been that of Blass's reconstructed β-text: οὐ μόνον τῷ γένει ἡμῶν ἀλλὰ σχεδὸν πάσῃ τῇ οἰκουμένῃ.[184]

At the close of 27.2 the majority of witnesses read: ὄντος σὺν ἡμῖν ᾿Αριστάρχου Μακεδόνος Θεσσαλονικέως. A number of Western witnesses conclude the verse: Θεσσαλονικέων δὲ ᾿Αρίσταρχος καὶ Σέκουνδος. These witnesses are: 614. 1518. (2147). 2495. syr[h] (D is lacking here, and it[55], which is extant for this passage, does not have the reading). The appearance of Secundus here is very probably to be explained by the mention of him in 20.4 as the companion of Aristarchus. What is not so readily explained is the form of the Western witnesses, in which Aristarchus appears twice: first alone, and then with Secundus. An explanation would be that a marginal note ᾿Αρίσταρχος καὶ Σέκουνδος has been incorporated. It should have been used to alter the sentence, but instead has been added to it, creating the redundant Western reading.

As a final example of redundancy, one may note the treatment of the end of Acts in the Western textual tradition. In 28.31 there occurs a Western reading, apparently represented by the words 'saying that this is Jesus Christ the Son of God, by whom the whole world is about to be judged' (?λέγων ὅτι οὗτός ἐστιν ᾿Ιησοῦς ὁ υἱὸς τοῦ θεοῦ δι᾿ ὃν μέλλει ἡ οἰκουμένη κριθῆναι). This reading commended itself to several Vulgate copyists, and has found its way also into the text of the Harclean Syriac, although different witnesses have dealt with the material in different ways. Some witnesses have simply added the material to the end of the common text of 28.31, and this appears to have been the most primitive form of the reading.[185] Some scribes noticed that the content of Paul's preaching is thus given twice, and have amended the text accordingly. One group of witnesses has substituted the Western material for the account of Paul's preaching in the common text.[186] The scribe of it[54] has excised the first description of Paul's message, but has left the Western material rather awkwardly at the end of the passage.[187] As Ropes observed, the material seems to have originated in Greek, and to have been intended as a substitute for at least part of the passage τὰ περὶ ... ἀκωλύτως.[188] Here, too, the redundant Western reading may have arisen from the incorporation of a gloss.

Inconsistencies

As well as the redundancy they produce, marginal notes when introduced into a text can betray their origin by their inconsistency with their context. Such inconsistency has been noted at 1.5 (*until* Pentecost: pp. 113–15), 15.2 (pp. 137–40), and 17.1 (pp. 150–3). A narrative inconsistency was created by the introduction of 15.34 without the necessary consequent changes to 15.33 (pp. 142–61).

Further examples of inconsistency are to be found in the Western tradition. At 11.1 D has the reading: ἀκουστὸν δὲ ἐγένετο τοῖς ἀποστόλοις καὶ τοῖς ἀδελφοῖς οἳ ἐν τῇ Ἰουδαίᾳ.[189] The peculiar series τοῖς ... τοῖς ... οἳ ... could be explained if ἀκουστὸν δὲ ἐγένετο τοῖς ἀποστόλοις καὶ τοῖς ἀδελφοῖς had been taken into the text from a gloss, and the copyist then returned to the common text without noticing that his own adopted construction now required the dative, and not the common text's nominative.

Several witnesses at 18.21 give Paul's reason for leaving Ephesus: δεῖ με (δὲ D*; om. με vg[231a]) πάντως τὴν ἑορτὴν (+ ἡμέραν D) τὴν (om. D) ἐρχομένην ποιῆσαι εἰς Ἱεροσόλυμα D H L P Ψ Maj. it[5.51.58.59.61.63.] vg[(231a.).1266.1700.gk629] syr ndl ger[tepl] prov eth[mss]; Cass Chr Theoph. In D (diff. it[5]), it[58] and the Provençal, there is no connecting conjunction between the Western material and the following text. This anacolouthon makes the Western material look intrusive, and may suggest that it was originally a note which has been placed in the text.

Misplacements

Misplacement has been observed in the Western readings at Acts 1.5 (pp. 113–15), 14.2 (κατὰ τῶν δικαίων: pp. 126–31) and 14.27 (see p. 129, n. 83). It may also account for the Western reading at 19.1.[190]

A particular type of misplacement of material is the running-together of notes which were meant to be separate. This has been observed at 3.11 (pp. 115–19), 14.2 (two instances, ἀρχισυνάγωγοι' ἄρχοντες τ. συν. and αὐτοῖς διωγμόν + κατὰ τῶν δικαίων: pp. 126–31), and 15.2 (pp. 137–40). Quite possibly, 14.10 provides another example (see pp. 160f.).

A further example of misplacement occurs in 20.4. The whole

passage 20.1–7 appears to have undergone extensive revision in the Western version, and D in particular is rather confused. All witnesses agree in 20.3 in narrating Paul's decision to return to Syria through Macedonia, the Western version attributing the decision to the prompting of the Spirit. Before giving the list of Paul's companions on the journey, D adds μέλλοντος οὖν ἐξειέναι αὐτοῦ μέχρι τῆς 'Ασίας. The phrase μέλλοντος οὖν ἐξειέναι αὐτοῦ is witnessed by only it[5] and syr[hmg], while the second phrase, μέχρι τῆς 'Ασίας, had a much wider currency (other witnesses have ἄχρι: it is found in A D E H L P Maj it[5.50.51.62.] vg[1700] syr[p.hmg] geo prov; it is absent from p[74] ℵ B 33 pc vg sah boh). The list of Paul's companions follows the phrase ἄχρι/μέχρι τῆς 'Ασίας (although in D the necessary phrase συνείπετο δὲ αὐτῷ does not appear), making them accompany Paul only as far as Asia. In view of the fact that at least two of them did *not* accompany Paul to Asia (v. 5), and that at least two went on with Paul to Jerusalem (21.29, 27.2), it may be suspected that this phrase has itself been misplaced: perhaps it was originally intended to qualify διὰ (τῆς) Μακεδονίας in the previous verse. That is, Paul's projected itinerary was to return through Macedonia as far as Asia, and *then* to head for Syria, which is indeed the course which he takes in the narrative.

Annotated material in the Western tradition

The Western text of Acts, therefore, exhibits several characteristic features of interpolation from marginal or interlined notes. Twelve passages were considered on pp. 113–58 above. A further fourteen passages were considered more briefly on pp. 159–64. But the instances which have been studied here do not, of course, account for the entire stock of annotations. If the text of Acts had been extensively annotated at some early point, then many of the glosses could either have been lost, or have been incorporated quite smoothly. It would only be in those instances in which a note has been taken into the text ineptly that the process might be detected at all, and such instances might represent no more than a small fraction of the total. We can trace the incorporation of marginal material in some Western readings; we may suspect that it was also the origin of many more.

The annotating work which has been the object of study in this chapter clearly took place at an early stage in the text's history. The dissemination of these readings in the Old Latin and the presence of Western material in Irenaeus show at least that we have to do with a primitive development in the text.

It may be that more than one hand has been at work to produce these glosses. Acts, however, attracted very little attention in the pre-Irenaean period, if our meagre sources give a fair picture, and attracted little more after it. It is therefore all the harder to suppose that Acts, of all the books of the New Testament, should have been worked over by a series of glossators at a very early period. When the readings also occur in a quite well-defined and allied group of witnesses, then we may suspect that the glossing work on the text of Acts was confined to a particular point in the history of the book's transmission, if not to the work of one hand.

The literary character of the marginal material, as far as it may be judged, is not markedly non-Lucan. The Western version of 15.1–5 has often been supposed to depart from Luke's outlook, but it has here been argued that it does not in fact do so (see pp. 131–42 above). Linguistically, the material which has been considered here does indeed contain some non-Lucan words and expressions,[191] but they are not so striking or numerous as to preclude Lucan authorship, and on the other side, there are several characteristic features of Lucan thought and expression in the marginal material.[192]

An important constituent of the Western text in Acts, therefore, is material which originally stood in marginal or interlined notes on the text. Since it is likely that only a relatively small part of this material betrays its origins because of the way it has been incorporated, there must be a suspicion that a large part of the Western text may have begun in this form. This conclusion is consistent with the observations made earlier about the commentary-like nature of the Western text of Acts (pp. 41–7 above).

The annotated material could have been the work of a very early commentator on Acts. This is possible, but on the face of it, it is unlikely in view of the neglect of Acts in the early second century. The evidence suggests that there may be a relationship worth investigating between the author of Acts and the author of the Western annotations on Acts.

We are then brought back to consider the hypothesis of Blass, but in a significantly different sense. Blass thought that the Western form of the text was the work's first edition; that Luke annotated it with improved readings, which accounts for the occasionally mixed text of D, incorporating these readings; and that the final edition was the revised work as presented to Theophilus, the non-Western text. From the observations made here, though, it appears that the Western material is more likely to represent the annotations, and the non-Western text to represent the version on which the annotations were made. Blass also assumed that Luke published the work twice. It is important first to establish whether Luke ever published Acts at all.

The investigation of the relationship between Luke and the Western annotations will involve trying to establish the processes by which Luke is likely to have prepared his work for publication. It may then be possible, in the light of this investigation, to decide what part was played by the circumstances of Acts' publication in the production of its textual peculiarities.

5

THE COMPOSITION AND EDITING OF ACTS

The composition of books in antiquity

The observations made so far about the Western text of Acts have suggested that the origin of the distinctive stratum of Acts' Western text is to be sought in an extensive and meticulous process of annotation which took place at an early stage in the book's history. This conclusion raises a further question: how could a book such as Acts have acquired this layer of annotations?

Luke, more than any other New Testament author, seems to have been aware of the world of Hellenistic culture and its literary conventions.[1] We might expect him to have followed these conventions, and that what we may discover of the processes by which authors in antiquity brought their works to completion will tell us something of the way in which he is likely to have worked. There were several points in the process of compiling and disseminating a book which would have permitted annotation to have taken place.

Annotation by the author

An author in antiquity would begin work on a serious literary production by compiling notes (ὑπομνήματα or *commentarii*) which were to serve as its basis. A *commentarius* might carry the preliminary notes of a scholar.[2] Lucian advised the aspiring historian first to collect such notes, which would give him the information from which to work. It is the historian's art, according to Lucian, to turn these data into a literary product worth calling 'history'.[3] Lucian was not alone in his view of the preliminary nature of *commentarii*; Hirtius, who provided the eighth book of Caesar's *Gallic War*, noted that the reader would find in Caesar's *Commentarii* the material from which a proper history could be written.[4]

Josephus is known to have kept notes during the war of AD 66–70, perhaps already with a view to writing them up later.[5]

The writer's ὑπομνήματα would be rough in their composition and their expression. Galen helpfully distinguished ὑπομνήματα, which men write for their own reference and may in consequence be obscure, from σύγγραμματα, or properly written books.[6]

It is therefore likely that Luke, too, would have begun his work with the compilation of ὑπομνήματα of this sort. Whatever view is taken of the possibility of sources behind the book of Acts, the conventions of writing in Luke's day, and of historical writing in particular, would suggest that the author would first have compiled his notes before embarking on his work in its final form.

We are seldom in a position to know what an author's notes would look like, since in the nature of things, they were ephemeral productions. They might use a variety of media. It was quite common by Luke's time for literate people to carry notebooks with them to keep notes of their reading or ideas.[7] It was no more than efficient tradesmen had been doing for centuries.[8] Such notebooks might be in the form of waxed wooden tablets.[9] By the first century of the Christian era, they might have been of parchment or papyrus, and often in codex form.[10]

A few literary allusions to the process of writing help us to visualise what this early stage of an author's work would have looked like. Quintilian, for instance, advised students to leave alternate pages of their notebooks blank as they worked through them.[11] Space for annotation was evidently important. From Egypt there have survived some speeches of advocates in which the text has been drawn up with a wide margin for annotation. The notes which fill these margins are an abbreviated version of the speech, perhaps for reference during the presentation of the case.[12]

Poets, as their work progressed, were liable to fill the margins, and even the backs, of their rolls, according to an acid comment of Juvenal.[13] Aulus Gellius related that a friend of his had bought a copy of the second book of the *Aeneid* with interlined notes which he believed were those of the author.[14] Diogenes Laertius claimed to have seen the ὑπομνήματα of the dramatist and supposed philosopher, Epicharmus (*c.* 550–460 BC). According to Diogenes, these notebooks contained marginal annotations, which showed that they were indeed the author's own copies.[15] Whether or not these men were correct to believe that they had seen autograph copies of the authors' works, the state of the text was clearly what they expected of authors' own working copies of their notes. Marginal and interlined annotations were evidently common means by which authors revised drafts of their works.

Galen refers to another practice. He stated that it was customary for an author to write *currente calamo*, leaving more than one draft of some phrases standing in his manuscript. These might be in the body of the text or in the margin. When he had opportunity, the author would work over the material and decide which version he wished to retain. But, Galen said, a copyist dealing with a text like this might misunderstand the author's intention, and create a passage marked by redundancy because he had incorporated both versions when they were meant to be alternatives.[16] It is clear at least that authors' working drafts, obscure in expression, and confused in presentation, were well known in the literary world of antiquity.[17]

In a handful of cases we may be in possession of the sort of working drafts to which these references point. A possible example is contained in one of the papyri recovered from Herculaneum. Many of the works found there are the writings of Philodemus of Gadara, an Epicurean philosopher of the first century BC. Since Philodemus is known to have been under the patronage of Piso, who lived not far from Herculaneum, and since the Herculaneum library contained multiple copies of several of Philodemus' works, it has been conjectured that the library represents the literary deposit of an Epicurean circle which flourished under Piso's patronage, and among whom Philodemus was prominent.[18]

Of particular interest is papyrus 1021 of the Herculaneum collection, because it consists of part of a work of Philodemus with marginal and interlined corrections, which are found incorporated into the text of another witness of the same work, papyrus 164.[19] It has been suggested that papyrus 1021 is an author's draft, later worked up into the form shown by papyrus 164.[20]

More recent work has questioned the connection of Herculaneum with the Pisonian circle, and has cast doubt on the identification of papyrus 1021 as an annotated autograph.[21] In the light of this work, the papyrus appears more likely to be an example of scribal correction of a poor exemplar, rather than alteration by the author himself.

A more likely example of author's annotation is found in a late third-century papyrus from Oxyrhynchus. It is an anonymous encomium on an ἄρχων named Theon.[22] It was probably a prize

poem addressed to a local benefactor.[23] It has been extensively
altered by means of erasure and interlining. Part of the title has
been erased by sponge – it was apparently originally entitled
Ἑρμοῦ ἐνκώμιον, but has been retitled εἰς τὸν ἄρχοντα. In the
text itself, two types of alteration are to be seen. In some cases,
words or parts of words have been crossed out, and alternatives
interlined. In others, alternative drafts have been added above the
line without the words below being crossed out. So line 10 reads:

ιερω ενι   ω
ενθα σε και παις ουτος αναξ τιων ~ανα~ ~δημον~
and line 19

                        κενεαυχεα δωρα
πλουτου γαρ κενεοιο πελει μειλιγματα κεινα.

It is difficult to be certain whether the alterations were made by
the original writer. Hunt tentatively suggested that an amanuensis
first wrote the poem out, and that the author then made the
alterations which the poem now has.[24] Turner was apparently
willing to allow that the whole poem was the author's autograph.[25]
In either case, the papyrus gives a valuable idea of what an author's
draft would have looked like as work on it progressed.

Another example is provided by the surviving works of Dioscorus of Aphrodito (sixth century).[26] The significance of Dioscorus is
not the quality of his poetry, which is not great, but the fact that he
threw away several drafts of his poems which have survived.[27] Like
his predecessor, the anonymous encomiast, Dioscorus entered
corrections of his work, often without deletion or other marking to
indicate how he intended to develop his work.[28] Presumably he
either knew what he intended to do, or still had not decided what
form he wanted the poems to take, and so left the alternatives side
by side. The result is that it would be difficult to produce a definitive
edition of the remains of Dioscorus, because the text as the author
left it is ambiguous.

Dioscorus and the encomiast were poets, and Dioscorus at least
lived at the very end of Egypt's classical age. If their evidence stood
alone, it would be hazardous to argue from it to other forms of
literature, and to other ages of classical antiquity. But Quintilian,
Diogenes Laertius, Aulus Gellius, Juvenal, and Galen provide the
evidence that annotation of a manuscript by the author was a
common practice, and not confined to a particular place, time, or
genre of writing. The result of the annotating process would be a

confused text, comprehensible to its author, but more or less opaque to any other reader.

The role of the author's circle

The composition and production of literary works in antiquity was often more than a solitary affair. It would be difficult to overestimate the role of patrons and friends in the production and dissemination of literature in the ancient world. Ancient book-production has been fittingly called 'un commerce d'amitié'.[29]

An author's friends began to play a part before a work was completed. When an author had cast his work into a presentable, though not final, form, it was quite usual for him to distribute it to friends or to read it to them, in order to gain their comments.[30] Josephus made use of people he called 'co-workers' (συνεργοί) in producing the *Jewish Wars*. These are likely to have been friends to whom he circulated the manuscript.[31]

A patron was a particular type of 'friend' for these purposes. Augustus himself asked that a draft (ὑπογραφή) of the *Aeneid* be sent to him while he was on campaign.[32] Agrippa read the *Jewish Wars* of Josephus before its publication.[33]

While a work was still restricted to a small circle of readers around the author, it apparently did not need a title. Galen remarked that he did not give titles to the notes of his teaching which he gave to friends and pupils when they asked, because they were not for publication.[34]

The ties of friendship were also important in the dissemination of literature in the ancient world. Much has been made of the existence of a 'book trade' in antiquity, but the scale of this trade should not be exaggerated. Certainly, there were establishments which sold both luxury editions and more modest productions.[35] Rome had them, and so did Alexandria,[36] but beyond these cosmopolitan centres, little is certain. Pliny was surprised, or professed to be surprised, to be told that there was a bookseller in Lyons.[37] Pliny may not have been entirely serious, but his words suggest that provincial cities were not well supplied with bookshops.

If the book trade, such as it was, was concentrated only in the largest cities, it appears also to have dealt mainly with established classics. Certainly, some writers' work was in demand from booksellers even during their own lifetimes. The relationship between

Cicero and his 'publisher' Atticus is well known.[38] Pliny's works were available from the bookseller at Lyons, and Martial's poems could be bought from three different Roman shops.[39] But not every writer was a Cicero, a Pliny, or a Martial. It is unlikely that a bookseller would waste the time of his copyists on books unless they were commissioned, or likely to command a ready sale. Josephus circulated the *Jewish War* partly by giving presentation copies, and partly by direct sale.[40] Cicero had to tell his brother that some of the books he wanted for his library were simply unobtainable from commercial booksellers.[41]

These observations on the ancient book trade are of significance for Dibelius' hypothesis that Acts circulated through the medium of professional booksellers, and that the vagaries of its text are due to the fact that it was copied in commercial scriptoria, away from the protection of ecclesiastical control (see pp. 12 and 15f. above). It is questionable whether any bookseller would have been interested in the book of Acts. Dibelius' error was to suppose that because Luke intended to enter the literary world of his day, he would have had to do so through the book trade. In fact, works of literature, especially monographs of restricted interest, were more likely to circulate among groups of friends, in the form of copies made by members of the group.[42] That these works were not reproduced and offered for sale by booksellers by no means detracted from their claim to be serious literature.

Circulating work privately among friends did not guarantee that the work would remain out of other hands. Several writers found that works not ready for publication were pirated by friends or pupils without their consent.[43]

Later work on the text

Publication of a work did not ensure that a work would be preserved from alteration. The 'publication' of a work in antiquity meant only that it was no longer restricted to a private circle, and that anyone who wished was free to make a copy of it.[44] In only a few instances, such as those of Cicero and Martial noted above, would it have meant a commercial bookseller undertaking to produce multiple copies.

Works once published were open to alteration in numerous ways. The most blatant type of alteration was the publication of a revised text. This is known to have happened to Tertullian, who was prompted to issue a second edition of the *Adversus Marcionem* by the action of a 'lapsed brother', who had brought out an unauthorised second edition of his own.[45]

It is quite possible that alterations could enter the textual tradition of a book from annotations on the text. The British Museum papyrus 131, the celebrated copy of Aristotle's ᾽Αθη- ναίων Πολιτεία, is an example of a carefully annotated and corrected exemplar, which may have been 'a scholar's working copy'.[46] The annotation consists of interlined and marginal comments, reflecting a reader's thoughts on the text. With a text of this sort, it would be quite possible for a copyist working from it to assume that at least some of the marginal or interlined material had been brought in from a better exemplar, and represented 'corrections' to the text. Such a copyist might well suppose that he should try to insert this material into the text as he copied.

There were, therefore, various ways in which a work might acquire extensive annotations: first, during the process of composition, from the hand of the author himself; then, while the work was in the hands of the author's circle, from friends, pupils, or patron; and finally, when the work had passed into the wider public domain, from the book's eventual readers.

It is now necessary to ask at what point Acts itself received the annotations which appear to lie behind its distinctive Western text.

The annotations of the Western text of Acts

The work of a later annotator?

Several scholars have suggested that the Western text of Acts is derived from the work of a commentator (Lake and Cadbury, Haenchen), or from that of an editor preparing the book for publication to a wider readership, perhaps at Rome (Hanson), Antioch (Ropes), or Edessa (Zuntz). It might be supposed that annotation of the text was a stage in the work of the commentator or editor.

A hypothesis of this type was proposed by G. Salmon, in an early reaction to the Blass thesis. Salmon suggested that while Luke was in Rome he followed the custom of the day, in reading his work to a circle of hearers. He would often have been asked questions by those who listened. Others, too, would have supplied answers to questions about the book as it was read later. It is in these answers that the origin of the Western text of Acts lay. Such material as Acts 8.37 or 15.34 suggests the reflection of a perceptive hearer or reader of the text, although some passages which imply direct knowledge of events may have come from Luke himself.[47]

Salmon's proposal depended on a particular assumption about the identity of Luke. Taken more generally, though, it could still be argued that the Western annotations may have been the work of an early reader who had followed the text with great care, and had noted improvements which might be made to the work.

But two difficulties face any hypothesis which ascribes the Western material in Acts to a later reader, unrelated to Luke. There is in the first place the evidence of the Lucanism of the theology and the language of the Western readings (see pp. 57–106 above). This would be a remarkable achievement for a writer isolated from the author. In the second place there is the difficulty of supposing that the 'tunnel period' of Acts' transmission in the early second century produced a reader of Acts so attentive as to produce a virtual commentary on the book, more detailed than the first Patristic commentaries of the succeeding centuries. And for all the attention given to the book by the Western text, it does not bring the work into the second century, either by adding references to the theological problems of the day, or by completing the narrative with such well-known scenes as the martyrdom of Paul (see pp. 52–6 above).

If the Western text of Acts had been produced in the early second century, it would have arisen out of a minute concern for the text of Acts, and a scrupulous imitation of Luke's style, at a time when even bare knowledge of the book is hard to establish. It is, therefore, unlikely that the Western text's origin is to be found at such a distance from the author.

The work of the author's circle?

It has been seen (pp. 171f. above) that an author's friends would play a large part in preparing a work for publication. Pliny states that he circulated drafts of his work to friends so that they could annotate the text.[48] Is it possible that the Western annotated material in Acts represents the annotations made to the text by one of the author's circle, perhaps his comments on a draft sent to him preparatory to publication?

This hypothesis has several strong points. It would explain why a reader has taken such a close interest in the work. It might also account for the 'Lucanism' of the readings: the work of someone close to the author might be indistinguishable from Luke's own work.

The hypothesis is also open to some strong objections. One objection is that the 'Lucanism' of the readings is so marked that another hand is unlikely to have been responsible for them. This is the argument of Boismard and Lamouille, but it does not take into account the possibility of a contribution to the text from a source close to Luke in outlook, language, and style. It is therefore not as strong as the second objection, which arises from the nature and distribution of the readings. A friend or fellow-worker on the text might be expected to be concerned either with style or with content. Josephus, for example, seems to have had two sources of help: his 'collaborators', who helped with his Greek style, and his informants (such as Agrippa), who helped with the narrative.[49] The Western readings in Acts, however, make alterations of style and of content. A helper whose contribution was to the narrative might be expected to have more to add to some sections than to others, but the Western readings are scattered throughout the book. Finally, if the alterations were made by a member of the Lucan circle, he seems to have had nothing substantial to add to Luke's work. No new narrative material is given, and the readings restrict themselves to elucidating what is already in the alternative text.

For these reasons, then, it seems unlikely, though not entirely impossible, that a member of the Lucan circle was responsible for the Western annotations.

The work of the author?

The remaining possibility is that the copy of Acts from which the Western text was derived was an autograph annotated by the author. Annotated autographs, both genuine and spurious, were well known in antiquity (see pp. 168–71 above). When they were thought to be genuine, they were also highly prized. If such an annotated autograph lies behind the distinctive stratum of the Western text in Acts, the various characteristics of the text become comprehensible. Its Lucanism, its distribution throughout the work, and its cautious treatment of the existing text would all indicate the work of the author in improving what he had written.

If the Western annotated material were the work of the author, the incorporation of the material would evidently have been made by another hand. Only so can one explain the misunderstandings and misplacements of the marginal material which are the clue to revealing the material's origin (see pp. 158–66 above). An editor is responsible for combining the annotations with the text.

The hypothesis that the Western material began in the form of Lucan annotation of the text in fact pre-dates Blass's hypothesis. In 1886 a student of Zahn, Fr. Gleiss, produced a study, never published, entitled 'Untersuchung der sachlich bedeutsamen Eigentümlichkeiten des Codex D in der Apostelgeschichte' ('An Investigation of the Materially Significant Characteristics of Codex D in the Acts of the Apostles').[50] Gleiss's conclusion was that the Western text of Acts represents 'either the author's draft before publication, or the author's own copy with his supplementary marginal annotations'. [51] Gleiss's arguments persuaded Zahn himself, until Blass's work began to appear.[52] It is now impossible to know precisely what Gleiss's arguments were, since his work has apparently not been preserved,[53] but it can be guessed that Gleiss produced strong evidence, since Zahn says only that the superiority of Blass's thesis was to have been 'more definitely conceived and more thoroughly elaborated'.[54] Had Blass not written, Zahn's own extensive work on Acts might well have proceeded along the lines indicated by Gleiss in his study.

Gleiss's hypothesis, as Zahn summarised it, posits two possibilities. Either the Western material represents drafts considered and rejected in the final definitive form of the work, or the material originated as annotations on the author's own copy. If the second possibility is accepted, then it may be that this working copy was the only one Luke produced. Did Luke himself leave two forms of Acts, the 'finished' (non-Western), and the annotated (Western) forms? Or did he leave only a rough draft of his projected second volume, from which editors have produced the two textual traditions which we have today? The study of the text of Acts thus leads to a consideration of the processes by which Acts was edited and published.

The editing of Acts

The Book of Acts as a posthumous edition

A possible explanation for the textual confusion of the book of Acts is that there never was a definitive edition of the book at all, that

Luke never completed his second volume, and that the editing and publication of the work were undertaken by others.

The possibility that Acts was a posthumous edition has been raised by a few scholars, and there is indeed evidence, apart from the textual history of the book, that Luke did not complete it. This possibility was first raised by H. Ewald, who noted the abrupt ending of the book, and was struck by the numerous examples of difficult and even impossible wording which evidently existed before the text of Acts began to develop into 'longer' and 'shorter' forms. Ewald concluded that the work must have been left incomplete at the author's death, and was published by a friend, possibly Theophilus.[55] Ewald was followed by Harnack, who was also impressed by the 'roughness' of Acts, and suggested that different textual versions of the book were able to establish themselves precisely because no authentic version had been published by the author.[56]

R. B. Rackham suggested that the textual variety in Acts' textual tradition might be ascribed to the circulation of early drafts of Luke's work, or that Luke's death 'may have cut short the work of revision, so that the Acts never did appear in a fixed and final form'.[57]

De Zwaan argued in a study published in 1924 that Acts was edited and published after Luke's death.[58] De Zwaan's main concern was with the literary arrangement of the work, which he argued showed that it had not been given the same care as the Gospel of Luke. After summarising the theses of Harnack, Loisy, and Goguel concerning the authorship and composition of Acts, he continued:

> In my opinion none of these theories is satisfactory, and the evidence seems rather to support the hypothesis that our Acts is a sketch left unfinished by Luke, and afterwards edited by some friend or friends. He left it, as it appears, roughly outlined in his preface ... a skeleton-history filled in with extracts and notes in various stages of redaction, some gaps being left, and the whole by no means ready for the scriptorium.[59]

The weakness of de Zwaan's study was his failure to deal in detail with what he described as the unevenness of the book of Acts. Although he stated that some sections, for example Stephen's speech in Acts 7, were mere drafts,[60] he did not substantiate his assertions by close attention to the text. Similarly, his treatment of the supposed literary structure of Acts was rather cavalier, and his detection of a literary pattern, which allowed him to make the deduction that Luke planned a third volume, was more confident than his method justified.[61]

Lake and Cadbury were also willing to entertain the idea that the book of Acts had not reached its final form. Some remarks in their *Commentary* show that they believed there was evidence for this in the text.[62] But their remarks appear to have remained at the level of general conjecture.

The possibility that the book of Acts was unfinished was raised indirectly in two studies by H. W. and C. F. D. Moule, published in 1940 and 1954 respectively.[63] The articles suggested that the author of Acts had in places written out alternative drafts of a passage, and had neither removed the unsatisfactory drafts nor clearly indicated which version was the preferred one. The result was a confused text. H. W. Moule's observations were based on Acts 4.25: C. F. D. Moule applied his father's observation also to Acts 3.16, 10.36–8, 19.40, 20.34, 23.30, and 27.10. H. W. Moule's proposal reflects precisely the habit of composition referred to by Galen.[64]

The preliminary observations outlined here can in fact be taken further. There is more evidence that Acts was not brought to completion and publication by Luke himself, evidence which is to be found both in the internal witness of its contents and in the external witness of its early history.

The publication of Acts

At first sight, the most obvious piece of evidence for the incompleteness of Acts is the ending. The reader is left without any explicit information about what happened to Paul after the 'two years' of 28.30. But various explanations are possible to account for the ending of Acts in the form in which we now have it. There may be historical reasons for the book to end where it does: in particular, the possibility that it had brought the narrative to the present day.[65] Numerous literary proposals have been made to account for the ending; among them those of J. Dupont, that the true conclusion of the book is Paul's arrival and preaching in 28.16–28, with 28.30f. a mere epilogue,[66] and of P. Davies, that the ending of Acts is modelled on that of 2 Kings.[67] It is widely held that the ending of Acts can be satisfactorily explained without recourse to the notion that it is incomplete,[68] and it cannot therefore be taken as firm evidence that the book was not completed.

Stronger evidence that Acts may not have been published with the Gospel by Luke comes from the fate of the book in the course of the second century. The Gospel of Luke was almost certainly in circulation before Marcion used it in the 140s. The first certain evidence for Acts, on the other hand, is Irenaeus. How may this divergence between Luke and Acts be accounted for?

The answer most commonly accepted is that given by Haenchen, among others, that Acts was not a Gospel and so had no place in the church's worshipping life. While Luke was accepted as an ecclesiastical reading-book, Acts was neglected until the end of the second century, when in the hands of Irenaeus it proved its usefulness in combating heresy.[69]

But it is only a supposition that the emergence of the category 'Gospel' severed Luke from Acts, excluding Acts from ecclesiastical use, and it is unsatisfactory in several respects. For one thing, Gospels were not the only material read in Christian assemblies. Marcion's division of his scriptures into 'Gospel' and 'Apostle' reflected the types of writing read in Christian assemblies other than his own. Letters had been read in these assemblies at least from the time of Paul, and continued to be read apparently without a break.[70] That there was also lively interest among second-century Christians in the apostles and their doings is attested by Papias and Hegesippus, as well as by the growth of the apocryphal *Acts*. All of which prompts the question: if Acts found a home in the 'Apostle'-section of the emerging canon in the third century, why did it not find it in the second century? It is not enough to say, with Haenchen: 'In Acts the Christian reader encountered a book unlike any he had previously known, and one which was neither necessary nor customarily used in preaching or instruction.'[71] Acts is as unique in the contemporary canon as it would have been to a second-century reader, and the reading of 'Apostle' alongside 'Gospel' from the earliest times would have provided a potential life-setting for the book in the church.

J. C. O'Neill offered another explanation for the silence of Acts: that both Luke and Acts were published much later than has generally been supposed, at some time between approximately AD 115 and AD 130.[72] O'Neill arrived at the first of these dates by arguing that theologically Luke–Acts shows affinities with Justin Martyr, but that since Justin does not show knowledge of Luke–Acts, then he and Luke must have been drawing on a common fund of contemporary thinking.[73] The second date O'Neill established by the observation that Marcion in the 140s knew Luke, and that it is therefore unlikely to have been published much after 130.[74]

O'Neill's argument relies heavily on Justin's supposed ignorance of Luke–Acts as a literary work, combined with the similarities between his thought and that of Luke. But was Justin really ignorant of at least Luke's Gospel? O'Neill examined with great attention to detail the passages in Justin which appear to show knowledge of Luke.[75] His conclusion was that particular differences of wording and presentation show that Justin was following a parallel tradition, and not Luke's Gospel itself.

But it is by no means certain that Justin's use of the Gospel tradition will lend itself to such close verbal scrutiny. For Justin, the scriptures are the Old Testament, to which he refers frequently and which he cites explicitly throughout his work. The Christian writings which he calls ἀπομνημονεύματα of the apostles (1 Apol. 66.3; Dial. 103.8) are seldom, if ever, cited by him explicitly. This may be either because to do so would not have served his apologetic purpose, or, as is quite likely, because for him they did not have the full status of 'scripture'.[76] The result is that he alludes to the Gospel material, rather than attempting to quote it exactly, and one can therefore only safely argue from the general content of his material, and not from the precise wording of his text.

It seems quite clear that Justin knew the Gospel of Luke, possibly in its Western form.[77] It is less clear whether Justin was aware of Acts. Haenchen has argued that he was, because of his words in 1 Apol. 50.12, where Justin wrote of the passion in words reminiscent of Luke 23.49, then of Jesus' post-resurrection appearances in a way which shows dependence on Luke 24.25, 44f., and finally of the ascension and coming of the Spirit in terms, so Haenchen has argued, drawn from Acts 1.8 (Justin: δύναμιν ... λαβόντες; Acts: λήμψεσθε δύναμιν).[78] But Justin could have drawn the entire contents of 1 Apol. 50.12 from Luke 24.44–53. The Gospel itself contains references to being clothed with power from on high (24.49), to the ascension (24.51),[79] and to the beginning of the worldwide mission of the apostles (24.47). Indeed, the phrase εἰς πάντα τὰ ἔθνη (Luke 24.47: cf. Justin, εἰς πᾶν γένος ἀνθρώπων ἐλθόντες), and the insistence that the power they receive is sent by Jesus himself (Luke 24.49), are elements shared by Justin, and lacking in Acts. Justin was probably relying on Luke's Gospel alone.

The remaining possible allusions to Acts in Justin may all be accounted for as religious commonplaces, and it would appear, therefore, that while Justin knew and used Luke, he did not use Acts and may not have known it.

Another source from which knowledge of Acts might have been expected is the longer Marcan ending (Mark 16.9–20). This appears to be an early second-century compilation.[80] Some of its material may have been drawn, like Justin's, from Luke's Gospel, and there are close links between its narrative and that of Luke.[81] The longer ending may, though, have drawn on parallel tradition. The ending's summary of the apostolic work (vv. 15–18) does not seem dependent on Acts; it is more likely to have drawn on a stock of miracle stories such as those known to Papias.[82] The longer Marcan ending is another example of an early second-century text which had the opportunity to demonstrate an acquaintance with Acts, but did not do so.

From the very scanty evidence available, what is true of Justin appears to have been true of other sources in the period before Irenaeus. While Luke was known, Acts was not. The combination Luke–Acts is a familiar part of present-day scholarship, and the study of both works together is common, but it is necessary to be reminded that there is no strong evidence to suppose that the two works were issued or ever circulated together.

Luke–Acts would not have fitted a single roll.[83] As a matter of physical necessity, therefore, the Gospel and Acts would at first have existed in separate volumes. Even when the rise of the codex form permitted longer texts to appear together, the connection of Acts with Luke was not always obvious. The papyrus p[53] (third century) contains fragments of Matthew and Acts. It may originally have contained Luke also, but in view of its size it is quite possible that it only ever contained Matthew and Acts.[84] There is no early manuscript of the New Testament which places Acts with Luke. The separation of the two was established at a primitive stage, and ran very deeply in the tradition.

Irenaeus pressed his opponents by using the connection between Luke's Gospel, on which they depended, and Acts, which contained material harmful to their case. If they accepted one, then they must also accept the other.[85] But he did not accuse them of suppressing Acts. It was merely that he was in possession of a work which they did not recognise.

The early history of the book of Acts therefore is consistent with the possibility that it was not published at the same time as the

Gospel of Luke. Irenaeus urged that Luke and Acts belonged together, but Christian practice from the second century separated them. Acts was not known to Clement;[86] it was probably not used by the author of the longer Marcan ending, or by Justin. Its clandestine existence for the better part of a century suggests that it may not have been published.

In addition to the external evidence for the posthumous publication of Acts, there is the evidence from within the work itself. Most of the scholars mentioned in pp. 177f. above, who have concluded that Acts was not brought to completion by Luke, were impressed by the roughness of the text, either in its construction (de Zwaan), or in specific points of expression (Harnack, Rackham, Lake and Cadbury, H. W. and C. F. D. Moule). Rackham produced a short list of passages which he considered evidence of such roughness.[87] Lake and Cadbury referred frequently to passages at which the text, particularly the common, non-Western text, was poorly constructed, ungrammatical, or impossible.[88]

No author ever writes consistently to his highest standard, and Luke can be no exception. However, the book of Acts is dotted with passages which are obscure and difficult, not because the thought is particularly convoluted, but simply because the chosen forms of expression are, so it would seem, carelessly put together. The last stage in an author's preparation of his work in antiquity was that of 'polishing' his text: Acts gives precisely the impression of being 'unpolished' in its detailed expression. Galen informs us that authors frequently placed alternative forms of expression side by side in their drafts: the studies of H. W. and C. F. D. Moule appear to have identified such duplicate passages in Acts (see p. 178 above). The internal evidence of the text of Acts points to an original form which had not been completely revised by the author.

The conclusion to which we are drawn is, then, that at Luke's death the first volume of his work had been published, but that the second had not. This second volume, near completion but still in draft form, remained in obscurity until published relatively late in the second century, perhaps in the third quarter. There were currents in the church's life in the third quarter of the second century which would have made the publication of Acts particularly timely. Marcion had produced a distinctive interpretation not only of Paul's teaching, but of the entire first generation of the Christian church. He accused all the earliest leaders of the church, apart from

Paul, of a lapse into Judaising practices. Marcion threatened the church by questioning its historical legitimacy in two ways: first, by appropriating the figure of Paul to himself, and secondly, by positing a radical disjunction between Jesus and Paul (with whom he identified) on the one hand, and the rest of the church's early leadership on the other.

Marcion was not alone in laying claim to Paul. The Valentinians similarly drew support from him. This had serious implications for the place of the apostle in the non-Gnostic church. Von Campenhausen detects a falling-off in enthusiasm for Paul in the mid second century.[89] But the tradition which maintained Paul's cause within the church seems an unbroken one (2 Peter, Clement, Ignatius, Polycarp, Irenaeus), and equally, those who declined to acknowledge Paul seem to have existed alongside this tradition throughout (Papias, Justin, Hegesippus). Yet it is no doubt true that the increasing use of Paul by heretics lent weight to the suspicion with which he had always been regarded in some quarters. And as the Marcionite challenge gained strength, the portrayal of Paul in Acts became proportionately more valuable to those who continued to claim him for the non-Gnostic church. The Marcionite Paul had no more solid opponent than the Lucan Paul.

Acts' value in the mid second century lay not only in its portrayal of Paul, but in its complete picture of the earliest years of the church. Acts gives the reader a presentation of the origins of the church as a seamless robe. The ministry of Jesus gives rise in Acts, not merely to the church in general, but specifically to the Jerusalem church. This church spreads its influence over the emerging new churches, as at Antioch. Paul himself is brought into the developing picture. Luke, like the other evangelists, bases the origin of the Twelve in the earthly ministry of Jesus. But he has gone beyond them in binding the Twelve to the Jerusalem church, and in linking Paul firmly to this Jerusalem nucleus. Acts simply leaves no room for the radical disjunction in the earliest years of the church which was the foundation for the Marcionite case. As a narrative, Acts served to undermine the historical basis of Marcionism.

These observations may explain why a work which had lain in obscurity for two generations should have acquired a new relevance in mid-century. There was a need to make Luke's Acts known after Marcion, which had not been so pressing before.

Posthumous edition and textual variation in antiquity

If Acts was edited and published posthumously, it would not have been the only work in antiquity to have appeared in this way. Posthumous editing was a not uncommon fate of literary works, and one which posed particular problems for editors, and gave opportunities for textual variation in the works' traditions.[90]

Plotinus gives an example of the textual problems which could arise from posthumous publication. Towards the end of his life, Plotinus committed his teaching to writing, but left it in the form of short and untitled notes.[91] He gave his student Porphyry the task of editing his work, a task which was only completed twenty-eight years after the master's death, and which resulted in the publication of the *Enneads*.[92] However, another student of Plotinus – Eustochius – also undertook the same task, and produced another edition of Plotinus' works, arranged on different principles, which was known and circulated alongside the *Enneads*.[93]

Among poets whose work left unpublished at their deaths is known to have been edited posthumously are Heraclitus,[94] Lucretius,[95] Virgil,[96] and Persius.[97] Virgil had two editors, Lucius Varius and Plotius Tucca.[98] Persius' *Satires* were edited by the author's friend, Caesius Bassus. According to Persius' biographer, the editor adopted the expedient of excising a section at the end of the work, in order to give an impression of completeness.[99]

According to Diogenes Laertius, Thucydides did not complete his *Peloponnesian War*, but some time after his death Xenophon took the manuscript in hand, and brought it to a fit state for publication.[100] This story is at least consistent with critical observations which suggest that the *Peloponnesian War* is incomplete.[101] It fails by six years, for example, to bring the story to the point which the author had set as its end (5.26.1). The last book lacks speeches, and incorporates source material in a way which is not characteristic of the author.[102] These, and other indications of lack of attention to detail, suggest strongly that at Thucydides' death the *War* was still only in a draft form, but near enough to completion to require no more than polishing to make it acceptable for public readership.[103]

Caesar's works, too, seem to have been the subject of posthumous editing and publication. Aulus Hirtius added an eighth book to the *Gallic War* in order to fill the gap between that work and the *Civil War*.[104] In the same passage in which Hirtius gave his reason for writing the additional volume, he also described the *Civil War* as 'unfinished' (*imperfectum*). He may have meant that it left the narrative incomplete, but there is evidence to suggest that the *Civil War* was not published in Caesar's lifetime. Externally, there is the fact that Cicero's *Brutus* contains no reference to the *Civil War*, an omission which is particularly significant if, as several scholars hold, *Brutus* was written very close to the time of Caesar's death.[105] Internally, the evidence consists of the gaps it contains, the relatively poor construction, and the contradictions within it.[106] There are cases in which expressions which appear to have been alternative drafts of the same passage have been incorporated into the text to produce overloaded and redundant expressions.[107] In consequence, the majority of scholars are of the opinion that the *Civil War* is a posthumous edition.[108]

A final example of posthumous publication is provided by Marcus Aurelius. His *Thoughts* are generally recognised to have been composed for his own reference, and to have been published only after his death.[109] Political considerations may have delayed publication until a considerable time after his death.[110]

It was not unusual, then, for a work to be published posthumously. Posthumous editors could treat their texts arbitrarily (as with Persius), and more than one editor could produce variant texts (as with Plotinus). If Acts was published posthumously, there would have been ample opportunity for textual variation from the outset.

The origin of the texts of Acts

A large part of the distinctive stratum of the Western text of Acts has its origin in marginal annotations which show every indication of having been the work of the author (see pp. 107–166 and 173–6 above). Gleiss proposed two possibilities which might account for the existence of material in this form: either the Western readings could be derived from Luke's draft before publication, or they might be taken from his own copy retained after publication, and containing further reflections on the text.[111] Rackham suggested a further possibility: that Luke may never have published Acts in a final form at all.[112] These theses raise a question: does the non-Western text represent a recognised and published version of Acts, with the Western having incorporated extra material (albeit Lucan), or are both forms of text derived from the work of different editors on a single, rough, and ambiguous Lucan original?

Several considerations make it unlikely that the Western text represents a supplementing of a published Lucan Acts, and probable that Western and non-Western texts represent versions of a text left unedited by Luke.

It has been seen that there is no reason to suppose that Acts was published along with the Gospel. There is no positive evidence for acquaintance with the book before Irenaeus, and there is some evidence that early second-century sources which might have shown knowledge of Acts do not do so. While Luke was known and used in the early second century, the evidence suggests that Acts only emerged into public use after the mid-century. Before that point there appears to have been no published and widely known version of Acts.

The roughness of the common text of Acts suggests further that Luke had not given the work his final attention. There are too many obscure and incoherent passages in the book for one to be satisfied that it represents his finished work. The textual evidence of Acts suggests that two editors worked on Luke's literary remains to present this book for publication, probably at some point in the third quarter of the second century.

The Western fulness of expression in Acts is the result of an editor's wish to preserve annotated and interlined marginal material, of the sort we might expect in an author's working copy. The occasional misplacements and inconsistencies to which this policy led him were the subject of Chapter 4. The development of the Western tradition has tended to smooth out these awkward passages, but where they can be traced, they are our clearest indication of the approach taken by this 'Western' editor.

The non-Western text is also the result of posthumous editing. Two characteristics may be discerned in it. The first is its cautious treatment of Luke's narrative. The non-Western editor did not, as far as may be seen, include the annotated material in his version. In a similarly cautious way, he allowed obscure narrative passages to stand, but occasionally tried to clear them up. This aspect of his work only becomes clear when he departs from Luke's manner of expression or pattern of thought, as in the two following examples. In 11.2 (see pp. 77–87 above) the Western version is awkward, but Lucan in style, and yields a consistent meaning in the context of Acts as a whole. The non-Western version looks like an attempt to simplify an obscure passage by abstracting a plain meaning from it. The result, though, is to create difficulties in the development of the narrative. Another example of the same phenomenon is 19.14. In that verse, in the Western version, the narrative moves forward: 'At that time' (ἐν οἷς),[113] some exorcists (probably Gentile) tried, to copy the activity of the Jewish exorcists already mentioned (19.13). But the non-Western version seems to derive from a misunderstanding of ἐν οἷς as 'among whom'. When understood in this way, v. 14 as it is in the Western version becomes largely redundant repetition of v. 13, and the non-Western version appears to be an abbreviated rewriting of v. 14 in order to eliminate the perceived redundancy. However, as with 11.2, the Western version of 19.14 gives a better and more Lucan text. The non-Western reading is the result of an ill-judged attempt to simplify a difficult passage.[114] The non-Western editor in general, therefore, attempted to reproduce the narrative as it lay in Luke's text, but on a few occasions he betrayed his hand by his attempts at removing obscurities.

The second characteristic of the non-Western editor was his cautious treatment of some issues which had become sensitive matters for the mid-second-century church.

On matters of church discipline, for instance, it has already been argued that the non-Western editor, in accordance with the growing sensitivity of his age, decided to withdraw the catechetical scene of 8.37 from public scrutiny (pp. 69–77 above). In the so-called 'Apostolic Decree', he added the gloss τὸ πνικτόν in order to make the meaning of the blood-prohibition more explicit, again in accordance with the tendency of contemporary thinking (pp. 100f.). In 27.35 he seems to have understood Paul's breaking of bread on board ship as a eucharist, and therefore he took offence at the statement that 'he also gave [the bread] to us'.[115] This reaction is not surprising when we recall that the dominical saying 'Give not that which is holy to the dogs' had been a guiding principle of eucharistic discipline from the time of the *Didache* (Mt. 7.6, *Did.* 9.5). On matters of doctrinal significance, we have the example of 2.30, where some Western witnesses (together with Byzantine witnesses which have borrowed from the Western tradition) include the phrase τὸ κατὰ σάρκα ἀναστήσειν τὸν Χριστόν.[116] Luke's concern to demonstrate the physical characteristics of the resurrected body of Christ is clear in several passages, and is particularly evident in his presentation of the resurrection (Lk. 24.39, Acts 10.41, 13.34–7). The flesh of Christ is at the centre of Luke's attention in Acts 2. He has altered the reading of Ps. 16.10

to introduce a reference to flesh (2.31), and one of his main aims in Peter's speech is to demonstrate that the flesh of Jesus did not see corruption, in accordance with the words of scripture. The Western reading appears quite Lucan in outlook. But this passage might seem questionable to a mid-second-century scribe, aware of the contemporary debate over the physical nature of the future resurrection (Justin, *Dial.* 80). The phrase τὸ κατὰ σάρκα ἀναστήσειν τὸν Χριστόν might seem to open the door to the sort of views of a physical resurrection being put forward by the followers of Cerinthus (see Eusebius, *HE* 3.28.2, 7.25.3). The non-Western editor seems therefore to have taken the opportunity to eliminate a potentially misleading phrase.[117]

The depiction of Paul in Acts must have been one of the major points of interest for its second-century readers. Indeed, it may be that the publication of the book was an attempt to acquaint the church at large with the Lucan Paul in order to combat the Gnostic Paul. Here again the non-Western editor displays a cautious approach.

In 21.25 Paul's position with regard to the 'zealots for the law' is being considered by the Jerusalem elders. In the Western version there is a continuity of thought, as the elders conclude their speech to Paul: 'But concerning the believing Gentiles, they [the zealots] have nothing to say to you, for we have written to them, judging that they should keep nothing of that sort [i.e. the demands of the Law], except to abstain from meat sacrificed to idols, from blood, and from fornication.'[118] The non-Western version, by omitting the phrase 'they have nothing to say to you, for ... ' makes the conclusion of the elders' speech introduce the Gentile believers as an unconnected afterthought. The editor appears to have had a purpose in making this omission: an attempt to liberate Paul from the implied protection of the Jerusalem church. The phrase 'that they should keep nothing of that sort, except ... ' may have seemed objectionable because it allowed a Marcionite interpretation. The second-century church observed many provisions of the Law apart from those of the Apostolic Decree, and to a reader with the example of Marcion before him, the Western reading may have seemed far too sweeping in its apparent dismissal of the value of the scriptures.

At 17.18 the non-Western text again seems to be guarding against the Gnostic interpretation of Paul. The Epicureans and Stoics on the Areopagus say of Paul that 'he seems to be a preacher of foreign deities (δαιμόνια)', after which most witnesses give the explanatory clause: 'for he was preaching Jesus and the resurrection'. This last clause, though, is omitted by D and it[51]. It is hard to explain why it should have been omitted, if genuine. But it would be a useful clarification to the text by a copyist who was concerned that the reference to Paul preaching strange δαιμόνια should not become the growth point for Gnostic speculation. By spelling out what he understood to be the content of Paul's preaching, the non-Western editor was trying to rescue Paul from his Gnostic interpreters. The editor responsible for the non-Western text seems to present a substantially Lucan text. But despite this, the non-Western text has been affected by the process of posthumous publication; the editor had too high a regard for Luke's work to allow it either to offend his contemporaries or to give potential support for Gnostic sects.

The enigma of the text of Acts has produced a wide variety of interpretations and proposed solutions. The solution proposed here is that Acts suffered the fate, not uncommon in antiquity, of posthumous publication. The uncertain state of the draft copy from which its editors worked has given rise to the two great textual traditions present in our witnesses, both of which have Lucan traits, but neither of which is Lucan in all its readings. Our access to Luke's second volume is by way of his editors, who were also his earliest interpreters.

It was the achievement of these editors to put into the hands of the late second-century church a key to the interpretation of many of the most difficult problems it faced. The book of Acts tied 'Gospel' and 'Apostle' together. Against Marcion, it placed Paul within a wider apostolic fellowship. Against the claims of the Gnostics, it bound the church to the earthly ministry of Jesus, calling into question the possibility or the necessity of a secret tradition. The polemical work of Irenaeus demonstrated how effectively the publication of Acts could serve the needs of the church in the last quarter of the century.

It is the legacy of these editors with which readers of Acts have to deal today. The editors' methods have left us a problematic bequest, but one whose value has not diminished since the time of Acts' belated publication.

Appendix

TEXTUAL WITNESSES

Greek

Papyri

Sigla	Description	Date
p^{29}	Oxf.Bodl.Lib.Gr.bibl.g.4(P)	3rdC
p^{38}	Univ.Mich.Inv.1571	c.300
p^{45}	Dublin P.Chester Beatty 1	3rdC
p^{48}	Flor.Bibl.Laur.PSI 1165	3rdC
p^{53}	Univ.Mich.Inv.6652	3rdC
p^{74}	Cologny/Gen. P.Bodmer XVII	7thC
p^{91}	P.Mil.Vogl.Inv.1224	3rdC

Fourteen papyri contain parts of the book of Acts, but of these, only p^{74} contains any continuous substantial portion of text.[1] p^{74} is a relatively late papyrus and exhibits an Alexandrian text of Acts. Of the earlier papyri, three exhibit Western characteristics ($p^{29.}$ $p^{38.}$ p^{48}),[2] and three $p^{45.53.91}$ (all 3rdC), exhibit Alexandrian characteristics.[3]

Uncials

Sigla	Description	Gr/Al No.	Date
א	Sinaiticus: Lond.Br.Lib.Add.43725	01	4thC
A	Alexandrinus: Lond.Br.Lib.Roy.		
	1D.VIII	02	5thC
B	Vaticanus: Rom.Bibl.Vat.Gr.1209	03	4thC
C	Ephraemi: Par.Bibl.Nat.Gr.9	04	5thC
D	Bezae: Cambr.Bibl.Univ.Nn.II 41	05	5thC
E	Laudianus: Oxf.Bibl.Bodl.Laud.		
	Gr.35	08	6thC

Sigla	Description	Gr/Al No.	Date
H	Mutinensis: Modena.Bibl. Estens.		
	G 196	014	9thC
L	Angelicus: Rom.Bibl.Angelica 39	020	9thC
P	Porphirianus: Leningr.Bibl.Pub.		
	Gr.225	025	9thC
Φ	Beratinus: Tirana, Nat.Archive 1	043	6thC
Ψ	Athous Laurae: Athos Lavra β'52	044	8/9thC
048	Rom.Bibl.Vat.Gr.2061	048	5thC

Of the uncial witnesses, the most striking are D and E, because of their frequent departures from the Majority text.

D is the major witness to the Western text of Acts, and has probably as much secondary material devoted to its study as any New Testament manuscript.[4] It must be recalled that D has several lacunae in Acts (8.29–10.14, 21.2–10, 16–18, 22.10–20, 22.29–end).

E has peculiarities of its own. It contains a number of Western readings, but differences between the wording of E and of other Western witnesses, especially D, have led to a suspicion that E's Western material is a retranslation from Latin, although this has recently been questioned.[5]

The other uncial witnesses to Acts stand outside the Western textual tradition, but they may occasionally exhibit Western readings, as C does at 14.10,19, 15.34. The uncials ℵ and B are the major witnesses to the non-Western textual tradition.

Minuscules

The evidence of minuscules for the text of Acts is far from being fully explored. The very quantity of manuscripts concerned has inhibited a comprehensive collection of the minuscule data. Only one edition of an individual minuscule witness for Acts has been published, but collations of others have appeared.[6] The most comprehensive collections of evidence so far available remain the editions of Tischendorf (8th edition) and von Soden,[7] while some further collating work has been done by Boismard and Lamouille.[8]

The list given below indicates the minuscule witnesses whose evidence, when it can be ascertained from the sources mentioned above, is given in the apparatus to readings. Minuscules are here cited by their Gregory–Aland numbers.

Sigla	Description	Date
6	Par.Bibl.Nat.Gr.112	13thC
33	Par.Bibl.Nat.Gr.14	9thC
36	Oxf.New Coll.58	12thC
81	Lond.Brit.Lib.Add.20003	1044
88	Naples Bibl.Nat.II.Aa7	12thC
104	Lond.Brit.Lib.Harley 5537	1087
181	Rom.Bibl.Vat.Reg.Gr.179	11thC
242	Moscow Hist.Mus. V 25	12thC
257	(Lost) Berlin St-Bibl.MSGr.Qu 40	13/14thC
307	Par.Bibl.Nat.Coislin Gr.25	10thC
323	Gen.Bibl.Publ & Univ.Gr.20	11thC
383	Oxf.Bodl.Clarke 9	13thC
431	Strasb.Priester-Sem.1	11thC
453	Rom.Bibl.Vat.Barb.Gr.582	14thC
467	Par.Bibl.Nat.Gr.59	15thC
522	Oxf.Bodl.Canonici Gr.34	1515/16
536	Mich.Univ.Lib. NT Ms.24	13thC
614	Mil.Bibl.Amb. E97sup.	13thC
876	Mich.Univ.Lib.NT.Ms.16	12thC
913	Lond.Brit.Lib.Egerton 2787	14thC
915	Escorial T.III.12	13thC
945	Athos Dionysiu 124	11thC
1108	Athos Esphigmenu 64	13thC
1175	Patmos Joannu 16	11thC
1518	Const.Patr.Jerus.	15thC
1522	(Lost) London, Lambeth Palace 1184	14thC
1611	Athen.Nat.Bibl. 94	12thC
1704	Athos Kutlumusiu 356	1541
1739	Athos Lavra β'64	10thC
1765	Lond.Brit.Lib.Add.33214	14thC
1799	Princeton Univ.Lib.Garrett Ms.8	12/13thC
1838	Grottaferrata Bib.Badia A'β'6	11thC
1891	Jerus.Saba 107	10thC
2138	Moscow Univ.Lib. 1	1072
2147	Leningr.Bibl.Publ.Gr.224	11thC
2298	Paris Nat.Gr.102	11thC
2401	Chic.Univ.Lib.Ms.142	*c.* 1200
2412	Chic.Univ.Lib.Ms.922	12thC
2464	Patmos Joannu 742	10thC
2495	Sinai St.Cath. 1992	14/15thC

Lectionaries

lec[6]   Leiden Univ.Bib.Or.243   13thC

Latin

It is in the citation of Latin witnesses that most confusion is likely to arise, because of the haphazard allocation of letters (following Lachmann) to designate manuscripts. In several cases, the same letter has been used to designate quite different witnesses. An example is A. C. Clark's choice of q to designate the Vulgate MS Paris Nat.Lat.343, when q already conventionally designated the Old Latin Gospel MS, Codex Monacensis (13 in the Vetus Latina list). E. J. Epp later designated the same Paris MS it[q]. Both scholars made clear the identity of their q, but the potential for confusion in idiosyncratic systems of naming MSS is clear.

The system adopted here is to designate Old Latin MSS by the numbers allocated to them by the Vetus Latina Institute at Beuron.[9] This system has the disadvantage of not being as familiar as the alphabetic convention (particularly in the loss of the immediately recognisable pairs Dd and Ee), but has the advantage that it is less ambiguous.

For the Vulgate, Wordsworth and White provided an alphabetic convention which is widely recognised.[10] Wordsworth and White's system has two limitations: it invites confusion between Vulgate MSS and Greek uncials (for instance D represents both Codex Bezae and Codex Armachanus), and it covers only a handful of Vulgate MSS. For this reason, Vulgate MSS are here cited according to Gregory's numeric system wherever possible.[11] In three cases, as the list shows, this has not been possible, and new sigla have been created, adapted from Boismard and Lamouille (vg[BG] vg[MM] vg[gk629]). As with the Old Latin, this convention entails sacrificing familiarity for clarity and a greater degree of comprehensiveness.

Old Latin

VL No.	Description	Other sigla (W&W = *)	Date
it[5]	Camb.Bibl.Univ.Nn.II 41 (Bezae)	d	5thC
it[6]	Par.Nat.Fond.Lat.254 (Colbertinus)	c	12thC

VL No.	Description	Other sigla (W&W=*)	Date
it⁵⁰	Oxf.Bibl.Bod.Laud Gr 35 (Laudianus)	e	6thC
it⁵¹	Stockh.Kung.Bibl. (Gigas)	g, gig	13thC
it⁵²	Milan Bib.Amb.B.168 Sup (Frag.Med.)	g²	?8thC
it⁵³	Naples Bib.Naz.Cod.Lat.2 (Bobbiensis)	s	5/6thC
it⁵⁴	Par.Nat.Fond.Lat.321 (Perpinianus)	p	13thC
it⁵⁵	Par.Nat.Fond.Lt.6400G (Floriacensis)	h	5thC
it⁵⁶	Par.Nouv.Acq.Lt.2171 (Lib.Comicus)	t	11thC
it⁵⁷	Seles. B.Mun.1093 (Schlettstadtensis)	r	7/8thC
it⁵⁸	Prag.Com.Ev.th.Fac. (Wernigerodensis)	w	15thC
it⁵⁹	Lost (Demidovianus)	dem	12/13thC
it⁶¹	Dublin Trin.Coll.52 (Armachanus)	D*	9thC
it⁶²	Par.Nat.Fond.Lat.6 (Bible de Rosas)	r R*	10thC
it⁶³	Univ.Michigan Ms. 146		12thC
it⁶⁷	Léon Cathd.MS 15 (Pal.Legionensis)	l	7thC
it⁶⁹	Léon Cathd.MS 2 (Liber Comicus)	τ⁶⁹	11thC

Vulgate

Greg.	Description	Other sigla (W&W=*)	Date
vgᵃᵐ	Flor.Bibl.Laur. (Amiatinus)	A*	7thC
vg^BG	(Brev. Goth.)¹²		9/10thC
vgᶜᵃᵛ	La Cava MS 14 (Cavensis)	C*	9thC
vgˡᵘˣ	Par.Nat.Lat.9247 (Luxueilensis)		8thC
vg^MM	Missale Mixtum¹²		?11thC
vgᵗᵒˡ	Madr.Bibl.Nat.Tol.2.1,vitr.4 (Toletanus)	T*	10thC
vgᵛᵃˡⁱᶜ	Rome Valicella Bibl.Or.B6 (Valicellanus)	V*	9thC
vg²³¹ᵃ	Lond.Br.Lib.Royal 1.B (Sarisburiensis)	W*	13thC
vg²⁴³	Lond.Brit.Lib.Add.11852	U*	9/10thC
vg⁴²²	Oxf.Bibl.Bodl.Canon.Bibl.Lat.76		12thC
vg⁴⁹³	Oxf.Bibl.Bodl. 3418	O*	8thC

Greg.	Description	Other sigla (W&W=*)	Date
vg[654]	Vienna Nat.1190		9thC
vg[1186]	Par.Nat.Lat.4		9/10thC
vg[1188]	Par.Nat.Lat.6		10thC
vg[1189]	Par.Nat.Lat.7		11thC
vg[1192]	Par.Nat.Lat.10		12/13thC
vg[1193]	Par.Nat.Lat.11		13thC
vg[1199]	Par.Nat.Lat.93		9thC
vg[1213]	Par.Nat.Lat.202		14thC
vg[1240]	Par.Nat.Lat.305		11thC
vg[1242]	Par.Nat.Lat.309		11thC
vg[1243]	Par.Nat.Lat.315		12/13thC
vg[1258]	Par.Nat.Lat.341		13thC
vg[1259]	Par.Nat.Lat.342		13thC
vg[1260]	Par.Nat.Lat.343	q	13thC
vg[1266]	Par.Nat.Lat.9380 (Theodulfianus)	Θ*	9thC
vg[1274]	Par.Nat.Lat.11533		9thC
vg[1276]	Par.Nat.Lat.11553	G*	8thC
vg[1277]	Par.Nat.Lat.11932		13/14thC
vg[1282]	Par.Nat.Lat.16262		13thC
vg[1396]	Bamberg Bibl.Mun.A.I.5	B*	9thC
vg[1700]	Munich Bay.StBibl.Clm.6230 (Monacensis)	M*	9thC
vg[1897]	Berne Bongar.Bibl.A.9		10thC
vg[1985]	Léon Cathd. MS.6		10thC
vg[2084]	Milan Bibl.Ambr.E.53 inf.		10thC
vg[gk629]	Bibl.Vat.Otto.Gr.298[13] (= Greg/Al min629)		14thC

Other versions

Syriac

syr[c]	Curetonian	5thC
syr[p]	Peshitta	5thC
syr[h]	Harclean	
	Oxf.New Coll. 333	11thC
	Camb.Bibl.Univ.Add. 1700	12thC
syr[h**]	Harclean reading marked with obelus in Oxf.MS 333.	
syr[hmg]	Reading of Harclean margin in Oxf.MS 333	

Coptic

sah	Sahidic	[3rdC]
boh	Bohairic	[4thC]
cop	Sahidic + Bohairic	
cop^{G67}	New York Bibl.Pier.Morg.G.67	4/5thC

Other

arm	Armenian	[4/5thC]
arm^{osc}	Edition of Oscan	1666
geo	Georgian	[5thC]
bohem	Bohemian	[14thC]
nedl	Dutch	[13thC]
nedl^1	Lond.Brit.Mus.Add. 26663	
nedl^2	Bruss.Bibl.Reg. 2849–51	
ger^{tepl}	Codex Teplensis	14thC
prov	Provençal	[12thC]
prov^1	Par.Bibl.Pal.St-P. 36	
eth	Ethiopic	

Fathers and other writings

Sigla

Ambr	Ambrose of Milan	(d. 397)
Ambstr	Ambrosiaster	(4thC)
Amph	Amphilochius of Iconium	(d.c. 394)
App	Apponius	(5thC)
Ath	Athanasius	(d. 373)
AuctPel	Pelagian Author	(5thC)
Aug	Augustine of Hippo	(d. 430)
(?Ps)Aug^{cath}	*Epistula ad Catholicos* (= *De Unitate Ecclesiae*)	
Ps-Aug^{DS}	Pseudo-Augustine, *Liber de Divinis Scripturis*	(5thC)
Ps-Aug^{sol}	Pseudo-Augustine, *Solutiones*	(5thC)
Ps-Aug^{spec}	Pseudo-Augustine, *Speculum*	(427)
BarS	Dionysius Bar Salibi	(d. 1171)
Bede	Bede	(d. 735)
Cass	Cassiodorus	(d. 575)

Chr	John Chrysostom	(d. 407)
Chrom	Chromatius of Aquilea	(d. 407)
Clem	Clement of Alexandria	(d.*c.* 215)
ConstAp	*Constitutiones Apostolorum*	(?4thC)
Cyp	Cyprian of Carthage	(d. 258)
CyrJ	Cyril of Jerusalem	(d. 386)
Did	Didymus the Blind	(d. 398)
(?Ps-)Did	(?Pseudo-)Didymus *De Trinitate*	
Didasc	*Didascalia Apostolorum*	(3rdC)
Ephr	Ephraem Syrus	(d. 373)
Ephr[cat]	Ephraem's commentary found in Armenian catena	
Epiph	Epiphanius	(d. 403)
Eus	Eusebius of Caesaraea	(d.*c.* 340)
Ps-EusV	Pseudo-Eusebius Vercellensis	(unknown)
Evag	Evagrius	(*c.* 423)
Fulg	Fulgentius of Ruspe	(d. ?533)
Gaud	Gaudentius of Brescia	(4/5thC)
Hes	Hesychius of Jerusalem	(5thC)
Hil	Hilary of Poitiers	(d. 367)
Iren	Irenaeus of Lyons	(2ndC)
Iren[lat]	Readings of Irenaeus found only in Latin translation	
Jer	Jerome	(d. 420)
Jul	Julian of Toledo	(d. 690)
Lucif	Lucifer of Cagliari	(d. 371)
Max	Maximus of Turin	(d.*c.* 423)
Meth	Methodius of Olympus	(3rdC)
(?Ps-)Oec	(?Pseudo-)Oecumenius	(8thC)
Or	Origen	(d. 254)
Pac	Pacian of Barcelona	(4thC)
Porph	Porphyry	(d.*c.* 303)
Tert	Tertullian	(d.*c.* 225)
Theod	Theodoret of Cyrrhus	(d. 466)
Theoph	Theophylact	(11thC)
Ps-Vig	Pseudo-Vigilius of Thapsus	(d.*c.* 480)
Zeno	Zeno of Verona	(d.*c.* 375)

Patristic references

This list contains details of Patristic texts referred to in the critical apparatus, arranged verse by verse.

1.5

Ambrosiaster, *Quaestiones Veteris et Novi Testamenti* 93.1 (CSEL 50, p. 163, lines 16–18)

Augustine, *Contra Cresconium* 2.14(17) (CSEL 52, p. 376, lines 12–15)

   Contra Epistulam Manichaei 9 (CSEL 25.1, p. 203, lines 21–3)

   Contra Felicem 1.4 (CSEL 25.2, p. 804, lines 15–17)

   Contra Litteras Petiliani 2.32.76 (CSEL 52, p. 65, lines 8–11)

   Epistula 265.3 (CSEL 57, p. 640, lines 6–14)

(?Ps-) Augustine, *Epistula ad Catholicos* (= *De Unitate Ecclesiae*) 11.27 (CSEL 52, p. 262, lines 20–3)

Cyril of Jerusalem, *Catecheses ad Illuminandos* 17.14 (Reischl–Rupp, II, p. 268)

(?Ps-)Didymus the Blind, *De Trinitate*, 2.5.24 (Hönscheid and Seiler, II, p. 96, lines 22–4)

Ephraem, *Comm. in Eph.* 4.10 (*Commentarii in Epistolas D.Pauli*, p. 150)

Hilary of Poitiers, *De Trinitate* 8.30 (CChr.SL 62A, p. 341, lines 7–10)

Maximus of Turin, *Sermo 44*, 4 (CChr.SL 23, p. 180, lines 79–82)

Origen, *Contra Celsum* 7.51 (SC 150, p. 134, lines 12f.)

   Hom.Luc. 24 (GCS 49[35], p. 148, lines 12f.)

Ps-Vigilius of Thapsus, *Contra Varimadum* 38 (CChr.SL 90, p. 49, lines 39–41)

2.41

Augustine, *De Fide et Operibus* 8.13 (CSEL 31, p. 50, lines 3–5)

Bede, *Retractatio* 2.41 (CChr.SL 121, p. 118 lines 280–2)

Chrysostom, *Comm.in Act.* Hom.7.1 (Migne, PG 60, col. 64)

Ps-Eusebius Vercellensis, *De Trinitate* 12.125 (CChr.SL 9, p. 191, lines 967–9)

3.13

Ephraem (Conybeare, p. 398)

Ephraem[cat] (Conybeare, p. 399)

Irenaeus, *Adv. Omn. Haer.* 3.12.3 (SC 211, p. 186, lines 79f.)

Jerome, *In Esaiam* 14.52.13/15 (CChr.SL 73A, p. 567, lines 28f.)

4.31
Augustine, *Sermo* 356.1 (PL 39, col. 1574)
Bede, *Retractatio* 4.31
(CChr.SL 121, pp. 125f., lines 79–80)
Ephraem (Conybeare, p. 400)
Irenaeus, Fr.Gr.17 (= *Adv. Omn. Haer.* 3.12.5) (SC 211, p. 198,
    Fr.Gr.17, lines 16f.)
  Adv. Omn. Haer. 3.12.5 (SC 211, p. 198, lines 161f.)

4.32
Ambrose, *De Isaac* 7.59 (CSEL 32.1, p. 683, lines 16–18)
Bede, *Retractatio* 4.31 (CChr.SL 121, pp. 125f., lines 80–5)
Cyprian, *Ad Quirinium* 3.3 (CChr.SL 3, p. 91, lines 36–40)
  De Opere et Eleemosynis 25 (CChr.SL 3A, p. 71, lines 516–20)
Zeno, *Tractatus* 2.1.19 (CChr.SL 22, p. 149, lines 152–5)

5.15
Ambrose, *Expositio Ps. 118*, 19.5 (CSEL 62, p. 424, lines 25–7)
Chromatius, *Sermo* 31.3 (CChr.SL 9A, p. 141, lines 90–3)
Lucifer of Cagliari, *De non Parcendo* 17 (CChr.SL 8, p. 227, lines
    32–5)

6.10
Bede, *Retractatio* 6.10 (CChr.SL 121, p. 131, lines 44–8)
Didymus the Blind, *Liber de Spiritu Sancto*, 9 (Migne PG 39, col.
    1041B = Migne PL 23, col. 111C)
Julian of Toledo, *De Comprobatione Sextae Aetatis Oratio* 2.12
    (CChr.SL 95.1, p. 189, lines 7–9)

8.1
(?Ps-) Augustine, *Epistula ad Catholicos* (= *De Unitate Ecclesiae*)
    11.30 (CSEL 52, p. 267, lines 20–2)
Bar Salibi, *In Actus* 8.1 (CSCO.SS 101, p. 45, lines 29–32)

8.37
Ambrosiaster, *Quaestiones Veteris et Novi Testamenti*, 91.6 (CSEL
    50, p. 155, line 25–p. 156, line 1)
Augustine, *De Fide et Operibus* 8.14 (CSEL 31, p. 50, lines 24–6)
Ps-Augustine, *Liber de Divinis Scripturis*, 2 (CSEL 12, p. 308, line
    14–p. 309, line 1)
Bede, *Expositio* 8.36 (Laistner, 1939, p. 40, lines 21–6)
Chromatius of Aquilea, *Sermo* 2.7 (CChr.SL 9A, p. 11, lines 124–7)

Cyprian, *Ad Quirinium* 3.43 (CChr.SL 3, p. 134)

Fulgentius, *De Veritate Praedestinationis et Gratiae* 19 (CChr.SL 91A, p. 471, lines 459–61

   Ep.XII. Ad Ferrandum 14 (CChr.SL 91, p. 370, lines 282f.)

Irenaeus, Fr.Gr.20 (= *Adv. Omn. Haer.* 3.12.8) (SC 211, p. 214, Fr.Gr.20, lines 2–4)

   Adv. Omn. Haer. 3.12.8 (SC 211, p. 214, lines 286–8)

(?Ps-)-Oecumenius, *Commentarius in Acta Apostolorum* (PG 118, cols. 164f.)

Pacian, *De Baptismo* 6.4 (Fernandez, *Obras*, p. 170, lines 20f.)

Theophylact, *Expositio in Acta Apostolorum* (Migne PG 125, col. 637 (text a), col. 928 (text b)

8.39

(?Ps-) Augustine, *Epistula ad Catholicos* (= *De Unitate Ecclesiae*) 11.30 (CSEL 52, p. 268, lines 8f.)

Bar Salibi, *In Actus* 8.39 (CSCO.SS 101, p. 49, lines 6 and 11–14)

Cassiodorus, *Complexiones* 18 (Migne PL 70, col. 1387)

Didymus the Blind, in Cramer, *Catena*, p. 147, lines 21f.

   Liber de Spiritu Sancto, 56 (Migne PG 39, col. 1080C = Migne PL 23 col. 149A)

Ephraem and Ephraem^cat^ (Conybeare, pp. 408f.)

Fulgentius, *De Veritate Praedestinationis et Gratiae* 19 (CChr.SL 91A, p. 471, lines 461f.)

   Ep.XII. Ad Ferrandum 14 (CChr.SL 91, p. 370, line 283)

Jerome, *Dialogus contra Luciferianos* 9 (Migne PL 23, col. 165B)

   In Esaiam 17.63.11/14 (CChr.SL 73A, p. 729, lines 43f.)

9.40

Ambrose, *De Joseph* 3.17 (CSEL 32.2, p. 84, lines 9f.)

Ps-Augustine, *Solutiones* 51 (SChr.SL 90, p. 192, lines 11f.)

   Speculum 82 (CSEL 12, p. 586, lines 3f.)

Cassiodorus, *Complexiones* 21 (Migne PL 70, col. 1388)

Cyprian, *De Opere et Eleemosynis* 6 (CChr.SL 3A, p. 59, lines 126f.)

11.1

Augustine, *Enarrationes in Psalmos* 96.13 (CChr.SL 39, p. 1365, lines 25–7)

11.17
Augustine, *De Trinitate* 15.35 (CChr.SL 50A, p. 512, lines 111f.)
Bar Salibi, *In Actus* 11.17 (CSCO.SS 101., p. 61, lines 26–9)
(?Ps-)Didymus the Blind, *De Trinitate* 2.6.8.4 (Hönscheid and
    Seiler, II, p. 144, line 20)

11.28
Augustine, *De Sermone Domini* 2.17.57 (CChr.SL 35, p. 151, lines
    1292–6)

13.8
Bede, *Retractatio* 13.8 (CChr.SL 121, p. 145, lines 24f.)

14.2
Bede, *Expositio* 14.2 (Laistner, 1939, p. 59, lines 10f.)
Cassiodorus, *Complexiones* 31 (Migne PL 70, col. 1392)
Ephraem (Conybeare, p. 418)

14.7
Bede, *Expositio* 14.6 (Laistner, 1939, p. 59, lines 13–15)

15.1
Apostolic Constitutions 6.12.2 (SC 329, p. 326, line 9–p. 328, line
    12)
Didascalia 6.12.3 (Funk, I, p. 326, line 28–p. 328, line 2)
Irenaeus, *Adv. Omn. Haer.* 3.12.14 (SC 211, p. 238, lines 473f.,
    and 476–8)

15.2
Ephraem and Ephraem[cat] (Conybeare, pp. 420f.)

15.4
Ambrose, *Expositio Ps. 118*, 10.23 (CSEL 62, p. 217, lines 8–10)
Cassiodorus, *Complexiones* 35 (Migne PL 70, col. 1393)

15.20
Apostolic Constitutions 6.12.13 (SC 329, p. 331, line 32–p. 333,
    line 1)
Ps-Augustine, *Speculum* 28 (CSEL 12, p. 198, lines 13f.)
Chrysostom, *Comm.in Act.* Hom.15.1 (Migne, PG 60, col. 239)
Didascalia 6.12.13 (Funk, I, p. 330, line 25–p. 332, line 1)

202 *Appendix*

Ephraem (Conybeare, p. 426)
Irenaeus, *Adv. Omn. Haer.* 3.12.14 (SC 211, p. 242, lines 501–3)

15.28,29
Ambrosiaster, *Ad Galatas* 2.2.4 (CSEL 81.3, p. 19, lines 6–11)
Amphilochius, *Contra Haereticos* 20 (CChr.SG 3, p. 205, lines 767–70)
Apostolic Constitutions 6.12.15 (SC 329, p. 336, lines 106–10)
Apponius, *In Cant. Exp.* 3.13 and 9.20 (CChr.SL 19, p. 67, lines 216–19 and p. 223, lines 226–8
Augustine, *Contra Faustum* 32.13 (CSEL 25.1, p. 772, lines 3–8)
Ps-Augustine, *Speculum* 28 (CSEL 12, p. 198, lines 15–18)
Chrysostom, *Comm.in Act.* Hom.15.1 (Migne, PG 60, col. 240)
Clement of Alexandria, *Paedagogos* 2.17.2 and 2.56.2 (GCS 12, p. 166, lines 13f. and p. 191, lines 13–16)
    Stromata 4.97.3 (GCS 52[15], p. 291, lines 11–13)
Cyprian, *Ad Quirinium* 3.119 (CChr.SL 3, pp.178f., lines 11–15)
Cyril of Jerusalem, *Catecheses ad Illuminandos* 4.28 (Reischl–Rupp, I, p. 120 and II, p. 286)
Didascalia 6.12.15 (Funk, I, p. 332, lines 12–16)
Ephraem (Conybeare, p. 426)
Epiphanius, *Panarion* Haer. 29.8.6 (GCS 25, p. 331, lines 18–20)
Ps-Eusebius Vercellensis, *De Trinitate* 12.181 (CChr.SL 9, p. 204, lines 1431–5)
Evagrius, *Altercatio* 5 (CChr.SL 64, p. 276, lines 71–4)
(?Ps-)Fulgentius, *Pro Fide Catholica* (= Anon, *De Trinitate*) 9 (C.Chr.SL 90, p. 253, lines 419–21)
Gaudentius, *Tractatus de Machabaeis Martyribus* 15.21 (CSEL 68, p. 135, lines 141f.)
Hesychius of Jerusalem, *Homilies on Job* 15, Job 12,20b (PO 42.2, p. 389, lines 18–20) Cf. Hesychius, *Commentarius in Leviticum* 4 and 5 (PG 93, cols. 941B and 1005A)
Irenaeus, *Adv. Omn. Haer.* 3.12.14 (SC 211, p. 224, lines 514–19) (See also K. Lake and S. New (eds.), *Six Collations*, pp. 195f.)
Jerome, *Comm. in Ep. ad Gal.* 5.2 (Migne PL 26, col. 395B)
Methodius of Olympus, *Distinction of Foods*, 6.7 (GCS 27, p. 435, lines 9–12)
Origen, *Comm. in Matt.* 23.10 (GCS 38, p. 19, lines 11–13)
    Comm. in Rom. 9.28 (Migne PG 14, col. 1227f.)
    Contra Celsum 8.29 (SC 150, p. 236, lines 25–7)
    Hom. in Rom. 2.13 (Migne PG 14, col. 905)

Pacian, *Paraenesis ad Paenitentiam* 4.2 (Fernandez, *Obras* p. 140, lines 25–30)
Pelagian Author (Caspari, 1890, p. 18)
Tertullian, *De Pudicitia* 12.4 (CChr.SL 1:2, p. 1302, lines 11–15)
Theodoret, *Interpretatio Epist. ad Gal.* 2 (Migne PG 82, col. 469)

15.34
Cassiodorus, *Complexiones* 37 (Migne PL 70, col. 1393)
Ephraem (Conybeare, p. 426)
(?Ps-) Oecumenius, *Commentarius in Acta* PG 118, col. 221
Theophylact, *Expositio in Acta Apostolorum* Text b (PG 125, col. 980)

16.4
Ephraem (Conybeare, p. 428)

17.4
Cassiodorus, *Complexiones* 41 (Migne PL 70, col. 1395)

17.26
Irenaeus, *Adv. Omn. Haer.* 3.12.9 (SC 211, p. 218, lines 314f.)

18.8
Ephraem[cat] (Conybeare, p. 435)

18.21
Cassiodorus, *Complexiones* 44 (Migne PL 70, col. 1396)
Chrysostom, *Comm.in Act.* Hom.40.1 (Migne, PG 60, col. 281)
Theophylact, *Expositio in Acta Apostolorum* Texts a and b (PG 125, cols. 756f., 1001)

19.1
Ado of Lyons, *Martyrology*, 6 July (Dubois and Renaud, p. 216)
Ephraem[cat] (Conybeare, p. 441)

21.25
Augustine, *Epistula* 82.9 (CSEL 33, p. 359, lines 11–14)
Ps-Augustine, *Speculum* 28 (CSEL 12, p. 199, lines 15–17) (cf. *Speculum* 28 CSEL 12, p. 199, lines 23–5)

24.24
Cassiodorus, *Complexiones* 62 (Migne PL 70, col. 1402)

27.15
Bede, *Expositio* 27.15 (Laistner, 1939, p. 85, lines 11f.)
Cassiodorus, *Complexiones* 68 (Migne PL 70, col. 1403)

28.29
Cassiodorus, *Complexiones* 72 (Migne PL 70, col. 1405)

NOTES

1 The study of the text of Acts

1 See F. H. Scrivener, *Bezae Codex Cantabrigiensis, Being an Exact Copy in Ordinary Type* (Cambridge, 1864), pp. ixf. From the time of Bede to the era of the printed text, there is little evidence of concern with the problems of Acts' text. For the study of Acts before the sixteenth century see: P. F. Stuehrenberg, 'The Study of Acts before the Reformation. A Bibliographic Introduction', *NT* 29 (1987), 100–36.

2 J. Leclerc (Clericus), *Défense des sentimens de quelques théologiens d'Hollande sur l'histoire critique du Vieux Testament contre la réponse du Prieur de Bolleville* (Amsterdam, 1686), pp. 451–3. The passage occurs in a letter, written eighteen months previously by Leclerc (Critobulus Hieropolitanus) to Richard Simon (Origen) about Simon's project for a new Polyglott. A. C. Clark stated mistakenly that the passage was found in Leclerc's earlier work, *Sentimens de quelques théologiens d'Hollande* (Amsterdam, 1685): Clark, *The Acts of the Apostles* (Oxford, 1933), p. xxi, n. 1. Clark's reference has been repeated in later works.

3 R. Simon, *Histoire critique du Nouveau Testament* (Rotterdam, 1689), pp. 369–77, esp. p. 376 on the text of Acts.

4 A. Arnaud [Arnaldus], *Dissertation critique touchant les exemplaires grecs sur lesquels M. Simon prétend que l'ancienne Vulgate a esté faite, et sur le judgement que l'on doit faire du fameux manuscrit de Bèze* (Cologne, 1691).

5 F. A. Bornemann, *Acta Apostolorum ab Sancto Luca conscripta ad Codicis Cantabrigiensis* . . . (Grossenhain and London, 1848); Bornemann's thesis that Acts has been interpolated from a Lucan notebook is on pp. Xf., his argument that the non-Western text has suffered from abbreviation on pp. XI–XIV, and his general view of the classification of witnesses on pp. XXVIIIf. His thesis of abbreviation in the Majority text anticipated that of Clark (who refers to Bornemann's work), and the notion of interpolation from a separately preserved diary or notebook was taken up by A. Pott, *Der abendländische Text der Apostelgeschichte und die Wir-Quelle* (Leipzig, 1900).

6 See the comments of Eberhard Nestle in his *Introduction to the Textual Criticism of the Greek New Testament* (London, 1901), p. 222.

7 Scrivener, *Bezae Codex.*

8 B. F. Westcott and F. J. A. Hort, *The New Testament in the Original Greek* II (London, 2nd edn, 1896), pp. 122–6.
9 Ibid., pp. 174f.
10 F. Blass, 'Die Textüberlieferung in der AG', *ThStKr* 67 (1894), 86–119.
11 Blass, *Acta Apostolorum sive Lucae ad Theophilum liber alter, Editio Philologica* (Göttingen, 1895).
12 Ibid., p. 31
13 Ibid., p. 31.
14 Ibid., p. 31.
15 Ibid., p. 32.
16 Ibid., p. 32.
17 T. Zahn, *Introduction to the New Testament* (Eng. translation from 3rd German edition), III (Edinburgh, 1909), pp. 8–41; E. Nestle, *Textual Criticism*, p. 224. Also convinced by Blass were the British scholars F. C. Conybeare (see 'Two Notes on Acts', *ZNW* 20 (1921), 41f.) and J. M. Wilson, *The Acts of the Apostles Translated from the Codex Bezae* (London, 1923).
18 Among them: P. Corssen, 'Acta Apostolorum ed. F. Blass', *GGA* 158 (1896), 425–48; B. Weiss, *Der Codex D in der Apostelgeschichte. Textkritische Untersuchung* (TU 17.1, Leipzig, 1897); T. E. Page, *CR* 11 (1897), 317–20; H. Coppieters, 'De Historia Textus Actorum Apostolorum' (diss. Louvain, 1902).
19 J. H. Ropes, *The Text of Acts*. Vol. III of *Beg.* (London, 1926).
20 Ibid., p. viii.
21 Ibid., pp. ccxxivf.
22 Ibid., p. ccxxxiii.
23 Ibid., p. ccxxxv; among the other texts which Ropes was willing to accept are 11.1 (see p. 102), 15.29 (see pp. 265–8), 17.4 (see p. 162), 18.26 (see p. 178), and 28.14 (see p. 251).
24 Ibid., pp. ccxxxv-ccxxxviii.
25 Ibid., pp. ccxlivf.
26 G. Zuntz, 'On the Western Text of the Acts of the Apostles' in his *Opuscula Selecta* (Cambridge, 1972), pp. 189–215.
27 Ropes, *Beg.* III, p. ccxl.
28 Zuntz, 'Western Text', p. 189.
29 Ibid., pp. 190–2.
30 Ibid., pp. 201–5.
31 Ibid., pp. 207–12; see F. H. Chase, *The Old Syriac Element in Codex Bezae* (London, 1893).
32 Zuntz, 'Western Text', pp. 206f.
33 Ibid., pp. 193–6.
34 K. Lake and H. J. Cadbury, *Translation and Commentary*. Vol. IV of *Beg.* (London, 1933).
35 Ibid., p. ix.
36 The fullest discussion of Lake's views occurs in his comments on Acts 15.1–5, *Beg.* IV, pp. 169f.
37 The Western readings which Lake was willing to consider as possibly genuine were those at: 7.55, 8.24, 8.39, 9.22, 10.40, 11.12, 13.8, 14.13,

17.27, 17.28, 18.4f., 18.24,25, 19.9, 20.15, 21.1, 21.12, 21.22, 22.5, 22.28, 24.7, 26.6. Also to be noted is Lake and Cadbury's treatment of the text of 3.1–12 (pp. 31–5).

38 Lake and Cadbury, *Beg.* IV, p. ix.

39 Clark, *Acts*.

40 A. C. Clark, *The Primitive Text of the Gospels and Acts* (Oxford, 1914); *The Descent of Manuscripts* (Oxford, 1918).

41 Clark, *Primitive Text*, pp. 21, 57.

42 Ibid., pp. 92–105.

43 Ropes, *Beg.* III, p. ccxxvii.

44 Clark, *Acts*, pp. xlvf.; Clark's own copy of Ropes, *Beg.* III, which is now in the library of The Queen's College, Oxford, shows, by its heavy marking, the close attention which Clark paid to the work, even though his notes contain few detailed comments.

45 B. H. Streeter, 'The Primitive Text of the Acts' [Review of Clark's *Acts*], *JThS* 34 (1933), 232–41; see also S. New, 'The Michigan Papyrus Fragment 1571', in *Beg.* V (London, 1933), pp. 262–8. New proposed a similar development to account for the origin of p³⁸ (a Western witness), taking its readings to be an intermediate stage in the development of the Western into the Neutral text (p. 268).

46 The phrase is that of W. C. van Unnik, 'Luke–Acts, A Storm-Center in Contemporary Scholarship', in *SLA* (London, 1968), p. 16.

47 *Bulletin of the Bezan Club*, twelve numbers (Leiden, 1925–37).

48 See F. G. Kenyon, *Recent Developments in the Textual Criticism of the Greek Bible* (Schweich Lectures, 1932; London, 1933), pp. 44f.; C. A. Philips, 'Rendel Harris', *ET*, 52 (1941), 349–52.

49 F. G. Kenyon, 'The Western Text in the Gospels and Acts' *PBA* 24 (1938), 287–315.

50 G. D. Kilpatrick, 'An Eclectic Study of the Text of Acts', in *Biblical and Patristic Studies in memory of Robert Pierce Casey*, ed. J. N. Birdsall and R. W. Thomson (Freiburg, 1963), p. 64.

51 M. Dibelius, 'The Text of Acts: An Urgent Critical Task', *JR* 21 (1941), pp. 421–31, reprinted in M. Dibelius, *Studies in the Acts of the Apostles* (London, 1956), pp. 84–92 (to which reference is here made).

52 Dibelius, 'Text', in *Studies*, pp. 89f.

53 Ibid., pp. 88f.

54 G. D. Kilpatrick, 'Western Text and Original Text in the Gospels and Acts', *JThS* 44 (1943), 24–36.

55 See C. H. Turner, 'Historical Introduction to the Textual Criticism of the New Testament', *JThS* 10 (1908–9), 13–28, 161–82, 354–74; 11 (1909–10), 1–27, 180–210; 'A Textual Commentary on Mark 1', *JThS* 28 (1926–7), 145–58.

56 Kilpatrick, 'Western Text', 36.

57 See n. 50 above.

58 Kilpatrick, 'Eclectic Study', 64.

59 The approach is exemplified in his studies of particular texts and textual problems, e.g.: 'Acts 7.56, the Son of Man', *ThZ* 21 (1965), 209; 'ἐπιθύειν and ἐπικρίνειν in the Greek Bible', *ZNW* 74 (1983), 151–3;

'The Two Texts of Acts', *Studien zum Text und zur Ethik des Neuen Testaments. Festschrift zum 80. Geburtstag von Heinrich Greeven* (BZNW 47; Berlin and New York, 1986), pp. 188–95.

60 A. J. Wensinck, 'The Semitisms of Codex Bezae and their Relation to the non-Western Text of the Gospel of Saint Luke', *BBezC* 12 (1937), 11–48.

61 M. Black, *An Aramaic Approach to the Gospels and Acts* (Oxford, 3rd edn, 1967).

62 Ibid., pp. 277–80.

63 M. Wilcox, *The Semitisms of Acts* (Oxford, 1965).

64 Ibid., p. 185.

65 E. Haenchen, 'Zum Text der Apostelgeschichte', *ZThK* 54 (1957), 46; *The Acts of the Apostles* (Eng. trans. from 14th German edn, 1965, Oxford, 1971), pp. 50–60.

66 J. D. Yoder, 'Semitisms in Codex Bezae', *JBL* 78 (1959), 317–21.

67 E. Richard, 'The Old Testament in Acts: Wilcox's Semitisms in Retrospect', *CBQ* 42 (1980), 330–41, concentrated his detailed criticism on Wilcox's identification of variant OT texts in Acts, but left aside the more general problems of Semitisms in Acts, and particularly in the Western tradition.

68 A. F. J. Klijn, 'A Survey of the Researches into the Western Text of the Gospels and Acts (1949–59)', *NT* 3 (1959), 169–71.

69 L. Cerfaux, 'Citations scripturaires et tradition textuelle dans le livre des Actes', in *Aux sources de la tradition chrétienne. Mélanges offerts à M. Maurice Goguel* (Bibliothèque Théologique; Neuchâtel and Paris, 1950), pp. 43–51. A. F. J. Klijn, 'In Search of the Original Text of Acts', in Keck and Martyn (eds.), *SLA*, pp. 103–10; see also Kilpatrick's reply, 'Some Quotations in Acts', in *Actes*, ed. J. Kremer (EThL.B 48; Gembloux, 1979), pp. 81–97.

70 G. D. Fee, 'Rigorous or Reasoned Eclecticism – Which?', in *Studies in New Testament Language and Text: Essays in Honour of G. D. Kilpatrick on his Sixty-Fifth Birthday*, ed. J. K. Elliott (NT.S 44; Leiden, 1976), pp. 174–97.

71 Dibelius, 'Text', in *Studies*, pp. 88–90.

72 A. D. Nock, 'Martin Dibelius: Aufsätze zur Apostelgeschichte. Göttingen, 1951', *Gn.* 25 (1953), 501f.

73 Cicero, *Ad Q.Fr.* 3.5.6; Strabo, *Geog.* 13.1.54 fin.; Martial, *Ep.* 2.8.3–4; Aulus Gellius, *Noct.Att.* 5.4.

74 Haenchen, *Acts*, pp. 50–60.

75 Ibid., p. 9.

76 Ibid., p. 51.

77 Ibid., pp. 51–3.

78 Ibid., pp. 52f., and discussions of particular readings, e. g. 1.9 (p. 149), 1.23 (p. 162,n. 1).

79 Ibid., pp. 53–6.

80 J. Rendel Harris, *Codex Bezae. A Study of the So-called Western Text of the New Testament* (Texts and Studies 2.1; Cambridge, 1891), pp. 148–53.

81 Page, *CR* 11 (1897), 317–20.

82 Ropes, *Beg.* III, p. ccxxxiii.
83 P. H. Menoud, 'The Western Text and the Theology of Acts', *Studiorum Novi Testamenti Societas, Bulletin*, 2 (1951), 19–32; reprinted in his *Jesus Christ and the Faith: A Collection of Studies by P. H. Menoud* (Pittsburgh, 1978), pp. 61–83 (to which reference is here made).
84 Menoud, 'Western Text', in *Jesus Christ*, p. 64.
85 Ibid., p. 64.
86 Ibid., p. 78.
87 E. Fascher, *Textgeschichte als hermeneutisches Problem* (Halle, 1953).
88 Ibid., pp. 12f.
89 Ibid., p. 27; although Fascher also detected theologically motivated alterations in the Western text of Acts (see p. 143 n. 133 below).
90 E. J. Epp, 'The "Ignorance Motif" in Acts and Anti-Judaic Tendencies in Codex Bezae', *HThR* 55 (1962), 51–62.
91 E. J. Epp, *The Theological Tendency of Codex Bezae Cantabrigiensis in Acts* (MSSNTS 3; Cambridge, 1966).
92 Ibid., p. 165; the quotation is from B. H. Streeter, 'Codices 157, 1071 and the Caesaraean Text', in *Quantulacumque. Studies Presented to Kirsopp Lake*, ed. R. P. Casey, S. Lake, and A. K. Lake (London, 1937), p. 150. For Streeter's own view of the text of Acts, see Streeter, 'Primitive Text'.
93 Epp, *Theological Tendency*, pp. 12–21; see Fascher, *Textgeschichte*, and D. W. Riddle, 'Textual Criticism as a Historical Discipline', *AThR* 18 (1936), 220–33.
94 Epp, *Theological Tendency*, pp. 41–164.
95 Ibid., pp. 22–4.
96 Streeter, 'Primitive Text', p. 235.
97 J. Crehan, 'Peter according to the D-Text of Acts', *ThSt* 18 (1957), 596–603; C. M. Martini, 'La figura di Pietro secondo le varianti del codice D negli Atti degli Apostoli', in *San Pietro* (Atti della XIX Settimana Biblica; Brescia, 1967), pp. 279–89.
98 W. Thiele, 'Ausgewählte Beispiele zur Charakterisierung des "westlichen" Textes der Apostelgeschichte', *ZNW* 56 (1965), 51–63.
99 Ibid., 52.
100 Ibid., 58.
101 Ibid., 58–60.
102 Ibid., 60–2.
103 R. P. C. Hanson, 'The Provenance of the Interpolator in the "Western" Text of Acts and of Acts itself', *NTS* 12 (1966), 211–30.
104 Ibid., 215f.
105 Ibid., 216.
106 Ibid., 219–23.
107 Ibid., 228f.
108 Ibid., 224.
109 E. Grässer, 'Acta-Forschung seit 1960', *ThR* 41 (1976), 176f.
110 Ibid., 141–96, of which pp. 175–81 deal with the text.
111 Ibid., 175f.

112 Ibid., 176.
113 Ibid., 176–9.
114 Ibid., 179.
115 *TCGNT*.
116 Ibid., pp. 259–72.
117 Ibid., pp. 271f.
118 Ibid., p. 272.
119 Three times the UBS Committee allowed into the text readings which might be called 'Western': 2.43, where the reading is supported by B (*TCGNT*, p. 302); 18.26, where two words omitted by D and it[51] are placed in brackets (*TCGNT*, p. 467); and 20.5, where προελθόντες is read, but here it is clear that the presence of the reading in p[74] was the deciding factor (*TCGNT*, pp. 476f.). Distinctively Alexandrian readings were rejected at 3.16 (p. 313), 4.18 (p. 320), 11.23 (p. 390), and 21.23 (p. 484).
120 Metzger, *TCGNT*, pp. 279, 282 (quoting D. Plooij), 285, 296, 303, 450, 458 (quoting Lake and Cadbury), 462, 465–7, 469.
121 Ibid., pp. 466 (18.25), 470 (19.9); see p. 4 above.
122 See pp. 25f. (M. Black), and p. 27 (C. M. Martini).
123 See K. Aland and B. Aland, *Der Text des Neuen Testaments* (Stuttgart, 1982), pp. 63f., 78f.
124 *TCGNT*, pp. 442f. (16.9), 456 (17.26), 467 (18.26), 472 (19.20), 476 (20.4), 482 (21.1), 490 (24.6–8).
125 N–A[26], pp. 4*–5*; see also H.-W. Bartsch, 'Ein neuer Textus Receptus für das Neue Testament?', *NTS* 27 (1981), 585–92, and K. Aland, 'Ein neuer Textus Receptus für das griechische Neue Testament?', *NTS* 28 (1982), 145–53.
126 In addition to the works discussed on pp. 25–7, see also the detailed review of Epp's *Theological Tendency* by R. P. C. Hanson: 'The Ideology of Codex Bezae in Acts', *NTS* 14 (1968), 282–6.
127 Ropes, *Beg.* III, p. viii.
128 M. Black, 'Notes on the Longer and Shorter Texts of Acts', in *On Language, Culture and Religion: In Honour of Eugene A. Nida*, ed. M. Black and W. A. Smalley (Approaches to Semiotics 56; The Hague and Paris, 1974), pp. 119–31; M. Black, 'The Holy Spirit in the Western Text of Acts', in *NTTC*, ed. Epp and Fee, pp. 159–70.
129 Black, 'The Holy Spirit', p. 170.
130 Ibid., p. 160, n. 7.
131 See E. C. Colwell, *Studies in Methodology in Textual Criticism of the New Testament* (NTTS 9; Leiden, 1969), p. 150.
132 C. K. Barrett, 'Is there a Theological Tendency in Codex Bezae?', in *Text and Interpretation; Studies Presented to Matthew Black*, ed. E. Best and R. McL. Wilson (Cambridge, 1979), pp. 15–27.
133 Ibid., p. 26.
134 Ibid., p. 27; see also C. K. Barrett, *Luke the Historian in Recent Study* (London, 1961), p. 15; Zuntz had already made a similar suggestion to account for the characteristics of what he described as the late, degenerate element in the Western text ('Western Text', pp. 206f.).

135 C .M. Martini, 'La Tradition textuelle des Actes des Apôtres et les tendances de l'Eglise ancienne', in *Actes*, ed. Kremer, pp. 21–35.
136 Ibid., pp. 29–32.
137 Ibid., p. 26.
138 Ibid., pp. 27f.; on the Apostolic Decree, see below, pp. 87–105.
139 Ibid., pp. 28f.
140 Ibid., p. 35.
141 Ibid., p. 34; for Hanson, see above, pp. 21–3.
142 M. Wilcox, 'Luke and the Bezan Text of Acts', in *Actes*, ed. Kremer, pp. 447–55; analysis of readings, pp. 448–54.
143 Ibid., p. 455.
144 R. S. MacKenzie, 'The Western Text of Acts: Some Lucanisms in Selected Sermons', *JBL* 104 (1985), 637–50.
145 Ibid., 646, 650.
146 Delebecque has published nineteen studies of particular passages in Acts. For details see Bibliography.
147 E. Delebecque, *Les Deux Actes des Apôtres* (Etudes bibliques, n.s. 6; Paris, 1986).
148 Ibid., p. 212.
149 Ibid., pp. 184,211.
150 Ibid., pp. 301–12 (secondary characters), 313–70 (Paul).
151 Ibid., p. 336.
152 Ibid., pp. 373f.
153 Ibid., pp. 375f.
154 Ibid., pp. 376–9.
155 Ibid., p. 380; see also p. 417.
156 Ibid., p. 380.
157 Ibid., pp. 11–13, 22.
158 M.-E. Boismard and A. Lamouille, *Le Texte occidental des Actes des Apôtres. Reconstitution et réhabilitation*, 2 vols. (Synthèse 17; Paris, 1984). (Although the title page bears the date 1984, printing did not take place until 1985.)
159 M.-E. Boismard, 'The Texts of Acts: A Problem of Literary Criticism?', in *NTTC*, ed. Epp and Fee, pp. 147–57.
160 Ibid., pp. 153, 157.
161 Boismard and Lamouille, *Texte occidental*, I, p. 9.
162 Ibid., pp. 97–118.
163 Ibid., pp. 115–17.
164 Ibid., p. 117.
165 Ibid., pp. 97–104.
166 Ibid., pp. 119–22.
167 On Pott see n. 5 above, and pp. 110f. below.
168 Boismard and Lamouille, *Texte occidental*, I, p. 9.
169 See pp. 48–50, pp. 58–63, and discussions of particular variants in Chapter 4.
170 See, e.g., E. J. Epp, 'The Ascension in the Textual Tradition of Luke–Acts', in *NTTC*, ed. Epp and Fee, pp. 131–45; I. M. Ellis, 'Codex Bezae and Acts 15', *IrBibSt* 2 (1980), 134–40; B. Withering-

ton, 'The Anti-Feminist Tendencies of the "Western" Text in Acts', *JBL* 103 (1984), 82–4; R. I. Pervo, 'Social and Religious Aspects of the Western Text', in *The Living Text. Essays in Honor of Ernest W. Saunders*, ed. D. E. Groh and R. Jewett (Lanham, New York, and London, 1985), pp. 229–41.

171 B. Aland, 'Entstehung, Charakter und Herkunft des sog. westlichen Textes untersucht an der Apostelgeschichte', *EThL* 62 (1986), 5–65.
172 Ibid., 22f., 31–6.
173 Ibid., 43–56.
174 Aland argues that the marginal material, and that marked by critical signs, in the Harclean Syriac represents material current in Syrian ecclesiastical usage, but not found by Thomas in the MS which he consulted in the Henaton.
175 Aland, 'Entstehung', 64.
176 Ibid., 6.
177 Ibid., 6–9.
178 Ibid., 52f.

2 The nature of the Western text of Acts

1 See A. F. J. Klijn, *A Survey of the Researches into the Western Text of the Gospels and Acts* (Utrecht,1949); Klijn, 'A Survey (1949–1959)', 1–27, 161–73.
2 K. and B. Aland, *Der Text*, p. 79.
3 See, e.g., the comments of B. Fischer on the likely provenance of D: 'Das Neue Testament in Lateinischer Sprache', in *Die alten Übersetzungen des Neue Testaments, die Kirchenvaterzitate und Lektionare*, ed. K. Aland (ANTT 5; Berlin, 1972), pp. 39–41.
4 Ropes, *Beg.* III, pp. ixf.
5 Martini, 'Tradition textuelle', p. 35.
6 E. Grässer, 'Acta-Forschung', 175.
7 E. Plümacher, 'Acta-Forschung 1974–82', *ThR* 49 (1984), 116f.
8 M. W. Holmes, 'Early Editorial Activity and the Text of Codex Bezae in Matthew' (Ph.D. thesis, Princeton Theological Seminary, 1984), esp. 238–49.
9 G. E. Rice, 'The Anti-Judaic Bias of the Western Text in the Gospel of Luke', *AUSS* 17 (1979), 203–8; 18 (1980), 51–7.
10 Holmes, 'Editorial Activity', 89–94; Metzger, *TCGNT*, p. 53.
11 J. Jeremias, *Unknown Sayings of Jesus* (London, 2nd edn, 1964), pp. 61–5.
12 Lohse, *TDNT*, VII, pp. 23f.; W. Käser, 'Exegetische Erwägungen zur Seligpreisung des Sabbatarbeiters Lk. 6,5D', *ZThK* 65 (1968), 414–30; E. Bammel, 'The Cambridge Pericope. The Addition to Luke 6.4 in Codex Bezae', *NTS* 32 (1986), 404–26.
13 See pp. 16f. above.
14 Haenchen, *Acts*, p. 51.
15 Ibid., p. 51–3.
16 Ibid., pp. 53–6.
17 Ibid., p. 56.

18 Kenyon reckoned the Western text of Acts to be 8.5 per cent longer than the Westcott and Hort text by comparing Clark's edition (19,983 words) with Westcott–Hort (18,401 words): Kenyon, 'The Western Text in the Gospels and Acts', 310, n. 1. An alternative way of reckoning the relative sizes of the two texts is to compare the number of words in Acts D (14,062) with the number of words in the parts of N–A^{26} parallel to the extant parts of D in Acts (13,236). On this reckoning, D is 6.24 per cent longer than N–A^{26}.

19 Although Zahn argued for its authenticity: Zahn, *Die Apostel-geschichte des Lucas* (2 vols., Leipzig, 1919, 1921), II, pp. 614–16; and see the comments of B. Aland, 'Entstehung', 52f., discussed above, pp. 32f.

20 E.g., Haenchen (see pp. 16f.). Epp (pp. 19–21), Thiele (p. 21, Hanson (pp. 21–3), and Martini (p. 27).

21 W. M. Ramsay, *St. Paul the Traveller and the Roman Citizen* (London, 1895), pp. 24–7.

22 Lake and Cadbury, *Beg.* IV, p. 36.

23 Haenchen, *Acts*, p. 53.

24 The Latin witnesses it^{58} and vg^{1260} have *In Caesaream*, which may be a remnant of the Western reading.

25 Lake and Cadbury, *Beg.* IV, p. 117. See also C. S. C. Williams, *Alterations to the Text of the Synoptic Gospels and Acts* (Oxford, 1951), p. 59: 'the additional matter seems to be due to the Oriental belief that a literal forerunner was needed to go before any important person'. Clark, though, held that the omission of this material in most witnesses shows an abbreviator's 'contempt for minute details', *Acts*, p. ix; see also *Acts*, p. 346.

26 For a more substantial discussion of the textual problems of this verse, see below, pp. 126–31.

27 On Clark's view, this was a clear instance of the omission of στίχοι: *Acts*, p. xxv.

28 J. H. Ropes, 'Three Papers on the Text of Acts. 1. The Reconstruction of a Torn Leaf of Codex Bezae', *HThR* 16 (1923), 163–8. Ropes based his reconstruction on collations of the text made in the eighteenth century, before the MS suffered successive mutilations at this point.

29 F. Prat, 'Récents travaux de critique textuelle', *RSR* 5 (1914), 483; Zahn, *Introduction* III, p. 18; Lake and Cadbury, *Beg.* IV, pp. 269f.; Metzger, *TCGNT*, p. 483 (cautiously), E. Delebecque, 'La Dernière Etape du troisième voyage missionnaire de saint Paul selon les deux versions des Actes des Apôtres (21,16–17)', *RThL* 14 (1983), 446–55.

30 Corssen, 'Acta', 438–40; Weiss, *Codex D*, pp. 101ff.; Ropes, *Beg.* III, p. 204; Williams, *Alterations*, p. 62; Haenchen, *Acts*, p. 607, n.6; Martini 'Tradition textuelle', 33.

31 Ropes (*Beg.* III, p. 204) objected that a journey of such length would have to be broken more than once, so that the Western additional material is inadequate, as well as 'inherently highly improbable'. However, the reference to hosts in the plural in D (πρὸς οὓς ξενισθῶμεν) may well imply more than one stopping-place.

32 Lake and Cadbury, *Beg.* IV, p. 270.

33 This reading is dealt with in more detail below: see pp. 115–19.
34 This reading is dealt with in more detail below: see pp. 142–6.
35 Weiss, *Codex D*, p. 109; Ropes, *Beg.* III, pp. ccxxxv, 195; Lake and Cadbury, *Beg.* IV, p. 258; Williams, *Alterations*, p. 64.
36 Haenchen, *Acts*, p. 52.
37 See W. A. Strange, 'The Text of Acts 19.1', *NTS* 37 (1991).
38 Notably those of Menoud, Epp, and Hanson: see above, pp. 18, 19–21, 21–3.
39 Page, *CR* 11 (1897), 317–20.
40 Boismard and Lamouille, *Texte occidental* I, p. 107.
41 Ibid., pp. 111–18.
42 Ibid., p. 118.
43 The examples are: 'Jesus Christ'/'Jesus': 2.38, 3.6, 4.10, 8.12, 10.48, 11.17, 15.26, 16.18, 28.31; 'the Lord Jesus'/'Jesus': 4.33, 8.16, 15.11, 19.5,17, 20.24,35. Boismard and Lamouille, *Texte occidental* I, p. 107.
44 The occurrences are: 1.21, 2.38, 4.33, 5.42, 6.8(om.ὁ), 8.16, 10.48, 11.17 (common text), 11.20, 13.33, 14.10, 15.11, 16.4, 16.31, 19.5(om.ὁ), and 21.13. But note also 11.17b, where D has αὐτῷ and other Western witnesses have τὸν κύριον Ἰησοῦν Χριστόν. D in that instance maintains Luke's distinction between Gentiles (who come to believe in God), and Jews (who come to believe in Jesus): see Epp, *Theological Tendency*, pp. 88–90.
45 The occurrences are: 15.26 (common text), 18.8, and 20.21.
46 This is a passage in which D is supposed to have conflated the Majority reading with the Western reading, preserved by it[55]: Ropes, *Beg.* III, p. 172; Boismard and Lamouille, *Texte occidental* II, p. 126.
47 The textual problems of 18.8 are discussed below, pp. 154–6.
48 Boismard and Lamouille, *Texte occidental* I, p. 117.
49 Ropes, *Beg.* III, p. ccxxv.
50 1 Clem. 5.7 ; Ign., *Eph.* 12.2; Dionysius of Corinth in Eusebius, *HE* 2.25.8.
51 Martini, 'Tradition textuelle', 35.
52 Crehan, 'Peter'; Martini, 'La figura di Pietro'.
53 Ὁ μακάριος Παῦλος, 1 Clem 47.1; Παῦλος ... ὁ ἡγιασμένος, ὁ μεμαρτυρημένος, ἀξιομακάριστος, Ign., *Eph.* 12.2; ὁ μακάριος καὶ ἔνδοξος Παῦλος, Pol., *Philip* 3.2.
54 Streeter, *JThS* 34 (1933), 234.
55 1 Clem. 44; Ign., *Trall.* 2f., 12.2f., *Philad.* 5.1, *Smyrn.* 8.1.
56 Euseb., *HE* 5.24.1–5.25.1.
57 Irenaeus, *Adv. Omn. Haer.* 3.3.4.
58 Rendel Harris, *Codex Bezae*, pp. 148–53.
59 Barrett, 'Codex Bezae', 27.
60 *Acts of Paul*, 7.
61 *Acts of Paul*, passim.
62 *Acts of Paul*, 25.
63 The positive evidence for allusions to Acts is considered in *The New Testament in the Apostolic Fathers*, by A Committee of the Oxford Society of Historical Theology (Oxford, 1905), and in Haenchen, *Acts*, pp. 3–9. Negatively, note the way in which Clement, for instance, does

not appear to rely for his summary of Paul's ministry (1 Clem. 5.5–7) on the narrative of Acts, but on 2 Cor. 11.23–33 (notwithstanding the singular Ἀναλάβετε τὴν ἐπιστολὴν τοῦ μακαρίου Παύλου, 1 Clem. 47.1). D. A. Hagner, *The Use of the Old and New Testaments in Clement of Rome* (NT.S 34; Leiden, 1973), pp. 209–13, accepts that Clement may have known and used 2 Corinthians, although certainty is not possible. Clement's description may even be purely conventional: see R. Hodgson, 'Paul the Apostle and First-Century Tribulation Lists', *ZNW* 74 (1983), 59–80. Clement's dependence on Acts here is unlikely. The reasons for Acts' obscurity in the pre-Irenaean period will be examined below, pp. 178–83.

64 Irenaeus, *Adv. Omn. Haer.* 3.12–14.

3 Lucanism and the Western text of Acts

1 See the work of Wilcox, Delebecque, MacKenzie, and Boismard and Lamouille referred to on pp. 28–32, above.

2 Martini, 'Tradition textuelle', 34.

3 A. von Harnack, *Lukas der Arzt. Der Verfasser des Dritten Evangeliums und der Apostelgeschichte* (Beiträge zur Einleitung in das Neue Testament, I; Leipzig, 1906); J. C. Hawkins, *Horae Synopticae* (Oxford, 2nd edn, 1909); H. J. Cadbury, *The Style and Literary Method of Luke* (HThS 6; Cambridge, Mass., 1920); N. Turner, *A Grammar of New Testament Greek* (by J. H. Moulton), Vol. IV *Style* (Edinburgh, 1976), pp. 45–63.

4 The literature is large and rapidly increasing. Since Conzelmann's pioneering study in redaction criticism which took Luke as its basis – *Die Mitte der Zeit* (BHTh 17; Tübingen, 1954) – Luke's work has been a favourite field for the exercise of redaction criticism.

5 Leclerc, *Défense des sentimens*, pp. 451–3; Simon, *Histoire critique*, pp. 369–77.

6 Boismard and Lamouille, *Texte occidental* I, p. 9.

7 See above, pp. 30–2.

8 Boismard and Lamouille, *Texte occidental* II, pp. 195f.

9 Ibid., II, pp. 197–335.

10 Ibid., I, pp. 8–10.

11 Ibid., I, p. 98.

12 Ibid., I, p. 97.

13 See J. D. Yoder, 'The Language of the Greek Variants of Codex Bezae', *NT* 3 (1959), 247; Yoder, 'Semitisms', 318f.

14 See, for example, Delebecque's comments on Luke's 'Hellenism', in 'La Dernière Etape', 455.

15 F. Neirynck and F. van Segbroeck, 'Le Texte des Actes des Apôtres et les caractéristiques stylistiques lucaniennes', *EThL* 61 (1985), 312–14.

16 Ibid., 314f.

17 Ibid., 334f.

18 See Chapter 2 above.

19 E.g. Boismard and Lamouille, *Texte occidental* II, p. 169, choosing the most Lucan vocabulary in retroverting from Syriac.

20 W. L. Knox, *St. Paul and the Church of Jerusalem* (Cambridge, 1925), pp. xvii-xxvi.
21 Menoud, 'The Western Text' (see p. 18 above).
22 See pp. 19–21 above.
23 Epp, *Theological Tendency*, p. 165.
24 Ibid., pp. 165f.
25 Ibid., pp. 21, 165.
26 Ibid., p. 170.
27 Barrett, 'Codex Bezae', pp. 25–7.
28 Black, 'The Holy Spirit', p. 170.
29 Martini, 'Tradition textuelle', p. 26.
30 Metzger, *TCGNT*, pp. 360f.; see also E. Haenchen and P. Weigandt, 'The Original Text of Acts?', *NTS* 14 (1968), 477.
31 Black, 'The Holy Spirit', 166.
32 Ibid., 167; Boismard and Lamouille, *Texte occidental* II, p. 61.
33 See Haenchen, *Acts*, p. 313.
34 See M. Black, 'Notes on the Longer and Shorter Texts', 123. E. Schweizer also noted the untypical portrait of the Spirit in the Majority text, and inclined towards accepting the reading of A etc. He suspected either doctrinal interference, or accidental omission to account for πνεῦμα κυρίου: 'πνεῦμα, πνευματικός', Kittel, *TDNT* VI (Grand Rapids, 1968), p. 409.
35 These Old Testament parallels were not lost on Acts' earliest known commentator, Didymus the Blind (*c.* 313–398). His surviving comment on 8.39, for which he had the shorter reading, is entirely concerned with a discussion of Old Testament parallels.
36 O. Cullmann, *Baptism in the New Testament* (English edn, London, 1950), p. 71.
37 J. D. G. Dunn, *Unity and Diversity in the New Testament* (London, 1977), p. 55.
38 Metzger, *TCGNT*, p. 360.
39 Pliny, *Ep.* 10.96; Athenagoras, *Legatio* 3 and 31; Tertullian, *Apologeticum* 2, 7f. and 39; Minucius Felix, *Octavius* 9.
40 Justin, *1st Apology* 66; Tertullian, *De Baptismo* 20, *De Praescr. Haer.* 41.
41 Origen, *Contra Celsum* 1.1; and note the comments put into the mouth of the pagan spokesman Caecilius by Minucius Felix (*Octavius* 10.1–2).
42 Ibid., 1.1; 1.7; 3.50–8.
43 Ibid., 1.7.
44 Irenaeus, *Adv. Omn. Haer.* 1.2.3; Tertullian, *De Praescr. Haer.* 13.
45 Origen, *Contra Celsum* 1.3.
46 *Didache* 9.5.
47 Justin, *1st Apology* 61 and 66; *Ad Diognetem* 11.2; perhaps also already in Acts itself, Acts 16.15: Εἰ κεκρίκατέ με πιστὴν τῷ κυρίῳ εἶναι.
48 Justin, *1st Apology* 61–6.
49 Wilcox, *Semitisms*, p. 68.
50 Cullmann, *Baptism*, p. 71.
51 D. Daube, *The New Testament and Rabbinic Judaism* (London, 1956), pp. 111f.

52 See also Wilcox's comment on the 'ultimate Aramaic roots' of this passage: *Semitisms*, p. 174.
53 Matt. 4.4–Lk. 4.4; Matt. 13.11–Mk. 4.11–Lk. 8.10; Matt. 14.16–Mk. 6.37–Lk. 9.13; Matt. 17.4–Mk. 9.5–Lk. 9.33; Matt. 11.25–Lk. 10.21; Matt. 12.38–Lk. 11.29; Matt. 22.1–Lk. 14.16; Matt. 19.27–Mk. 10.28–Lk. 18.28; Matt. 25.26–Lk. 19.22; Matt. 21.27–Mk. 11.33–Lk. 20.7; Matt. 22.29–Mk. 12.24–Lk. 20.34; Matt. 22.41–Mk. 12.35–Lk. 20.41; Matt. 24.2–Mk. 13.2–Lk. 21.5; Matt. 24.4–Mk. 13.5–Lk. 21.8; Matt. 26.33–Mk. 14.29–Lk. 22.33; Matt. 26.55–Mk. 14.48–Lk. 22.52; Matt. 27.21–Mk. 15.12–Lk. 23.20.
54 Matt. 11.4–Lk. 7.22; Matt. 16.16–Mk. 8.29–Lk. 9.20; Matt. 17.17–Mk. 9.19–Lk. 9.41; (?) Matt. 25.12–Lk. 13.25; Matt. 21.24–Mk. 11.29–Lk. 20.3.
55 Matt. 4.10–Lk. 4.8; Matt. 9.4–Mk. 2.8–Lk. 5.22; Matt. 9.12–Mk. 2.17–Lk. 5.31; Matt. 12.3–Mk. 2.25–Lk. 6.3; Matt. 12.49–Mk. 3.34–Lk. 8.21; Matt. 16.14–Mk. 8.28–Lk. 9.19; Mk. 9.38–Lk. 9.49; Matt. 22.37–Mk. 12.29–Lk. 10.27; Matt. 26.52–Lk. 22.51.
56 Lk. 1.19,35,60, 3.11, 4.12, 5.5, 7.40,43, 10.41, 11.7,45, 13.2,8,14, 14.3, 15.29, 17.17,37, 19.40, 20.39, 24.18.
57 Dunn, *Unity and Diversity*, p. 55.
58 Ibid., p. 55.
59 See J. N. D. Kelly, *Early Christian Creeds* (London, 2nd edn, 1960), p. 94.
60 Metzger, *TCGNT*, p. 359.
61 Souter in W. Sanday and C. H. Turner, *Novum Testamentum Sancti Irenaei Episcopi Lugdunensis* (Old Latin Biblical Texts, 7; Oxford, 1923), p. cxxxiii.
62 Boismard and Lamouille, *Texte occidental* I, p. 152.
63 The phenomenon is analysed by, among others, H. Flender, *Luke, Theologian of Redemptive History* (London, 1967), pp. 8–35; C. H. Talbert, *Literary Patterns, Theological Themes, and the Genre of Luke–Acts* (SBL.MS 20; Missoula, 1974), pp. 15–50.
64 Clark, *Acts*, p. 347.
65 Metzger, *TCGNT*, p. 383.
66 Ropes, *Beg.* III, p. 102.
67 Boismard and Lamouille, *Texte occidental* II, p. 77. Boismard and Lamouille considered the more distinctively Lucan εὐλογεῖν τὸν Θεόν to be original. But δοξάζειν τὸν Θεόν is also perfectly Lucan (Lk. x8, Acts x3).
68 Cop^G67 has two verbs: 'He went forth, and coming out into the country ...'. See T. C. Petersen, 'An Early Coptic Manuscript of Acts: An Unrevised Version of the Ancient So-Called Western Text', *CBQ* 26 (1964), 238.
69 Petersen, 'Coptic MS', 238f.
70 Metzger, *TCGNT*, p. 383, n. 1.
71 Delebecque, 'La Montée de Pierre de Césarée à Jérusalem selon le *Codex Bezae* au chapitre 11 des Actes des Apôtres', *EThL* 58 (1982), 109f.
72 Zahn, *Die Urausgabe der Apostelgeschichte des Lucas* (Forschungen

zur Geschichte des neutestamentliche Kanons und altkirchlichen Literatur, 9 Teil; Leipzig, 1916), p. 348, where he noted also the 'Lucanism' of αὐτοῦ, and described καταντᾶν as 'echt lukanisch'.

73 Ropes, *Beg.* III, p. 102, note to verses 1 and 2.

74 Boismard, 'The Texts of Acts', p. 149.

75 Ropes, *Beg.* III, p. 102, note to v. 2; Kilpatrick considered D defective here, while αὐτοῦ he regarded as uncertain, and suggested tentatively that εἰς αὐτούς might have been expected: 'The Two Texts', pp. 189f.

76 F. Preisigke, *Wörterbuch der Griechischen Papyrusurkunden, mit Einschluss der griechischen Inschriften, Aufschriften, Ostraka, Mumienschilder usw. aus Ägypten*, I (Berlin, 1925), col. 760; although it is to be noted that Preisigke's example depends on a conjectured reading.

77 Wilcox, 'Luke and the Bezan Text', 451.

78 Boismard, 'The Texts of Acts', 150–3; Boismard and Lamouille, *Texte occidental* I, pp. 97f. Boismard and Lamouille also found Lucan traits in 11.1 TO: *Texte occidental* II, pp. 77, 299.

79 Delebecque, 'La Montée', 107f.

80 Ibid., 108; Ropes, *Beg.* III, p. 102.

81 Metzger, *TCGNT*, p. 382.

82 Ibid., p. 383.

83 Clark, *Acts*, p. 347.

84 Among them: J. M. Wilson, *Acts*, p. 63; B. W. Bacon, 'Some "Western" Variants in the Text of Acts', *HThR* 21 (1928), 127; Crehan, 'Peter', 597.

85 Delebecque, 'La Montée', 108.

86 This phenomenon of redundancy is a conspicuous feature of the Western text of Acts. See below, pp. 158–62.

87 See Mk. 2.18–22–Lk. 5.33–9; Mk. 2.23–8–Lk. 6.1–5; Mk. 3.20–30–Lk. 11.14–23; Mk. 11.27–33–Lk. 20.1–8; Mk. 12.13–17–Lk. 20.20–6; Mk. 12.18–27–Lk. 20.27–40; Mk. 12.28–34–Lk. 10.25–8. Luke sometimes appends sayings in the imperfect after controversies in the aorist (as at Lk. 5.36 and 6.5).

88 Luke may use continuous tenses to introduce the action, but keeps introductions to speeches in the aorist: Acts 2.12–14, 4.7f., 5.27–9, 6.1f., 6.13–7.2; 13.45f.; 18.12–14; 23.1; 24.2,10.

89 αἱ χῶραι or αἱ χῶραι τῆς Ἰουδαίας is a Lucan phrase for Judaea (Lk. 21.21, Acts 8.1). The portrayal in the Western reading of a countryside particularly suspicious of the Gentile mission may preserve a recollection of the nationalism of rural Judaea: see G. Theissen, *The First Followers of Jesus* (London, 1978), pp. 50–2, 55.

90 The Western description of Peter's opponents as *brethren* tells against the thesis of a wholly consistent anti-Judaic attitude in the Western text.

91 The most complete bibliography on the Decree (up to the time of the book's publication) is J. Sagi, *Textus Decreti Concilii Hierosolymitani Lucano Opere et Antiquioris Ecclesiae Disciplina Illustratus* (TeT 25; Rome, 1977), pp. 153–7.

92 The most comprehensive guide to this feature is Boismard and Lamouille, *Texte occidental* II, pp. 106f.

93 Menoud, 'Western Text', *SNTS Bulletin* 2 (1951), 26f.; Epp, *Theological Tendency*, pp. 110f.
94 M. J. Lagrange, 'Les Papyrus Chester Beatty pour les Evangiles', *RB* 43 (1934), 168.
95 Boismard and Lamouille, *Texte occidental* II, p. 106.
96 W. G. Kümmel, 'Die älteste Form des Aposteldekrets', in *Spiritus et Veritas* (Festschrift für K. Kundsin), ed. Auseklis Societas Theologorum Universitatis Latviensis (Eutin, 1953); reprinted in Kümmel, *Heilsgeschehen und Geschichte: Gesammelte Aufsätze 1933–64* (Marburg, 1965), pp. 280f. (to which reference is here made).
97 Kümmel, 'Älteste Form', in *Spiritus*, p. 282.
98 Ibid., p. 283.
99 Ibid., p. 280, n. 7.
100 Ibid., p. 281f.
101 Ibid., p. 284f.
102 Epp, *Theological Tendency*, pp. 109f.
103 Metzger, *TCGNT*, p. 432.
104 G. Resch, *Das Aposteldekret nach seiner außerkanonischen Textgestalt* (TU 36.2; Leipzig, 1905).
105 Ibid., p. 52.
106 Ibid., pp. 153–61.
107 A. von Harnack, *The Acts of the Apostles* (London, 1909), p. 251.
108 K. Lake, 'The Judaistic Controversy, and the Apostolic Council', *CQR* 71 (1910–11), 355f., 360; K. Lake in *Beg.* V, p. 205.
109 Ropes, *Beg.* III, pp. 265–9.
110 T. Boman, 'Das textkritische Problem des sogennanten Aposteldekrets', *NT* 7 (1964), 26–36.
111 Y. Tissot, 'Les Prescriptions des presbytres (Actes,xv,41,D), *RB* 77 (1970), 321–46.
112 Ibid., 344f.
113 Ibid., 344.
114 Ibid., 337.
115 Ibid., 328.
116 S. G. Wilson, *Luke and the Law* (MSSNTS 50; Cambridge, 1983), pp. 68–102, esp. p. 92 on the possible Alexandrian addition of πνικτόν.
117 F. Manns, 'Remarques sur Actes 15,20.29', *Ant.* 53 (1978), 443–51.
118 Ibid., 445f.
119 Ibid., 449–51.
120 Boismard and Lamouille, *Texte occidental* II, pp. 106–8.
121 Lake, *Beg.* V, p. 207.
122 Haenchen, *Acts*, pp. 449f.
123 Lake, 'Judaistic Controversy', 359f.
124 R. M. Grant, 'Dietary Laws among Pythagoreans, Jews and Christians', *HThR* 73 (1980), 299–310.
125 H. J. Schoeps, *Theologie und Geschichte des Jüdenchristentums* (Tübingen, 1949), pp. 188–96; E. Molland, 'La Circoncision, le baptême et l'autorité du décret apostolique (Actes XV,28sq.) dans les milieux judéo-chrétiens des Pseudo-Clémentines', *StTh* 9 (1955), 32.

126 K. Böckenhoff, *Das Apostolische Speisegesetz in den ersten fünf Jahrhunderten* (Paderborn, 1903), p. 39.

127 The possible relationship has been investigated by Molland, 'La Circoncision', and by A. F. J. Klijn, 'The Pseudo-Clementines and the Apostolic Decree', *NT* 10 (1968), 305–12.

128 Resch, *Das Aposteldekret*, p. 18 and n. 1; Ropes, *Beg.* III, p. ccxxx; Kenyon, 'Western Text', 311; Martini, 'Tradition textuelle', 26–8.

129 Among those drawing attention to Lev. 17 and 18 are: C. Waitz, 'Das Problem des sogennanten Aposteldekrets', *ZKG* 55 (1936), 227; Boman, 'Das textkritische Problem', 28; Haenchen, *Acts*, p. 469; D. R. Catchpole, 'Paul, James, and the Apostolic Decree', *NTS* 23 (1977), 429. Wilson argues that Lev. 17 and 18 are unlikely to be the true background of the Decree (*Luke and the Law*, pp. 84–94).

130 This partly answers Wilson's objection that there are other laws which apply to the 'resident alien' (*Luke and the Law*, p. 86). There *are* other laws, but this is the only *body* of relevant law.

131 Wilson, *Luke and the Law*, pp. 86f.

132 H. L. Strack and P. Billerbeck, *Kommentar zum Neuen Testament aus Talmud und Midrasch* II (Munich, 1924), p. 730; E. Nestle observed that πνικτόν was a term alien to Judaism ('Zum Erstickten im Aposteldekret', *ZNW* 7 (1906), 254) but little attention has been paid to his comment. The observation has been repeated by Wilson, *Luke and the Law*, pp. 88–92.

133 M. Jastrow, *A Dictionary of the Targumim, the Talmud Babli and Yerushalmi, and the Midrashic Literature* (New York, 1950), p. 485.

134 *Hullin* 2.4; see Strack–Billerbeck II, pp. 730–4.

135 Epp, *Theological Tendency*, p. 110. Virtually the only reference to strangled meat in a Jewish author is Philo, *Spec. Leg.* 4.122. This is not an exposition of the Law, but is a description of gluttony. See the discussion in Wilson, *Luke and the Law*, pp. 90f.

136 Molland, 'La Circoncision', 38.

137 See C. K. Barrett, 'Things Sacrificed to Idols', *NTS* 11 (1964–5), 150.

138 *Rec.* 4.36, 6.10, *Hom.* 8.23. See Molland, 'La Circoncision', 37f.

139 B. J. Malina, 'Does *Porneia* mean Fornication?', *NT* 14 (1972), 10–17.

140 Ibid., 12f.

141 The most thorough discussion is that of Wilson (*Luke and the Law*, pp. 89–92), who concludes that πνικτόν is probably a culinary term, but is possibly also used in Gentile religious practice.

142 F. C. Burkitt, Review of Ropes, *Beg.* III, *JThS* 28 (1927), 199.

143 Barrett, 'Things Sacrificed to Idols', 152f.

144 See F. C. Burkitt, 'St. Augustine's Bible and the *Itala*', *JThS* 11 (1909–10), 267f.; although Burkitt's own opinion concerning the original form of the Decree was in favour of the four-membered formula: *JThS* 28 (1927), 199. Ropes's comment (*Beg.* III, p. 268) that Amphilochius of Iconium supported the reading αἵματος πνικτοῦ was based on Ficker's 1906 edition. Amphilochius' more recent editor gives a different reading (C. Datema, *Amphilochii Iconiensis Opera* (CChr.SG 3; Tournhout and Louvain, 1978, p. 205). Note also the

reading of Hesychius of Jerusalem, *Homilies on Job* 15 (see Appendix: Textual witnesses under 15.28,29).

145 On the Levitical purity laws as a system, see M. Douglas, *Purity and Danger. An Analysis of the Concepts of Purity and Taboo* (London, 1966), pp. 41–57; M. Newton has argued that the concept of purity had a place in Paul's thought, as the community took the place in his Christian value-system which the Temple had occupied in his Jewish value-system: *The Concept of Purity at Qumran and in the Letters of Paul* (MSSNTS 53; Cambridge, 1985). Newton's argument is consistent with the observations about Paul made here.

146 *Did.* 6.2: a later interpolation according to Audet, *La Didachè* (Paris, 1958), pp. 350–7.

147 *Hom.* 7.8; cf. Lev. 15; see Douglas, *Purity*, p. 124.

148 Barrett, 'Things Sacrificed to Idols', 153.

149 Grant, 'Dietary Laws', 299–305.

150 *Apol.* 14.14f.; *Hom.* 7.4.4; see above, pp. 93–6.

151 Manns, 'Remarques', 445f., 450f.

152 W. Robinson, 'Historical Survey of the Church's Treatment of New Converts with Reference to Pre- and Post-Baptismal Instruction', *JThS* 42 (1941), 42–5; P. Borgen, 'The Golden Rule', in P. Borgen, *Paul Preaches Circumcision* (Trondheim, 1983), pp. 83, 100f., and n. 67.

153 See the list of early Christian references gathered in A. Dihle, *Die Goldene Regel. Eine Einführung in die Geschichte der antiken und frühchristlichen Vulgärethik* (SAW 7; Göttingen, 1962), p. 107.

154 See L. Cerfaux, 'Le Chapitre xve du Livre des Actes à la lumière de la littérature ancienne', in *Miscellanea Giovanni Mercati* (Studi e Testi 121; Rome, 1946); reprinted in *Recueil Lucien Cerfaux* II, (EThL.B 7; Gembloux, 1954), p. 116.

155 Kümmel, 'Älteste Form', in *Spiritus*, pp. 284f.

156 See Ropes, *Beg.* III, pp. 266f. on the reasons for supposing that the Rule entered the text at 15.29 before 15.20.

157 H.-W. Bartsch saw the presence of the Rule in the Decree as a response to the needs of the churches by giving a practicable rule of life. Luke himself, as Bartsch noted, does the same thing elsewhere (see Lk. 10.25–37, a story which makes concrete Jesus' instruction): 'Tradition-geschichtliches zur "goldenen Regel" und zum Aposteldekret', *ZNW* 75 (1984), 132.

158 Martini, 'Tradition textuelle', 26–8.

159 F. W. Grosheide proposed a similar distinction between the non-Western text of the Decree as the 'historical' form, recovered and used by Luke, and the Western text as the 'contemporary' form, to which scribes altered Luke's original': 'Acts 15[29] par., a Suggestion', *BBezC* 6 (1929), 15.

4 Marginal annotation and the origin of some Western readings in Acts

1 E.g. Metzger, *TCGNT*, pp. 457f. refers to Rendel Harris's explanation of 17.28.
2 F. H. A. Scrivener, *A Plain Introduction to the Criticism of the New Testament for the Use of Biblical Students*, ed. E. Miller (London, 4th edn, 1894), p. 369.
3 Blass, *Acta*, p. 26.
4 Ibid., p. 26.
5 Ibid., pp. 26f.
6 Galen, Kühn, XVII.1, p. 80; XVIII.2, pp. 863f.; see p. 169 below.
7 Blass, *Acta*, p. 32.
8 Ibid., p. 32.
9 Weiss, *Codex D*, p. 12.
10 Ibid., p. 12.
11 Ibid., pp. 12–14; see pp. 113–15 below, on 1.5.
12 Weiss, *Codex D*, p. 14; see pp. 126–31 below, on 14.2.
13 Weiss, *Codex D*, pp. 15f.; see pp. 115–19, below, on 3.11, pp. 120–2 on 3.13, pp. 146–501 on 16.4, pp. 150–3 on 17.1, pp. 154–6 on 18.8.
14 Boismard and Lamouille, *Texte occidental* I, pp. 115–17.
15 Harris, *Four Lectures*, pp. 70–4.
16 Ibid., pp. 75–9.
17 Ibid., pp. 79–81.
18 Harris [Editorial Article], *BBezC* 8 (1930), 6.
19 Corssen, 'Acta', 434–6.
20 See n. 1 above.
21 Pott, *Abendländische Text*.
22 See, for instance, the review by W. Bousset in *ThL* (1900), cols. 606–10.
23 A. V. Valentine-Richards, 'The Western Text of Acts. A Study by A. Pott', *JThS* 2 (1901), 439–47, esp. 445–7.
24 W. M. Ramsay, *SPT*, pp. 24f.
25 Ibid., pp. 25–7.
26 Clark treated the combined witness of 383 and 614 as particularly significant, and gave their shared readings a siglum of their own (δ).
27 Streeter, *JThS* 34 (1933), 234.
28 Ibid., 237f.
29 H. W. Moule, 'Acts iv.25', *ET* 51 (1940), 396; C. F. D. Moule, 'H. W. Moule on Acts iv.25', *ET* 66 (1954), 220f.
30 H. W. Moule, 'Acts iv.25', 396.
31 Weiss, *Codex D*, pp. 12–16; Ropes, *Beg.* III, p. clxxii; Clark, *Acts*, p. xlii; Epp, *Theological Tendency*, pp. 9–11; Boismard and Lamouille, *Texte occidental* I, pp. 115–17.
32 See preceding note; examples of 'fusion of texts' are given by Boismard and Lamouille at 3.11 (*Texte occidental* II, p. 21), 4.15 (pp. 28f.), 4.24 (p. 31), 7.26 (p. 49).
33 The words witnessed to by D* here are enclosed in small brackets in the MS. These brackets occur elsewhere in Acts in Codex D around

conspicuous Western readings (see also 6.1 and 7.26). They appear to be relatively late markings of the text (see Scrivener, *Bezae Codex*, p. xxix), and although here and in the apparatus of N–A[26] these readings have been designated D* (i.e. a reading of the first scribe, subsequently corrected), this should not be taken to mean that an early scribe has altered the reading.

34 Metzger, *TCGNT*, p. 280.
35 Weiss, *Codex D*, p. 14.
36 Metzger, *TCGNT*, p. 280.
37 Epp, *Theological Tendency*, p. 116.
38 Zahn, *Apg.*, I, p. 29; Zahn, *Urausgabe*, pp. 329f.
39 According to Haenchen and Weigandt, this ineptitude characterises the Western material as a 'typical late addition': 'Original Text?', 474.
40 Ropes, *Beg.* III, p. 4.
41 Metzger, *TCGNT*, p. 280.
42 *Bell.Jud.* 5.5.3.
43 *Middoth* 1.4; 2.6.
44 K. Lake in *Beg.* V, pp. 479–86; J. Duplacy, 'A propos d'une variante "occidentale" des *Actes des Apôtres* (III, 11)', *REAug* 2 (1956), 234f.
45 The implication is drawn from Josephus, *Bell.Jud.* 5.5.1.
46 K. Lake in *Beg.* V, p. 484; Duplacy, 'Variante', 236f.; F. F. Bruce, *The Acts of the Apostles* (London, 2nd edn, 1952), p. 106; Haenchen, *Acts*, p. 204, n. 2; Metzger, *TCGNT*, pp. 308f; D. Hamm has argued that ἱερόν in Luke and Acts consistently means 'Temple precincts', that the entry into the ἱερόν here is symbolic, not referential, and that the Western reading is a pedantic 'correction' which rests on a misunderstanding of Luke's meaning: 'Acts 3:1–10, The Healing of the Temple Beggar as Lucan Theology', *Bib* 67 (1986), 309–11.
47 K. Lake in *Beg.* V, p. 484; Metzger, *TCGNT*, p. 309.
48 Weiss, *Codex D*, p. 60; Bruce, *Acts*, p. 106; Duplacy, 'Variante', 236.
49 Metzger, *TCGNT*, p. 309.
50 Or it may, as Boismard and Lamouille suggest, be conformation to the Bezan Latin: *qui vocatur* (*Texte occidental* II, p. 21). Less likely is their suggestion that an archetype of D lacked τῇ καλουμένῃ, and that it has been inserted into D from the accompanying Latin. The extent to which D has undergone conformation to the Latin column is debatable: see D. C. Parker, 'A "Dictation Theory" of Codex Bezae', *JSNT* 15 (1982), 110f. The omission of τῇ καλουμένῃ in 1838 may be due, as von Soden suggested (*Die Schriften des neuen Testaments in ihrer ältesten erreichbaren Textgestalt hergestellt auf Grund ihrer Textgeschichte*, II (Göttingen, 1913), p. 500), to the influence of Acts 5.12.
51 Ropes, *Beg.* III, p. 28, was willing to consider the reading of it[55] as original, but it is more likely to be a clarificatory expansion.
52 See the discussion of 11.2 (pp. 77–87 above), and Haenchen and Weigandt, 'Original Text?', 470f.
53 Weiss, *Codex D*, p. 60.
54 This is implied by Metzger, who incorporates material from the non-Western text ('all the people ran together to them ...) in order to

make a comprehensible translation of the reading of D: *TCGNT*, p. 308.

55 Weiss, *Codex D*, p. 13; Boismard and Lamouille, *Texte occidental* II, p. 21.

56 Boismard and Lamouille, *Texte occidental* II, p. 214.

57 Blass, *Acta*, p. 67.

58 Ropes, *Beg.* III, p. 28; Lake and Cadbury, *Beg.* IV, p. 36.

59 Boismard and Lamouille, *Texte occidental* II, p. 22.

60 Boismard and Lamouille give Chrysostom as a witness to the reconstructed TO: θέλοντος ἀπολύειν αὐτόν. But Chrysostom is a difficult witness here. His lemma reads: κατὰ πρόσωπον Πιλάτου, κρίναντος ἐκείνου ἀπολύειν (i.e. the Majority text), and his comment runs: δύο τὰ ἐγκλήματα, καὶ ὅτι Πιλᾶτος ἤθελεν ἀπολύειν, καὶ ὅτι ὑμεῖς ἐκείνου θελήσαντος οὐκ ἠθελήσατε (*Hom in Act* Migne, *PG* 60, col. 75f.). Chrysostom's comment *may* be based on a text like that of TO (although the precise form would be hard to determine), but it may equally be an interpretation of the Majority text, or a reminiscence of Lk. 23.20.

61 The redundancy thus created seems to have been noticed by a scribe of unknown date (but probably early: see Scrivener, *Bezae Codex*, p. xxix), who cancelled the words τοῦ and θέλοντος by dots placed above the letters.

62 Boismard and Lamouille, *Texte occidental* II, p. 22.

63 This is, of course, part of the evidence for determining Luke's attitude to the Roman authorities. It is perhaps unfair to conclude, as R. Maddox does, that for Luke: 'Pilate is at best a weakling who gives in to pressure, when he knows quite well that his prisoner is innocent': *The Purpose of Luke–Acts* (Studies of the New Testament and its World (FRLANT 126); Edinburgh and Göttingen 1982), p. 95. Luke, after all, could scarcely deny that Pilate condemned Jesus to death, but Pilate's repetition of his willingness to release Jesus shows the reader who Jesus' 'real' enemies were, and what the representative of Roman authority would have done, left to himself.

64 Zahn, *Apg.* I, p. 229, n. 7.

65 Epp, *Theological Tendency*, p. 95.

66 Or possibly, 'to look after the accounts'. See Lake and Cadbury, *Beg.* IV, p. 64.

67 The incoherence of the account is noted by L. T. Johnson, *The Literary Function of Possessions in Luke–Acts* (SBL.DS 39; Missoula, 1977), pp. 211–13.

68 The reference in D and its allies in 2.45 to a daily distribution of alms to the needy seems to be due to a displacement of καθ' ἡμέραν from 2.46 (see below on 17.4, pp. 153f.).

69 So Haenchen, *Acts*, p. 268.

70 Phil. 3.5; for the wider use of 'Hebrew' with this connotation in Judaism of the Roman era, see Kittel, *TDNT* III, pp. 367–9. The point has been made with reference to Acts 6.1 by N. Walter, 'Apostelgeschichte 6.1 und die Anfänge der Urgemeinde in Jerusalem', *NTS* 29 (1983), 370–93.

71 This is the apparent implication of Acts 8.1; see also the good relations between James and the wider community implied both by Acts 21.18–25, and by Hegesippus in Eusebius, *HE* 2.23.4–7.
72 Lake and Cadbury, *Beg.* IV, p. 161; Bruce, *Acts*, p. 277.
73 Haenchen, *Acts*, p. 420, n. 3.
74 Ibid., p. 420, n. 3.
75 Conzelmann, *Apg.*, p. 87.
76 Boismard and Lamouille ascribe the redundancy to a fusion of two texts. But there are no witnesses to a clear Western text, and αὐτοῖς remains difficult: *Texte occidental* II, p. 97.
77 But see the remarks of J.-B. Frey (below, n. 78).
78 J.-B. Frey, *Corpus Inscriptionum Judaicarum* II (Rome and Paris, 1936), p. xcviii, n. 1.
79 Frey cites *CIJ* I, nos.265: Stafilus 'arch(h)on et archisynagogus' (Rome); ?281: Ισαακ '(αρχισυν)αγωγος (?και αρχων) συναγωγη(ς)' (Rome); 563: Alfius Juda 'arch(h)on et ar(ch)isynagogus' (Capua); to which he might have added 681: Joses 'Ioses arcisynagογος [*sic*] et principales' (Sofia).
80 Although note the uncertain reconstructed reading of *CIJ* I, no. 281 (above, n. 79).
81 Weiss, *Codex D*, p. 77.
82 Ibid., p. 15.
83 On 15.2D, see pp. 137–40 below. The αὐτοῖς of 14.27D has been accounted for as the reflection of an Aramaic proleptic pronoun (Ropes, *Beg.* III, p. 138), or as a literal retranslation from an Aramaic version of Acts (C. C. Torrey, *Documents of the Primitive Church* (New York, 1941), p. 146), or as a retranslation of an ethic dative (Wilcox, *Semitisms*, p. 155). It may, however, be a misplaced gloss, which should have been put after ἀνήγγελλον to give ἀνήγγελλον αὐτοῖς ὅσα ἐποίησεν κτλ.
84 ἐπήγαγον (D) seems to be an error for ἐπήγειραν, which is the reading of all other witnesses, including the Bezan Latin.
85 So Ropes, *Beg.* III, pp. 128, 138; Epp, *Theological Tendency*, p. 138.
86 Wilcox, *Semitisms*, p. 131; also Torrey, *Documents*, p. 147.
87 Unless, as is possible, οἱ δίκαιοι is a reference to Paul and Barnabas (see n. 92 below). The reading αὐτοῖς διωγμὸν κατὰ τῶν δικαίων would also exemplify a tendency to run such glosses together (cf. 3.11, pp. 115–19, and 15.2, pp. 137–40). If these glosses had stood in the margin, this coalescence would be an understandable error.
88 Among them it[61], vg[1260], prov; see Clark, *Acts*, pp. 284–6.
89 Clark, *Acts*, p. 357.
90 Clark, *Primitive Text*, pp. 92–105.
91 Clark, *Acts*, pp. xlvi, 357.
92 D. Hill has argued ('Δίκαιοι as a Quasi-Technical Term', *NTS* 11 (1964/5), 296–302) that in Matthean usage (as, for instance, Matt.10.41) δίκαιοι may be used 'with special reference to those in the community who witness, instruct and teach' (p. 302). This meaning would suit the context here. The proposed rewriting could have had the sense: 'The synagogue leaders stirred up a persecution against them

[i.e. the converts of the previous verse], and poisoned the minds of the Gentiles against the righteous [i.e. the missionaries].' This use of δίκαιος is not particularly congenial to D itself, which omits the relevant clause of Matt. 10.41. (But cf. the comments in pp. 72f. on the similarities between the Western text of Acts 8.37–9 and Matthew.)

93 Boismard and Lamouille, *Texte occidental* II, pp. 214, 231.
94 See the opinions referred to by Haenchen, *Acts*, p. 422, and by Ramsay, *SPT*, p. 108.
95 *Beg.* IV, p. 161; see also *Beg.* V, pp. 1–7.
96 Weiss, *Codex D*, p. 77; Ropes, *Beg.* III, p. 130; Lake and Cadbury, *Beg.* IV, pp. 161f.; Bruce, *Acts*, p. 277; Haenchen, *Acts*, p. 420, n. 3.
97 Irenaeus' reading is not a precise quotation, but appears to show knowledge of this variant: *et suaderent eis qui crediderant in Dominum circumcidi et reliqua secundum legis observationem perficere* (*Adv. Omn. Haer.* 3.12.14).
98 Lake and Cadbury, *Beg.* IV, p. 169.
99 Ropes, *Beg.* III, p. ccxxx.
100 Williams, *Alterations*, p. 60; Epp, *Theological Tendency*, pp. 101f.
101 Epp, *Theological Tendency*, p. 102.
102 Knox, *Church of Jerusalem*, p. xxiii; Williams, *Alterations*, p. 60.
103 Epp, *Theological Tendency*, p. 97.
104 Weiss, *Codex D*, p. 80; Ropes, *Beg.* III, p. ccxxx; Williams, *Alterations*, p. 60 (with the suggestion that ἔταξαν be taken as an impersonal plural); Epp, *Theological Tendency*, pp. 101f. (cautiously); Haenchen, *Acts*, p. 443, n. 6; Metzger, *TCGNT*, p. 427.
105 Ropes, *Beg.* III, pp. 139f.
106 This point is made by Clark, *Acts*, p. 359.
107 The text of syr^hmg is rather easier, but this may be partly accidental. Clark explained the phrase '*being* those who believed ...' as derived from ὄντες, itself a corruption of λέγοντες. This explanation seems highly probable: Clark, *Acts*, p. 359.
108 See, e.g., Ropes, *Beg.* III, p. lxxiv on Acts 18.21f.
109 See Ropes, *Beg.* III, pp. ccxxxv–ccxxxvii.
110 So Boismard and Lamouille, *Texte occidental* II, p. 103.
111 ἐξελθόντες is probably to be read with the majority of witnesses against B etc. It is unlikely that such a wide variety of witnesses should independently have added the word.
112 Zahn, *Introduction* III, pp. 32f.; Cerfaux, 'Le XVe Chapitre', in *Recueil LC* II, p. 121; C. F. D. Moule, *An Idiom-Book of New Testament Greek* (Cambridge, 2nd edn, 1959), p. 45.
113 Cerfaux, 'Le XVe Chapitre', in *Recueil LC* II, pp. 121f.
114 Williams, *Alterations*, p. 60.
115 Ropes, *Beg.* III, p. 139.
116 Ibid., p. 139. One might compare the suggestion of F. W. Grosheide that 1 Cor. had influenced the Western text of Acts 18.27 ('Acts 18:27, A Test Case', *BBezC* 8 (1930), 20). The influence of 1 Cor. on the textual tradition of Acts would be a reasonable assumption, since 1 Cor. appears to have been the most widely read of Paul's letters in the

early second century (see *The New Testament in the Apostolic Fathers*, by A Committee of the Oxford Society of Historical Theology, esp. Table 1, p. 137).

117 Note the reading of it[58], which *has* conformed Acts 15.2 to 1 Cor. 7.17–20, and has formalised what is said as Paul's *teaching* (1 Cor. 7.17), although it has also introduced Barnabas alongside Paul.

118 See above, n. 104.

119 Zahn, *Introduction* III, p. 33; Lake and Cadbury, *Beg.* IV, p. 170; Williams's suggestion (n. 104 above) of an impersonal plural is unlikely – the vagueness of the impersonal plural would be inappropriate to the context of Acts 15.1f.

120 This is one of the points of contact between Luke's thought and that of the Pastorals. See S. G. Wilson, *Luke and the Pastoral Epistles* (London, 1979), pp. 53–68.

121 Contra Haenchen, *Acts*, p. 444, n. 5, who argued that a disagreement exists between 15.24, where the 'certain men' are said to have no authority from Jerusalem, and 15.2D, which vests them with authority.

122 Ropes, *Beg.* III, p. 139.

123 Ibid., p. 139.

124 Wilcox, *Semitisms*, p. 132; Metzger favours the former explanation, *TCGNT*, p. 428.

125 E.g. Metzger's version: 'to give an account of themselves to the apostles and elders', *TCGNT*, p. 427.

126 See W. Bauer, W. F. Arndt, and F. W. Gingrich, *A Greek–English Lexicon of the New Testament* (Chicago and London, 2nd edn, 1979), art. κρίνω 4aα.

127 The corrector was identified by Scrivener as C, whom he placed in the seventh century (*Bezae Codex*, p. xxv).

128 Scrivener's corrector B, perhaps seventh century (*Bezae Codex*, p. xxv).

129 E.g. Metzger, *TCGNT*, p. 427.

130 Erasmus accepted only the first clause, which he took from the margin of one MS: see his *In Novum Testamentum Annotationes* (Basle, 1527), p. 292.

131 W. Bousset, *ThR* 1 (1897–8), 405ff.; Corssen, *Acta*, 428, 440; Williams, *Alterations*, p. 60; Metzger, *TCGNT*, p. 439.

132 Weiss, *Codex D*, pp. 82f.; Dibelius, 'Text', in *Studies*, p. 87.

133 Fascher, *Textgeschichte*, p. 35; Epp, *Theological Tendency*, p. 112.

134 Ramsay, *SPT*, pp. 174f.; Ramsay's interpretation of 15.33 was anticipated by Beza, *Jesu Christi Domini Nostri Novum Testamentum* (Cambridge, 1642), p. 343.

135 Blass, *Acta*, p. 173; also his 'On Acts xv.34 and xviiif.', *ET* 10 (1898–9), 89.

136 Clark, *Acts*, pp. 361f.

137 E. Delebecque, 'Silas, Paul et Barnabé à Antioche selon le texte "occidental" d'Actes 15,34 et 38', *RHPhR* 64 (1984), 48f.

138 Boismard and Lamouille, *Texte occidental* II, pp. 108f.

139 This was Scrivener's view: *Introduction* II, p. 374.

140 Weiss, *Codex D*, p. 84.
141 Fascher, *Textgeschichte*, p. 39.
142 Epp, *Theological Tendency*, p. 114.
143 Ropes, *Beg.* III, pp. 150f.; see also Thiele, 'Charakterisierung', 54f., and Epp, *Theological Tendency*, p. 113.
144 Boismard and Lamouille, *Texte occidental* II, p. 111.
145 Ropes, *Beg.* III, p. 428.
146 See pp. 48f. above.
147 Tissot, 'Les Prescriptions des presbytres', 323–45, esp. 330–2.
148 Lake and Cadbury, *Beg.* IV, p. 183.
149 E. Jacquier, *Les Actes des Apôtres* (Etudes bibliques; Paris, 1926), p. 477. (The reference is to 16.4.)
150 This interest shown by the Western text in the use of the Decree in instructing converts is probably the key to understanding the Western addition of the 'Golden Rule' to the Decree (see above pp. 101–4).
151 See above pp. 103f.
152 Weiss, *Codex D*, p. 16.
153 Haenchen, *Acts*, p. 506, n. 4.
154 The form Ἀπολλωνίδα in D is not certain. A dot has been placed over the δ. This may be from the hand of the original scribe, and it may be a mark of deletion. But it may equally well be accidental. See Scrivener, *Bezae Codex*, p. 445.
155 As was noticed by the corrector whom Scrivener called C, who seems to have intended moving καί to the other side of κατῆλθον (Scrivener, *Bezae Codex*, p. 445).
156 K. Lake, *The Earlier Epistles of St. Paul* (London, 2nd edn, 1930), p. 62, n. 1.
157 Lake and Cadbury, *Beg.* IV, p. 202.
158 *Itineraria Romana*, ed. O. Cuntz (Leipzig, 1929), pp. 48f., 99.
159 Cicero, *Prov.Cons.* 4: *via nostra militaris*, referring particularly to the Thracian section of the Egnatian Way. Note also the hint of military activity in laying out the eastern part of the Egnatian Way in Strabo, 7.322. See G. Radke, 'Viae Publicae Romanae', in *PRE* Suppl. Bd 13 (Munich, 1973), cols. 1666f.
160 Hierocles, *Synecdemus* 640.3.
161 See C. de Boor, 'Nachträge zu den Notitiae Episcopatuum', *ZKG* 12 (1890–1), p. 525; on Apollonia and its civic status, F. Papazoglu, *Makedonski gravodi u rimsko dobu* (*The Cities of Macedonia in the Roman Period*) (Skopje, 1957), pp. 149ff. (Serbian), 348 (French).
162 Compare the Western readings at Acts 16.12, 16.38–40, 20.4.
163 Blass, *Acta*, p. 186.
164 Clark, *Acts*, pp. 108, 366; for his view on the antiquity of the στίχοι, see *Acts*, pp. xxxvii–xli.
165 Boismard and Lamouille, *Texte occidental* II, p. 119.
166 Ropes, *Beg.* III, p. 162.
167 Weiss, *Codex D*, p. 13, n. 1.
168 Ropes, *Beg.* III, p. 173; Epp, *Theological Tendency*, p. 88, n. 2; Boismard and Lamouille, *Texte occidental* II, p. 127.
169 Weiss, *Codex D*, p. 16.

170 Epp, *Theological Tendency*, pp. 88–90.
171 The apparatus in N–A²⁶ is misleading in this respect, suggesting as it does that the Western reading is substituted for the Majority reading in the minuscule witnesses. See Valentine-Richards, *Codex 614*, p. 52; Boismard and Lamouille, *Texte occidental* II, p. 169.
172 See Boismard and Lamouille, *Texte occidental* II, pp. 168f.
173 So Haenchen, *Acts*, pp. 661f., n. 3.
174 'The "Western" text places the direct blame for Paul's prolonged imprisonment upon a *Jewess!*', Epp, *Theological Tendency*, p. 152.
175 A contrast in treatment seems implied, but see Haenchen's contrary opinion: *Acts*, p. 661, n. 3.
176 Compare Herod's use of Jesus' imprisonment (Lk. 9.9, 23.8, and see also Mk. 6.20).
177 The suggestion was made in Moulton and Howard, *Grammar* II, p. 473.
178 Weiss, *Codex D*, p. 14.
179 Ibid., p. 12.
180 Ibid., p. 12.
181 Boismard and Lamouille, *Texte occidental* II, p. 117.
182 The phrase has consequently been removed in sah.
183 Blass, *Acta*, p. 252; Clark, *Acts*, p. 153.
184 See Philo, *De Spec.Leg.* 2.163, for a somewhat parallel distinction between the Jewish nation and ἡ οἰκουμένη.
185 it⁽⁵⁹·⁶²⁾ vg¹¹⁸⁶·¹¹⁸⁸·¹¹⁸⁹·⁽¹²¹³⁾·¹²⁴³·¹²⁵⁹·¹²⁶⁰·⁽¹²⁶⁶⁾·¹²⁷⁶·¹²⁷⁷·¹²⁸² ger^tepl syr^h.
186 *et docens quoniam hic est Christus filius Dei per quem omnis mundus iudicabitur cum omni fiducia sine prohibitione*: vg⁽ᶜᵃᵛ⁾·ᵗᵒˡ·¹¹⁹²·¹¹⁹³·¹¹⁹⁹·¹²⁴⁰·¹²⁴²·⁽¹²⁵⁸⁾·¹⁸⁹⁷·¹⁹⁸⁵·²⁰⁸⁴.
187 *et dicens sine ulla proibicione quia hic est Iesus filius dei per quem incipiet totus mundus iudicari*.
188 Ropes, *Beg.* III, p. 255.
189 The substance of D's additional material here is also found in syr^p (although D's grammatical peculiarity is not reproduced). An alternative explanation to the one given above for this peculiarity would be that D has been influenced by the accompanying Latin: *apostoli et fratres qui erant in Iudaeam* (see Boismard and Lamouille, *Texte occidental* II, p. 77). D's omission of the verb, though, may tell against this possibility.
190 See Strange, 'The Text of Acts 19.1'.
191 τὸ δειλινόν (3.1), συνεκπορεύεσθαι, θαμβεῖσθαι (3.11), οἱ δίκαιοι (14.2), μεγάλως (15.4).
192 ἐπὶ τὸ αὐτό = ἐν τῇ ἐκκλησίᾳ (2.27, cf. 11.26), ἀπολύειν αὐτὸν θέλοντο (3.13), ἀρχισυνάγωγοι, ἄρχοντες τῆς συναγωγῆς (14.2; Lk. uses both expressions, Mk. only ἀρχισυνάγωγοι, Matt. neither), περιτμηθῆτε καὶ τῷ ἔθει Μωϋσέως περιπατῆτε (15.1), διϊσχυριζόμενος (15.2).

5 The composition and editing of Acts

1 See, for example, the studies of E. Plümacher, *Lukas als hellenistischer Schriftsteller, Studien zur Apostelgeschichte* (StUNT 9; Göttingen, 1972), and of W. C. van Unnik, 'Luke's Second Book and the Rules of Hellenistic Historiography', in *Actes*, ed. Kremer, pp. 37–60.

2 Seneca, *Ad Luc.Ep.Mor.* 108.32; Pliny, *Ep.* 3.5.15 and 17.

3 Lucian, *Hist.Consc.* 47f.

4 Hirtius, *Bell.Gall.*, Pref.

5 Josephus, *C.Ap.* 1.49.

6 Galen, *Hipp.Ep.6 et Gal.Comm.2* Kühn, XVII.1, p. 936.

7 Catullus, *Carmen* 42.5; Pliny, *Ep.* 3.5.15.

8 Demosthenes, *Or.* 49.5.30.

9 They were recommended by Quintilian because of the ease with which they could be reused (*Inst.Or.* 10.3.31). Luke was certainly familiar with them as everyday objects: Lk. 1.63.

10 See C. H. Roberts and T. C. Skeat, *The Birth of the Codex* (London, 1983), pp. 15–23.

11 *Inst.Or.* 10.3.32.

12 A. E. Hanson, 'Memorandum and Speech of an Advocate', *ZPE* 8 (1971), pp. 15–27.

13 Juvenal, *Satires* 1.1.4–6.

14 Aulus Gellius, *Noct.Att.* 2.3.5.

15 Diogenes Laertius, *Vit.Phil.* 8.78.

16 Galen, *Hipp.Ep.1 et Gal.Comm.1* Kühn, XVII.1, p. 80; *Hipp. de Med.Off.et Gal.Comm.3* Kühn, XVIII.2, pp. 863f.

17 The author's own annotations could add to the value of a copy of his work – at least in the owner's view – according to Martial (*Ep.* 7.11, and 7.17).

18 D. Comparetti, 'La Bibliothèque de Philodème', in *Mélanges offerts à E. Chatelain* (Paris, 1910), pp. 118–29; F. G. Kenyon, *Books and Readers in Ancient Greece and Rome* (London, 2nd edn, 1950), pp. 83f.

19 For pap. 1021, see *Herculanensium Voluminum quae supersunt Collectio Altera* I (Naples, 1862), pp. 162–97.

20 Comparetti, 'Bibliothèque', pp. 123f.

21 B. Hemmerdinger, 'La Prétendue Manus Philodemi', *REG* 78 (1965), 328–30; G. Cavallo, *Libri, Scritture, Scribi a Ercolano* (Primo Supplemento a *Chronache Ercolanesi*, 1983), pp. 26f.

22 A. S. Hunt, *P.Oxy* VII, no. 1015; E. G. Turner, *Greek Manuscripts of the Ancient World* (Oxford, 1971), p. 90, with a photographic facsimile, pl. 50.

23 Turner, *Greek MSS*, p. 90.

24 *P.Oxy* VII, p. 112.

25 Turner, *Greek MSS*, p. 90.

26 On Dioscorus, see R. Keydell in *PRE* Suppl. Bd 6 (Stuttgart, 1935), cols. 27–9; J. Maspero, 'Un dernier poète grec d'Egypte: Dioscore, fils d'Apollôs', *REG* 24 (1911), 426–81; H. I. Bell, 'An Egyptian Village in the Age of Justinian', *JHS* 66 (1944), 21–36; L. S. B. MacCoull, *Dioscorus of Aphrodito, His Work and His World* (The Trans-

formation of the Classical Heritage 16; Berkeley, Los Angeles, and London, 1988).

27 J. Maspero, *Papyrus grecs d'époque byzantine*, 3 vols. (Cairo and Leipzig, 1910–16), I, nos. 67055, 67097, 67120; II, nos. 67131, 67177–88.

28 An example is illustrated Ibid., I, pl. xxix.

29 R.Devréesse, *Introduction à l'étude des manuscrits grecs* (Paris, 1954), p. 76; E. J. Kenney, 'Books and Readers in the Roman World', in *The Cambridge History of Classical Literature*, ed. E. J. Kenney and W. V. Clausen (Cambridge, 1982), pp. 11f.

30 See: Apollonius of Perga, *Conicorum*, ed. I. L. Heiberg (Leipzig, 1891), p. 2; Ovid, *Tristia* 1.7.23–5; Pliny, *Ep.* 1.8.3, 7.20.1f., 8.19.2; Ausonius, Dedicatory poem of *Ludus Septem Sapientum*.

31 Josephus, *c.Ap.* 1.50; see T. Rajak, *Josephus, The Historian and his Society* (London, 1983), p. 63.

32 Donatus, *Vit.Virg.* 31.

33 Josephus, *Vit.* 366.

34 *De Lib.Prop.*, proem, Kühn, XIX, p. 10; see also E. Nachmanson, 'Der griechische Buchtitel. Einige Beobachtungen', *GHÅ* 47.19 (1941), 24f.

35 Lucian, *Adv.Indoct.* 1f., 24f.; Martial, *Ep.* 14.183–96.

36 Martial, *Ep.* 1.2; 1.117; 4.72; 13.3 (Rome); *P. Oxy* XVIII, no. 2192 (a letter arranging for the acquisition of books from an Alexandrian bookseller).

37 *Ep.* 9.11.2.

38 Th. Birt, *Das Antike Buchwesen in seinem Verhältnis zur Litteratur* (Berlin, 1882), pp. 348f.

39 Pliny, *Ep.* 9.11.2.; Martial, *Ep.* 1.2 (Secundus); 1.117 (Atrectus); 4.72, 13.3 (Trypho – who also published Quintilian's *Inst.Or.*).

40 Josephus, *c.Ap.* 1.51.

41 Cicero, *Ad Q.Fr.* 3.4.5.

42 This state of affairs is suggested by the contents of the Herculaneum library, and is reflected in Augustine's instructions for the publication of *De Civitate Dei*: see H.-I. Marrou, 'La Technique de l'édition à l'époque patristique', *VigChr* 3 (1949), 218–20.

43 Examples are: Quintilian, *Inst.Or.* 1, pr. 7; Galen, *De An.Adm.*, 1, Kühn II, p. 217; and Arrian (perhaps as a pretext for publication), *Disc.*, proem. Ovid was afraid it would happen to his *Metamorphoses* while he was in exile: *Tristia* 1.7.

44 See B. A. van Groningen, 'ΕΚΔΟΣΙΣ', *Mn.* 4.16 (1963), 4f.

45 Tertullian, *Adv.Marc.* 1.

46 E. G. Turner, *Greek Papyri, An Introduction* (Oxford, 1968), p. 94; Turner, *Greek MSS*, pp. 17, 102.

47 G. Salmon, *Some Thoughts on the Textual Criticism of the New Testament* (London, 1897), pp. 136–49.

48 Pliny, *Ep.* 8.19.2.

49 Josephus, *c.Ap.* 1.50; *Vit.* 366.

50 See T. Zahn, *Einleitung* II, p. 342 (Eng. trans., *Introduction* III, p. 25).

51 Ibid., p. 25.

52 Ibid., p. 25.
53 Enquiries at the University of Erlangen, at which the work was produced, failed to locate Gleiss's MS.
54 Zahn, *Einleitung* II, p. 342 (Eng. trans., *Introduction* III, p. 25).
55 H. Ewald, *Die Bücher des Neuen Bundes übersezt und erklärt* I, 2nd half (Göttingen, 2nd edn, 1871), pp. 4–13, 29f.
56 von Harnack, *Acts*, p. 48.
57 R. B. Rackham, *The Acts of the Apostles* (London, 9th edn, 1922), p. xxvi.
58 J. de Zwaan, 'Was the Book of Acts a Posthumous Edition?', *HThR* 17 (1924), 95–153.
59 Ibid., 98f. De Zwaan supposed that Luke would have continued the book beyond the point at which it now ends (106–10).
60 Ibid., 110.
61 Ibid., 106–10.
62 Lake and Cadbury, *Beg.* IV, p. 90 on 8.7: '[The lack of grammatical coherence in the verse] is one of the several indications in the text that it was never fully revised'; p. 161 on 14.2–7: 'It is easier to think that this is one of the passages which escaped final revision'; p. 329 on 27.10: 'The mistake is one which any writer might make and overlook in correcting his manuscript.'
63 H. W. Moule, 'Acts iv.25', 396; C. F. D. Moule, 'H. W. Moule on Acts iv.25', 220f.
64 Galen, Kühn, XVII.1, p. 80; XVIII.2, pp. 863f.; see above, p. 169.
65 This is the argument of Harnack, more recently revived by J. A. T. Robinson, *Redating the New Testament* (London, 1976), pp. 88–92.
66 J. Dupont, 'La Conclusion des Actes et son rapport à l'ensemble de l'ouvrage de Luc', in *Actes*, ed. Kremer, pp. 359–404.
67 P. Davies, 'The Ending of Acts', *ET* 94 (1983), 334f.
68 See the summary of approaches in G. Schille, *Die Apostelgeschichte des Lukas* (ThHNT 5; Berlin, 1983), pp. 481f.
69 Haenchen, *Acts*, p. 9.
70 See 1 Clem. 47.1; 2 Pet. 3.15; Eusebius, *HE* 4.23.11.
71 Haenchen, *Acts*, p. 9.
72 J. C. O'Neill, *The Theology of Acts* (London, 1961), p. 21.
73 Ibid., p. 17.
74 Ibid., pp. 18–20.
75 Ibid., pp. 28–53.
76 See H. von Campenhausen, *The Formation of the Christian Bible* (Philadelphia and London, 1972), pp. 168–70.
77 Justin, *Dial.* 103.8 refers to the 'bloody sweat' passage of Luke 22.43f. (Western). O'Neill argues that verbal differences from the Western reading in Luke show that Justin's 'apostles' memoirs' here are in fact an independent tradition from which the Western reading also entered Luke: *Theology*, pp. 40–2. This must be a possibility, but is only a strong possibility if one can rely on the exact wording of Justin as an indication of the wording of his source, and one probably cannot.
78 Haenchen, *Acts*, p. 8.

79 Even if, as was suggested above, Justin knew a Western form of Luke, without καὶ ἀνεφέρετο εἰς τὸν οὐρανόν, he might still have drawn the inference that Luke's διέστη ἀπ' αὐτῶν was a reference to the beginning of Jesus' heavenly session.
80 See K. Aland, 'Der Schluss des Markusevangeliums', in *L'Evangile selon Marc*, ed. M. Sabbe (EThL.B 34; Gembloux, 1974), p. 454; J. Hug, *La Finale de l'Evangile de Marc* (Etudes bibliques; Paris, 1978), pp. 173–5.
81 Hug, *Finale*, p. 21; Aland, 'Schluss', pp. 454f.
82 Eusebius, *HE* 3.39.9.
83 See T. C. Skeat, 'The Length of the Standard Papyrus Roll and the Cost-Advantage of the Codex', *ZPE* 45 (1982), 169–75; B. M. Metzger, *The Text of the New Testament, Its Transmission, Corruption, and Restoration* (Oxford, 2nd edn, 1968), pp. 5f.
84 H. A. Sanders, 'A Third Century Papyrus of Matthew and Acts', in *Quantulacumque*, ed. R. P. Casey, S. Lake and A. K. Lake (London, 1937), p. 153.
85 Irenaeus, *Adv. Omn. Haer.* 3.14.3, and 4.
86 See Chapter 2, n. 63.
87 Rackham, *Acts*, p. xxvi. The references are: 5.12–14,38f., 7.2–4, 8.7, 10.36, 12.25, 14.1–4, 15.33,40, 16.19–20, 17.8f., 18.18–21, 20.3–5, 27.9–12.
88 Lake and Cadbury, *Beg.* IV, pp. 38f. (3.24), 40 (4.2), 41 (4.5), 46 (4.25), 71 (7.5), 80 (7.45), 81 (7.48), 90 (8.7), 91 (8.11), 118 (10.30), 119 (10.36–8), 153 (13.27–9), 154 (13.33), 155 (13.34), 180 (15.28), 246 (19.26), 257 (20.12), 260 (20.24), 269f. (21.16ff.), 272 (21.23), 285 (22.29), 290 (23.9), 291 (23.15), 303 (24.19), 320 (26.20), 321 (26.22), 325 (27.1), 329 (27.10).
89 von Campenhausen, *Formation*, pp. 144f.
90 H. Emonds, *Zweite Auflage im Altertum. Kulturgeschichtliche Studien zur überlieferung der antiken Literatur* (KPS 14; Leipzig, 1941), pp. 17–19.
91 *Biography of Plotinus* 4.17.
92 Ibid., 24.2.
93 Scholion to σκεπτέον, *Enneads* 4.4.29.56; see Nachmanson, 'Griechische Buchtitel', 26f.
94 Tatian, *Ad Graecos* 3.1; see van Groningen, 'ΕΚΔΟΣΙΣ', 14.
95 Emonds, *Zweite Auflage*, pp. 355f.
96 Donatus, *Vit.Virg.* 37.
97 Valerius Probus, *Vit.Pers.* 8.
98 Donatus, *Vit.Virg.* 37.
99 Valerius Probus, *Vit.Pers.* 8.
100 Diogenes Laertius, *De Clar.Phil.Vit.* 2.57.
101 A. W. Gomme, A. Andrewes and K. J. Dover, *A Historical Commentary on Thucydides* V (Oxford, 1981), pp. 361–83.
102 Ibid., pp. 361f., 374.
103 Ibid., pp. 373f.
104 Hirtius, *Bell.Gall.* 8, pref.
105 H. Oppermann, 'Nachwort und bibliographische Nachträge', in *C.*

Iulii Caesaris Commentarii De Bello Civili, ed. H. Meusel (Berlin, 12th edn, 1959), p. 390.

106 A. Klotz, *C. Iulii Caesaris Commentarii* II, *Commentarii Belli Civilis* (Leipzig, 1957), pp. ix–xiv.

107 A. Klotz, 'Zur Caesars Bellum Civile', *RMP*, N.F. 66 (1911), 85–7.

108 Oppermann, 'Nachwort', p. 390.

109 J. Dahlfen (ed.), *Marci Aurelii Antonini Ad se ipsum* (Leipzig, 1979), p. xxv.

110 C. R. Haines, 'The Composition and Chronology of the *Thoughts* of Marcus Aurelius', *JP* 33 (1914), 294.

111 Gleiss in Zahn, *Introduction* III, p. 25.

112 Rackham, *Acts*, p. xxvii.

113 See S. New, 'The Michigan Papyrus Fragment 1571', in *Beg.* V, p. 268; Haenchen, 'Zum Text der Apostelgeschichte', 28f.

114 See W. A. Strange, 'The Sons of Sceva and the Text of Acts 19:14', *JThS* 38 (1987), 97–106.

115 ἐπιδίδους καὶ ἡμῖν: 614. 1611. 2147. 2401. 2412 syr[h*] sah.

116 (D*) P (Ψ) (33. 88. 104. 181. 242) 383. 614. 945. 2412. 2495. Maj l[6c] it[5] syr[h] Or.

117 The phrase seems to have troubled later copyists also, hence the readings ἀναστῆσαι τὸν Χριστὸν καὶ καθίσαι, E it[50], and ἀναστήσειν τὸν Χριστὸν καθίσαι, 1739 geo.

118 περὶ δὲ τῶν πεπιστευκότων ἐθνῶν ἡμεῖς ἐπεστείλαμεν κρίναντες φυλάσσεσθαι αὐτοὺς τό τε εἰδωλόθυτον καὶ αἷμα καὶ πνικτὸν καὶ πορνείαν: N–A[26]. After ἐθνῶν add οὐδὲν ἔχουσι λέγειν πρὸς σέ, ἡμεῖς γὰρ ἀπεστ.: D it[5.51.] sah. After κρίναντες (κρίνοντες: D*) add μηδὲν τοιοῦτον τηρεῖν αὐτοὺς εἰ μὴ φυλάσσεσθαι: D (C E) H L P S Ψ 104. 383. 614. 2412. (2495.) Maj it[5.51] syr[h] arm geo nedl[2] (eth) Aug. Omit καὶ πνικτόν: D it[5.51] geo Aug.

Appendix: textual witnesses

1 See R. Kasser (ed.), *Papyrus Bodmer XVII. Actes des Apôtres, Epîtres de Jacques, Pierre, Jean et Jude* (Cologny and Geneva, 1961).

2 See B. P. Grenfell and A. S. Hunt, *The Oxyrhynchus Papyri*, 13 (London, 1919), pp. 10–12 (p[29]); H. A. Sanders, 'A Papyrus Fragment of Acts the in Michigan Collection', *HThR* 20 (1927), 1–19; S. New, 'The Michigan Papyrus Fragment 1571', in *Beg.* V, pp. 262–8; H. A. Sanders, *Papyri in the University of Michigan Collection* III, ed. J. G. Winter (Ann Arbor, 1936), pp. 14–19 (on p[38]); Vitelli and Mercati, in *PSI* 10 (Florence, 1932), pp. 112–18 (on p[48]).

3 See F. G. Kenyon, *Chester Beatty Biblical Papyri* II.1, *The Gospels and Acts, Text* (London, 1933); *Plates* (London, 1934) (on p[45]); Sanders, 'A Third Century Papyrus of Matthew and Acts', 151–61 (on p[53]); C. Gallazzi, 'P.Mil.Vogl.Inv.1224: Novum Testamentum, Act,2,30–37 e 2,46–3,2', *BASP* 19 (1982), 39–42 (on p[91]).

4 The definitive edition of D remains: Scrivener, *Bezae Codex*; a photographic reproduction by P. Dujardin was published by Cam-

bridge University Press in 1899. Significant studies of the MS include: Ropes, *Beg.* III, pp. lvi–lxxiv; Clark, *Acts*, pp. 173–220; J. D. Yoder, 'The Language of the Greek Variants of Codex Bezae Cantabrigiensis' (unpublished Th.D. thesis, Princeton Theological Seminary, 1958); Yoder, 'The Language of the Greek Variants of Codex Bezae', 241–8; Yoder, 'Semitisms', 317–21; Boismard and Lamouille, *Texte occidental* I, pp. 11–21; J. N. Birdsall, 'The Geographical and Cultural Origin of the Codex Bezae Cantabrigiensis: A Survey of the *Status Quaestionis*, Mainly from the Palaeographical Standpoint', in *Studien zum Text und zur Ethik des Neuen Testaments. Festschrift zum 80. Geburtstag von Heinrich Greeven* (BZNW 47; Berlin and New York, 1986), pp. 102–14.

5 The most thorough edition of E is: O. K. Walther, 'Codex Laudianus G35. A Re-examination of the Manuscript; A Reproduction of the Text and an Accompanying Commentary' (unpublished Ph.D. thesis, University of St Andrews, 1979). See also Ropes, *Beg.* III, pp. lxxxiv–lxxxviii; Clark, *Acts*, pp. 234–46; Boismard and Lamouille, *Texte occidental* I, pp. 112–18.

6 Valentine-Richards, *Codex 614*. Among the published collations are those of: 81 in F. H. Scrivener, *An Exact Transcription of the Codex Augiensis ... to which is added a Full Collation of Fifty Manuscripts* (Cambridge, 1859); 383 in Pott, *Abendländische Text*; 1739 in K. Lake and S. New (eds.), *Six Collations of New Testament Manuscripts* (HThS 17; Cambridge, Mass., 1932).

7 C. Tischendorf, *Novum Testamentum Graece*, Editio octava critica maior, Vols. I and II (Leipzig, 1869–72), Vol. III, *Prolegomena*, by C. R. Gregory (Leipzig, 1894); von Soden, *Die Schriften*.

8 Boismard and Lamouille, *Texte occidental* I, pp. 25–7.

9 Erzabtei Beuron, *Vetus Latina: Die Reste der altlateinische Bibel; 1, Verzeichnis der Sigel* (Freiburg, 1949); see also B. M. Metzger, *The Early Versions of the New Testament, Their Origin, Transmission, and Limitations* (Oxford, 1977), pp. 302–5.

10 J. Wordsworth and H. J. White, *Novum Testamentum Domini Nostri Jesu Christi Latine secundum Editionem Sancti Hieronymi* I (Oxford, 1889–98), pp. x–xiv, xxxi–xxxiii; III (ed. H. F. D. Sparks and A. W. Adams, Oxford, 1954), pp. v–x.

11 C. R. Gregory, *Textkritik des Neuen Testaments* II (Leipzig, 1902), pp. 613–729.

12 The readings of vg^BG are drawn from Migne *PL* 86, *Breviarium Gothicum* (1862), which gives the text of a Gothic breviary following a text published by Alphonso Ortiz (1502) as reissued by Cardinal Lorenzanza (1775). The readings of vg^MM are drawn from Migne *PL* 85, *Missale Mixtum* (1862), which gives the text of a Mozarabic Missal following a text published by Ortiz (1500) as reissued by Alexander Lesleus (1755). In neither case, it appears, can the MS base of Ortiz's editions be identified: see H. Schneider, *Die Altlateinischen Biblischen Cantica* (Texte und Arbeiten 1.29–30; Beuron, 1938), p. 138. D. M. Férotin established that a portion of vg^MM may be identified with

Toledo Cabildo 35.5 (Beuron, 262): Férotin, *Le Liber Mozarabicus Sacramentorum et les manuscrits Mozarabes* (Monumenta Ecclesiae Liturgica 6; Paris, 1912), col. 738.

13 Collated by Boismard and Lamouille (*Texte occidental* I, p. 38). They give the reference as Bibl.Vat.Otto.Gr.325, but 298 is apparently intended.

BIBLIOGRAPHY

1 Editions

Belsheim, J. *Die Apostelgeschichte und die Offenbarung Johannis in einer alten lateinischen Übersetzung aus dem 'Gigas librorum' auf der königlichen Bibliothek zu Stockholm* (Christiania, 1879)

Berger, S. 'Un ancien texte latin des Actes des Apôtres retrouvé dans un manuscrit provenant de Perpignan', *Notices et extraits des manuscrits de la Bibliothèque Nationale* 25.1 (Paris, 1895 [1896])

Beza, T. *Jesu Christi Domini Nostri Novum Testamentum* (Cambridge, 1642)

Blass, F. *Acta Apostolorum sive Lucae ad Theophilum liber alter. Editio Philologica* (Göttingen, 1895)

'Neue Textzeugen für die Apostelgeschichte', *ThStKr* 69 (1896), 436–71

Boismard, M.-E. and A. Lamouille, *Le Texte occidental des Actes des Apôtres. Reconstitution et réhabilitation*, 2 vols. (I, *Introduction et textes*; II, *Apparat critique*: Synthèse 17; Paris, 1984)

Bornemann, F. A. *Acta Apostolorum ab Sancto Luca conscripta ad Codicis Cantabrigiensis . . .* (Grossenhain and London, 1848)

Clark, A. C. *The Acts of the Apostles* (Oxford, 1933)

Clédat, L. *Le Nouveau Testament traduit en XIIIe siècle en langue provençale suivi d'un rituel cathare* (Paris, 1887)

Dujardin, P. *Codex Bezae Cantabrigiensis quattuor Evangelia et Actus Apostolorum complectens Graece et Latine* Phototypice representatus (Cambridge, 1899)

Fischer, B. 'Ein neue Zeuge zum westlichen Text der Apostelgeschichte', in *Biblical and Patristic Studies in Memory of R. P. Casey*, ed. J. N. Birdsall and R. W. Thomson (Freiburg, 1963)

Gallazzi, C. 'P.Mil.Vogl.Inv.1224: Novum Testamentum, Act 2,30–37 e 2,46–3,2', *BASP* 19 (1982), 39–45

Garritte, G. *L'Ancienne Version géorgienne des Actes des Apôtres d'après deux manuscrits de Sinai* (Bibliothèque du *Muséon* 38; Louvain, 1955)

Gwynn, J. *Liber Ardmachanus. The Book of Armagh* (Dublin, 1913)

Kasser, R. (ed.). *Papyrus Bodmer XVII. Actes des Apôtres. Epîtres de Jacques, Pierre, Jean et Jude* (Cologny and Geneva, 1961)

Kenyon, F. G. *Chester Beatty Biblical Papyri* II.1, *The Gospels and Acts, Text* (London, 1933); *Plates* (London, 1934)

Lake, K., and S. New (eds.). *Six Collations of New Testament Manuscripts* (HThS 17; Cambridge, Mass., 1932)

Nestle, Eberhard, Erwin Nestle, K. Aland, M. Black, C. M. Martini, B. M. Metzger, and A. Wikgren (eds.). *Novum Testamentum Graece*, 26th edn (Stuttgart, 1979)

New, S. 'The Michigan Papyrus Fragment 1571', in *Beg.* V, pp. 262–8

Petersen, T. C. 'An Early Coptic Manuscript of Acts: An Unrevised Version of the Ancient So-called Western Text', *CBQ* 26 (1964), 225–41

Ropes, J. H. *The Text of Acts.* Vol. III of *Beg.*

Sanday, W. and C. H. Turner (eds.). *Novum Testamentum Sancti Irenaei Episcopi Lugdunensis* (Old Latin Biblical Texts, 7; Oxford, 1923)

Sanders, H. A. 'A Papyrus Fragment of Acts in the Michigan Collection', *HThR* 20 (1927), 1–19

'Acts XVII,27-XIX,6; XIX,12–16', in *Papyri in the University of Michigan Collection*, Vol. III, *Miscellaneous Papyri*, ed. J. G. Winter (Ann Arbor, 1936), pp. 14–19

'A Third Century Papyrus of Matthew and Acts', in *Quantulacumque. Studies Presented to K. Lake*, ed. R. P. Casey, S. Lake, and A. K. Lake (London, 1937), pp. 151–61

Scrivener, F. H. *An Exact Transcription of the Codex Augiensis ... to which is added a Full Collation of Fifty Manuscripts* (Cambridge, 1859)

Bezae Codex Cantabrigiensis, Being an Exact Copy in Ordinary Type (Cambridge, 1864)

Soden, H. von. *Die Schriften des Neuen Testaments in ihrer ältesten erreichbaren Textgestalt hergestellt auf Grund ihrer Textgeschichte*, 2nd edn, 2 parts in 4 vols. (Part 1, Berlin; Part 2, Göttingen, 1911–13)

Tischendorf, C. *Novum Testamentum Graece*, Editio octava critica maior, Vols. I and II (Leipzig, 1869–72); Vol. III, *Prolegomena* by C. R. Gregory (Leipzig, 1894)

Valentine-Richards, A. V. *The Text of Acts in Codex 614 (Tisch. 137) and its Allies* (Cambridge, 1934)

Walther, O. K. 'Codex Laudianus G35. A Re-examination of the Manuscript; A Reproduction of the Text and an Accompanying Commentary' (unpublished Ph.D. thesis, University of St Andrews, 1979)

Westcott, B. F. and F. J. A. Hort. *The New Testament in the Original Greek*, 2 vols. (I,Text; II,Introduction, Appendix; London, 1881–2)

Wordsworth, J. and H. J. White. *Novum Testamentum Domini Nostri Jesu Christi Latine Secundum Editionem Sancti Hieronymi* 3 vols. (Oxford, 1889–1954)

Zahn, T. *Die Urausgabe der Apostelgeschichte des Lucas* (Forschungen zur Geschichte des neutestamentlichen Kanons und altkirchlichen Literatur, 9 Teil; Leipzig, 1916)

2 Books and articles

Aland, B. 'Entstehung, Charakter und Herkunft des sog. westlichen Textes untersucht an der Apostelgeschichte', *EThL* 62 (1986), 5–65

Aland, K. *Kurzgefasste Liste der griechischen Handschriften des Neuen Testaments.* Vol. I, *Gesamtübersicht* (ANTT 1; Berlin, 1963)

'Der Schluss des Markusevangeliums', in *L'Evangile selon Marc*, ed. M. Sabbe (EThL.B 34; Gembloux, 1974), pp. 435–70

'Ein neuer Textus Receptus für das griechische Neue Testament?', *NTS* 28 (1982), 145–53

Aland, K., and B. Aland. *Der Text des Neuen Testaments* (Stuttgart, 1982)

Arnauld, A. [Arnaldus]. *Dissertation critique touchant les exemplaires grecs sur lesquels M. Simon prétend que l'ancienne Vulgate a esté faite, et sur le judgement que l'on doit faire du fameux manuscrit de Bèze* (Cologne, 1691)

Audet, J.-P. *La Didachè: Instructions des Apôtres* (Etudes bibliques; Paris, 1958)

Bacon, B. W. 'Some "Western" Variants in the Text of Acts', *HThR* 21 (1928), 113–45

Bammel, E. 'The Cambridge Pericope. The Addition to Luke 6.4 in Codex Bezae', *NTS* 32 (1986), 404–26

Barrett, C. K. *Luke the Historian in Recent Study* (London, 1961)

'Things Sacrificed to Idols', *NTS* 11 (1964–5), 138–53.

'Is there a Theological Tendency in Codex Bezae?', in E. Best and R. McL. Wilson (eds.), *Text and Interpretation: Studies Presented to Matthew Black* (Cambridge, 1979), pp. 15–27

Bartsch, H.-W. 'Ein neuer Textus Receptus für das Neue Testament?', *NTS* 27 (1981), 585–92

'Traditiongeschichtliches zur "goldenen Regel" und zum Aposteldekret', *ZNW* 75 (1984), 128–32

Bell, H. I. 'An Egyptian Village in the Age of Justinian', *JHS* 66 (1944), 21–36

Birdsall, J. N. 'The Geographical and Cultural Origin of the Codex Bezae Cantabrigiensis: A Survey of the *Status Quaestionis*, Mainly from the Palaeographical Standpoint', in *Studien zum Text und zur Ethik des Neuen Testaments. Festschrift zum 80. Geburtstag von Heinrich Greeven* (BZNW 47; Berlin and New York, 1986), pp. 102–14

Birt, Th. *Das Antike Buchwesen in seinem Verhältnis zur Litteratur* (Berlin, 1882)

Black, M. *An Aramaic Approach to the Gospels and Acts* (Oxford, 3rd edn, 1967)

'Notes on the Longer and Shorter Texts of Acts', in *On Language, Culture and Religion: In Honour of Eugene A. Nida*, ed. M. Black and W. A. Smalley (Approaches to Semiotics 56; The Hague and Paris, 1974), pp. 119–31

'The Holy Spirit in the Western Text of Acts', in *NTTC*, pp. 159–70

Blass, F. 'Die Textüberlieferung in der AG', *ThStKr* 67 (1894), 86–119

'On Acts xv.34 and xviiif.', *ET* 10 (1898–9), 88–90

Böckenhoff, K. *Das Apostolische Speisegesetz in den ersten fünf Jahrhunderten* (Paderborn, 1903)

Boismard, M.-E. 'The Texts of Acts: A Problem of Literary Criticism?', in *NTTC*, pp. 147–57

Boman, T. 'Das textkritische Problem des sogennanten Aposteldekrets', *NT* 7 (1964), 26–36

Boor, C. de. 'Nachträge zu den Notitiae Episcopatuum', *ZKG* 12 (1890–1), 303–22, 519–34; 14 (1893–4), 573–99

Borgen, P. *Paul Preaches Circumcision* (Trondheim, 1983)

Bruce, F. F. *The Acts of the Apostles. The Greek Text with Introduction and Commentary* (London, 2nd edn, 1952)

Burkitt, F. C. 'St. Augustine's Bible and the *Itala*', *JThS* 11 (1909–10), 258–68, 447–58

Review of Ropes, *Beg.* III, *JThS* 28 (1927), 194–9

Cadbury, H. J. *The Style and Literary Method of Luke* (HThS 6; Cambridge, Mass., 1920)

Campenhausen, H. von. *Die Entstehung der christlichen Bibel* (BHTh 39; Tübingen, 1968); Eng. trans., *The Formation of the Christian Bible* (Philadelphia and London, 1972)

Catchpole, D. R. 'Paul, James, and the Apostolic Decree', *NTS* 23 (1977), 428–44

Cavallo, G. *Libri, Scritture, Scribi a Ercolano* (Primo Supplemento a *Chronache Ercolanesi*, 1983)

Centre d'analyse et de documentation patristique. *Biblia Patristica. Index des citations et allusions bibliques dans la littérature patristique*, 3 vols. (Paris, 1975–80)

Cerfaux, L. 'Citations scripturaires et tradition textuelle dans le livre des Actes', in *Aux sources de la tradition chrétienne. Mélanges offerts à M. Maurice Goguel* (Bibliothèque Théologique; Neuchâtel and Paris, 1950), pp. 43–51

'Le Chapitre xve du Livre des Actes à la lumière de la littérature ancienne', in *Miscellanea Giovanni Mercati* (Studi e Testi 121; Rome, 1946), pp. 107–26; reprinted in *Recueil Lucien Cerfaux*, 2 vols. (EThL.B 6 and 7; Gembloux, 1954), II, pp. 105–24

Chase, F. H. *The Old Syriac Element in Codex Bezae* (London, 1893)

Clark, A. C. *The Primitive Text of the Gospels and Acts* (Oxford, 1914)
The Descent of Manuscripts (Oxford, 1918)

Colwell, E. C. *Studies in Methodology in Textual Criticism of the New Testament* (NTTS 9; Leiden, 1969)

Comparetti, D. 'La Bibliothèque de Philodème', in *Mélanges offerts à E. Chatelain* (Paris, 1910), pp. 118–29

Conybeare, F. C., 'Two Notes on Acts', *ZNW* 20 (1921), 36–42

Conzelmann, H. *Die Mitte der Zeit* (BHTh 17; Tübingen, 4th edn, 1962); Eng. trans., *The Theology of Saint Luke* (London, 1960)
Die Apostelgeschichte (Handbuch zum Neuen Testament 7; Tübingen, 2nd edn, 1972)

Coppieters, H. 'De Historia Textus Actorum Apostolorum' (diss. Louvain, 1902)

Corssen, P. 'Acta Apostolorum ed. F. Blass', *GGA* 158 (1896), 425–48

Crehan, J. 'Peter according to the D-Text of Acts', *ThSt* 18 (1957), 596–603

Cullmann, O. *Die Tauflehre des Neuen Testaments* (AThANT 12; Zurich, 1948); Eng. trans., *Baptism in the New Testament* (London, 1950)

Cuntz, O. *Itineraria Romana*, 2 vols. (Leipzig, 1929 and 1940)

Dahlfen, J. (ed.). *Marci Aurelii Antonini Ad se ipsum* (Leipzig, 1979)

Daube, D. *The New Testament and Rabbinic Judaism* (London, 1956)

Davies, P. 'The Ending of Acts', *ET* 94 (1983), 334f.

Delebecque, E. 'Les Deux Prologues des Actes des Apôtres', *RThom* 80 (1980), 628–34

'Saint Paul avec ou sans le tribun Lysias en 58 à Césarée (Actes, XXIV, 6–8): Texte courte ou texte long?', *RThom* 81 (1981), 426–34

'Ascension et Pentecôte dans les Actes des Apôtres selon le Codex Bezae', *RThom* 82 (1982), 79–89

'De Lystres à Philippes (Act 16) avec le *Codex Bezae*', *Bibl* 63 (1982), 395–405

'L'Eglise d'Antioche et le sanctuaire de Zeus à Lystres en l'année 45', *REG* 95 (1982), 74–84

'La Mésaventure des fils de Scévas selon les deux versions (Actes 19, 13–20)', *RSPhTh* 66 (1982), 225–32

'La Montée de Pierre de Césarée à Jérusalem selon le *Codex Bezae* au chapitre 11 des Actes des Apôtres', *EThL* 58 (1982), 105–10

'Paul à Thessalonique et à Bérée selon le texte occidental des Actes (XVII,4–15)', *RThom* 82 (1982), 605–15

'Saul et Luc avant le premier voyage missionaire. Comparaison des deux versions des *Actes* 11.26–8', *RSPhTh* 66 (1982), 551–9

'La Dernière Etape du troisième voyage missionnaire de Saint Paul selon les deux versions des Actes des Apôtres (21, 16–17)', *RThL* 14 (1983), 446–55

'Les Deux Versions du voyage de Saint Paul de Corinthe à Troas', *Bibl* 64 (1983), 556–64

'L'Embarquement de Paul, captif, à Césarée, pour Rome (Actes des Apôtres 27, 1–2)', *LTP* 39 (1983), 295–302

'La révolte des orfèvres à Ephèse et ses deux versions', *RThom* 83 (1983), 419–29

'Actes 20,3–6', *Bib* 65 (1984), 356

'L'Art du conte et la faute du tribun Lysias selon les deux versions des *Actes* (22,22–30)', *LTP* 40 (1984), 217–25

'Deux études de critique litteraire sur les deux versions du Concile de Jérusalem en 49', *RBPH* 72 (1984), 30–55

'Les Deux Versions du Discours de Saint Paul à l'Aréopage (*Actes des Apôtres* 17,22–31)', *Etudes classiques* 52 (1984), 233–50

'Paul entre Juifs et Romains selon les deux versions de Act.XXIII', *RThom* 84 (1984), 83–91

'Silas, Paul et Barnabé à Antioche selon le texte "occidental" des Actes 15,34 et 38', *RHPhR* 64 (1984), 47–52

Les Deux Actes des Apôtres (Etudes bibliques, n.s. 6; Paris, 1986)

Devréesse, R. *Introduction à l'étude des manuscrits grecs* (Paris, 1954)

Dibelius, M. 'The Text of Acts: An Urgent Critical Task', *JR* 21 (1941), 421–31

Aufsätze zur Apostelgeschichte, ed. H. Greeven (FRLANT 60; Göttingen 4th edn, 1961). Eng. trans., *Studies in the Acts of the Apostles* (London, 1956)

Dihle, A. *Die Goldene Regel. Eine Einführung in die Geschichte der antiken und frühchristlichen Vulgärethik* (SAW 7; Göttingen, 1962)

Douglas, M. *Purity and Danger. An Analysis of the Concepts of Purity and Taboo* (London, 1966)

Duplacy, J. 'A propos d'une variante "occidentale" des *Actes des Apôtres* (III, 11)', *REAug* 2 (1956), 231–42

Dupont, J. 'La Conclusion des Actes et son rapport à l'ensemble de l'ouvrage de Luc', in *Actes*, pp. 359–404

Ellis, I. M. 'Codex Bezae and Acts 15', *IrBibSt* 2 (1980), 134–40

Emonds, H. *Zweite Auflage im Altertum. Kulturgeschichtliche Studien zur Überlieferung der antiken Literatur* (KPS 14; Leipzig, 1941)

Epp, E. J. 'The "Ignorance Motif" in Acts and Anti-Judaic Tendencies in Codex Bezae', *HThR* 55 (1962), 51–62

The Theological Tendency of Codex Bezae Cantabrigiensis in Acts (MSSNTS 3; Cambridge, 1966)

'The Ascension in the Textual Tradition of Luke–Acts', in *NTTC*, pp. 131–45

Erasmus, *In Novum Testamentum Annotationes* (Basle, 1527)

Erzabtei Beuron, *Vetus Latina: Die Reste der altlateinische Bibel*, Vol. I, *Verzeichnis der Sigel* (Freiburg, 1949)

Ewald, H. *Die Bücher des neuen Bundes übersetzt und erklärt*, 3 vols. (Göttingen, 1857–72)

Fascher, E. *Textgeschichte als hermeneutisches Problem* (Halle, 1953)

Fee, G. D. 'Rigorous or Reasoned Eclecticism – Which?', in *Studies in New Testament Language and Text: Essays in Honour of G. D. Kilpatrick on his Sixty-Fifth Birthday*, ed. J. K. Elliott (NT.S 44; Leiden, 1976), pp. 174–97

Férotin, D. M. *Le Liber Mozarabicus Sacramentorum et les Manuscrits mozarabes* (Monumenta Ecclesiae Liturgica 6; Paris, 1912)

Fischer, B. 'Das Neue Testament in lateinischer Sprache', in *Die alten Übersetzungen des Neuen Testaments, Die Kirchenväterzitate und Lektionare* (ANTT 5; Berlin, 1972), pp. 1–92

Flender, H. *Heil und Geschichte in der Theologie des Lukas* (BETh 41; Munich, 1965); Eng. trans., *Luke, Theologian of Redemptive History* (London, 1967)

Frey, J. B. *Corpus Inscriptionum Judaicarum*, 2 vols. (Rome, 1936,1952)

Gomme, A. W. *A Historical Commentary on Thucydides*, 5 vols. (Vols. IV and V by A. W. Gomme, A. Andrewes, and K. J. Dover, Oxford, 1945–81)

Grant, R. M. 'Dietary Laws among Pythagoreans, Jews, and Christians', *HThR* 73 (1980), 299–310

Grässer, E. 'Acta-Forschung seit 1960', *ThR* 41 (1976), 141–94, 259–90; *ThR* 42 (1977), 1–68

Gregory, C. R. *Textkritik des Neuen Testaments*, 3 vols. (Leipzig, 1900–9)

Groningen, B. A. van. 'ΕΚΔΟΣΙΣ', *Mn.* 4.16 (1963), 1–17

Grosheide, F. W. 'Acts 15[29] par., a Suggestion', *BBezC* 6 (1929), 15f.

'Acts 18:27, A Test Case', *BBezC* 8 (1930), 18–20

Haenchen, E. 'Schriftzitate und Textüberlieferung in der Apostelgeschichte', *ZThK* 51 (1954), 153–67

'Zum Text der Apostelgeschichte', *ZThK* 54 (1957), 22–55

Die Apostelgeschichte (Kritisch-exegetischer Kommentar über das Neue Testament 3; Göttingen, 3rd edn, 1961); Eng. trans., *The Acts of the Apostles. A Commentary* (Oxford, 1961)

Haenchen, E. and P. Weigandt. 'The Original Text of Acts?', *NTS* 14 (1968), 469–81

Hagner, D. A. *The Use of the Old and New Testaments in Clement of Rome* (NT.S 34; Leiden, 1973)

Haines, C. R. 'The Composition and Chronology of the *Thoughts* of Marcus Aurelius', *JP* 33 (1914), 278–95

Hamm, D. 'Acts 3:1–10, The Healing of the Temple Beggar as Lucan Theology', *Bib* 67 (1986), 305–19

Hanson, A. E. 'Memorandum and Speech of an Advocate', *ZPE* 8 (1971), 15–27

Hanson, R. P. C. 'The Provenance of the Interpolator in the "Western" Text of Acts and of Acts itself', *NTS* 12 (1966), 211–30

'The Ideology of Codex Bezae in Acts', *NTS* 14 (1968), 282–6

Harnack, A. von. *Lukas der Arzt. Der Verfasser des Dritten Evangeliums und der Apostelgeschichte* (Beiträge zur Einleitung in das Neue Testament, 1; Leipzig, 1906)

The Acts of the Apostles (London, 1909)

Harris, J. Rendel. *Codex Bezae. A Study of the So-called Western Text of the New Testament* (Texts and Studies 2.1; Cambridge, 1891)

Four Lectures on the Western Text of the New Testament (London, 1894)

[Editorial Article], *BBezC* 8 (1930), 4–7

Hatch, E. and H. A. Redpath. *A Concordance to the Septuagint*, 2 vols. (Oxford, 1897)

Hawkins, J. C. *Horae Synopticae* (Oxford, 1899)

Hemmerdinger, B. 'La Prétendue Manus Philodemi', *REG* 78 (1965), 328–30

Herculanensium Voluminum Quae Supersunt. Collectio Altera, 11 vols. (Naples, 1861–75)

Hill, D. 'Δίκαιοι as a Quasi-Technical Term', *NTS* 11 (1964/5), 296–302

Hodgson, R. 'Paul the Apostle and First-Century Tribulation Lists', *ZNW* 74 (1983), 59–80

Holmes, M. W. 'Early Editorial Activity and the Text of Codex Bezae in Matthew' (Ph.D. thesis, Princeton Theological Seminary, 1984)

Hug, J. *La Finale de l'Evangile de Marc* (Etudes bibliques; Paris, 1978)

Jacquier, E. *Les Actes des Apôtres* (Etudes bibliques; Paris, 1926)

Jastrow, M. *A Dictionary of the Targumim, the Talmud Babli and Yerushalmi, and the Midrashic Literature* (New York, 1950)

Jeremias, J. *Unknown Sayings of Jesus* (London, 2nd edn, 1964)

Johnson, L. T. *The Literary Function of Possessions in Luke–Acts* (SBL.DS 39; Missoula, 1977)

Käser, W. 'Exegetische Erwägungen zur Seligpreisung des Sabbatarbeiters Lk. 6,5D', *ZTK* 65 (1968), 414–30

Kenney, E. J. 'Books and Readers in the Roman World', in *The Cambridge History of Classical Literature*, ed. E. J. Kenney and W. V. Clausen, 2 vols. (Cambridge 1985, 1982), II, pp. 3–32

Kenyon, F. G. *Recent Developments in the Textual Criticism of the Greek Bible* (Schweich Lectures, 1932; London, 1933)

'The Western Text in the Gospels and Acts', *PBA* 24 (1938), 287–315

Books and Readers in Ancient Greece and Rome (Oxford, 2nd edn, 1950)

Keydell, R. 'Dioscorus', *PRE* Suppl. Bd 6 (Stuttgart, 1935), cols. 27–9

Kilpatrick, G. D. 'Western Text and Original Text in the Gospels and Acts', *JThS* 44 (1943), 24–36

'An Eclectic Study of the Text of Acts', in *Biblical and Patristic Studies in memory of Robert Pierce Casey*, ed. J. N. Birdsall and R. W. Thomson (Freiburg, 1963), pp. 64–77

'Acts 7.56, the Son of Man', *ThZ* 21 (1965), 209

'Some Quotations in Acts', in *Actes*, pp. 81–97 'ἐπιθύειν and ἐπικρίνειν in the Greek Bible', *ZNW* 74 (1983), 151–3

'The Two Texts of Acts', in *Studien zum Text und zur Ethik des Neuen Testaments. Festschrift zum 80. Geburtstag von Heinrich Greeven* (BZNW 47; Berlin and New York, 1986), pp. 188–95

Klijn, A. F. J. *A Survey of the Researches into the Western Text of the Gospels and Acts* (Utrecht, 1949)

'A Survey of the Researches into the Western Text of the Gospels and Acts (1949–59)', *NT* 3 (1959), 1–27, 161–73

'In Search of the Original Text of Acts', in *SLA*, pp. 103–10

'The Pseudo-Clementines and the Apostolic Decree', *NT* 10 (1968), 305–12

Klotz, A. 'Zur Caesars Bellum Civile', *RMP*, NF 66 (1911), 81–93

C. Iulii Caesaris Commentarii, 2 vols. (Leipzig, 1957)

Knox, W. L. *St. Paul and the Church of Jerusalem* (Cambridge, 1925)

Kümmel, W. G. 'Die älteste Form des Aposteldekrets', in *Spiritus et Veritas* (Festschrift für K. Kundsin), ed. Auseklis Societas Theologorum Universitatis Latviensis (Eutin, 1953), pp. 83–98; reprinted in Kümmel, *Heilsgeschehen und Geschichte: Gesammelte Aufsätze 1933–64* (Marburg, 1965), pp. 278–88

Lagrange, M.-J. 'Les Papyrus Chester Beatty pour les Evangiles', *RB* 43 (1934), 168

Lake, K. 'The Judaistic Controversy, and the Apostolic Council', *CQR* 71 (1910–11), 345–70

The Earlier Epistles of St. Paul (London, 2nd edn, 1930)

Lake, K., and H. J. Cadbury. *Translation and Commentary*, Vol. IV, and *Additional Notes*, Vol. V, of *Beg.* (London, 1933)

Leclerc, J. [Clericus], *Sentimens de quelques théologiens d'Hollande* (Amsterdam, 1685)

Défense des sentimens de quelques théologiens d'Hollande sur l'histoire critique du Vieux Testament contre la réponse du Prieur de Bolleville (Amsterdam, 1686)

MacCoull, L. S. B. *Dioscorus of Aphrodito, His Work and His World* (The Transformation of the Classical Heritage 16; Berkeley, Los Angeles, and London, 1988)

MacKenzie, R. S. 'The Western Text of Acts: Some Lucanisms in Selected Sermons', *JBL* 104 (1985), 637–50

Maddox, R. *The Purpose of Luke–Acts* (Studies of the New Testament and its World (FRLANT 126; Edinburgh and Göttingen, 1982)

Malina, B. 'Does *Porneia* mean Fornication?', *NT* 14 (1972), 10–17

Manns, F. 'Remarques sur Actes 15,20.29', *Ant.* 53 (1978), 443–51

Marrou, H.-I. 'La Technique de l'édition à l'époque patristique', *VigChr* 3 (1949), 208–24

Martini, C. M. 'La figura di Pietro secondo le varianti del codice D negli Atti degli Apostoli', in *San Pietro* (Atti della XIX Settimana Biblica; Brescia, 1967), pp. 279–89

'La Tradition textuelle des Actes des Apôtres et les tendances de l'Eglise ancienne', in *Actes*, pp. 21–35

Maspero, J. *Papyrus grecs d'époque byzantine*, 3 vols. (Catalogue générale des antiquités égyptiennes du Musée de Caire 51,54,58,60,67,73; Cairo and Leipzig, 1910–16)

'Un dernier poète grec d'Egypte: Dioscore, fils d'Apollôs', *REG* 24 (1911), 426–81

Menoud, P. H. 'The Western Text and the Theology of Acts', *Studiorum Novi Testamenti Societas, Bulletin* 2 (1951), 19–32. Reprinted in *Bulletin of the Studiorum Novi Testamenti Societas*, nos. 1–3 (Cambridge, 1963) Also reprinted in *Jesus Christ and the Faith: A Collection of Studies by P. H. Menoud* (Pittsburgh, 1978), pp. 61–83

Metzger, B. M. *The Text of the New Testament, Its Transmission, Corruption, and Restoration* (Oxford, 2nd edn, 1968)

The Early Versions of the New Testament, Their Origin, Transmission, and Limitations (Oxford, 1977)

Molland, E. 'La Circoncision, le baptême et l'autorité du décret apostolique (Actes XV,28sq.) dans les milieux judéo-chrétiens des Pseudo-Clémentines', *StTh* 9 (1955), 1–39

Morgenthaler, R. *Statistik des Neutestamentlichen Wortschatzes* (Zurich and Frankfurt-on-Main, 1958)

Moule, C. F. D. 'H. W. Moule on Acts iv.25', *ET* 66 (1954), 220f.

An Idiom-Book of New Testament Greek (Cambridge, 2nd edn, 1959)

Moule, H. W. 'Acts iv.25', *ET* 51 (1940), 396

[Moulton, J. H.]. *A Grammar of New Testament Greek*, Vol. IV (by N. Turner), *Style* (Edinburgh, 1976)

Moulton, J. H., and W. F. Howard. *A Grammar of New Testament Greek*, Vol. II, *Accidence and Word-Formation* (Edinburgh, 1929)

Nachmanson, E., 'Der griechische Buchtitel. Einige Beobachtungen', *GHÅ* 47.19 (1941), 1–52

Neirynck, F., and F. van Segbroeck. 'Le Texte des Actes des Apôtres et les caractéristiques stylistiques lucaniennes', *EThL* 61 (1985), 304–39

Nestle, Eberhard. *Introduction to the Textual Criticism of the Greek New Testament* (London, 1901)

'Zum Ersticken im Aposteldekret', *ZNW* 7 (1906), 254–6

Newton, N. *The Concept of Purity at Qumran and in the Letters of Paul* (MSSNTS 53; Cambridge, 1985)

Nock, A. D. '[Review of] Martin Dibelius: Aufsätze zur Apostelgeschichte. Göttingen, 1951', *Gn.* 25 (1953), 497–506

O'Neill, J. C. *The Theology of Acts* (London, 1961)

Oppermann, H. 'Nachwort und bibliographische Nachträge', in *C. Iulii Caesaris Commentarii De Bello Civili*, ed. H. Meusel (Berlin, 12th edn, 1959)

Oxford Society of Historical Theology, A Committee of the, *The New Testament in the Apostolic Fathers* (Oxford, 1905)

Page, T. E. [Review of Blass, *Acta*] *CR* 11 (1897), 317–20

246   Bibliography

Papazoglu, F. *Makedonski gravodi u rimsko dobu* (*The Cities of Mace-donia in the Roman Period*: Serbian with French summary) (Skopje, 1957)

Parker, D. C. 'A "Dictation Theory" of Codex Bezae', *JSNT* 15 (1982), 97–112

Pervo, R. I. 'Social and Religious Aspects of the Western Text', in *The Living Text. Essays in Honor of Ernest W. Saunders*, ed. D. E. Groh and R. Jewett (Lanham, New York, and London, 1985), pp. 229–41

Philips, C. A. 'Rendel Harris', *ET* 52 (1941), 349–52

Plümacher, E. *Lukas als hellenistischer Schriftsteller, Studien zur Apostelgeschichte* (StUNT 9; Göttingen, 1972)

'Acta-Forschung, 1974–82', *ThR* 49 (1984), 105–69

Pott, A. *Der abendländische Text der Apostelgeschichte und die Wir-Quelle* (Leipzig, 1900)

Prat, F. 'Récents travaux de critique textuelle. 2.Le texte occidental des Actes des apôtres', *RSR* 5 (1914), 472–86

Preisigke, F. *Wörterbuch der Papyrusurkunde mit Einschluss der griechischen Inschriften, Aufschriften, Ostraka, Mumienschilder usw. aus Ägypten*, 4 vols. (Heidelberg and Berlin, 1924–44)

Rackham, R. B. *The Acts of the Apostles* (London, 9th edn, 1922)

Radke, G. 'Viae Publicae Romanae', *PRE* Suppl. Bd 13 (Munich, 1973), cols. 1415–1686

Rajak, T. *Josephus, The Historian and his Society* (London, 1983)

Ramsay, W. M. *St. Paul the Traveller and the Roman Citizen* (London, 1895)

Resch, G. *Das Aposteldekret nach seiner außerkanonischen Textgestalt* (TU 36.2; Leipzig, 1905)

Rice, G. E. 'The Anti-Judaic Bias of the Western Text in the Gospel of Luke', *AUSS* 17 (1979), 203–8; 18 (1980), 51–7

Richard, E. 'The OT in Acts: Wilcox's Semitisms in Retrospect', *CBQ* 42 (1980), 330–41

Riddle, D. W. 'Textual Criticism as a Historical Discipline', *AThR* 18 (1936), 220–33

Roberts, C. H. and T. C. Skeat. *The Birth of the Codex* (London, 1983)

Robinson, J. A. T. *Redating the New Testament* (London, 1976)

Robinson, W. 'Historical Survey of the Church's Treatment of New Converts with Reference to Pre- and Post-Baptismal Instruction', *JThS* 42 (1941), 42–53

Ropes, J. H. 'Three Papers on the Text of Acts. I. The Reconstruction of the Torn Leaf of Codex Bezae', *HThR* 16 (1923), 163–8; ' . . . III. The Greek Text of Codex Laudianus', *HThR* 16 (1923), 175–86

Šagi, J. *Textus Decreti Concilii Hierosolymitani Lucano Opere et Antiquioris Ecclesiae Disciplina Illustratus* (TeT 25; Rome, 1977)

Salmon, G. *Some Thoughts on the Textual Criticism of the New Testament* (London, 1897)

Schille, G. *Die Apostelgeschichte des Lukas* (ThHNT 5; Berlin, 1983)

Schneider, H. *Die altlateinischen Biblischen Cantica* (Texte und Arbeiten 1.29–30; Beuron, 1938)

Schoeps, H. J. *Theologie und Geschichte des Jüdenchristentums* (Tübingen, 1949)

Scrivener, F. H. A. *A Plain Introduction to the Criticism of the New Testament for the Use of Biblical Students*, ed. E. Miller (London, 4th edn, 1894)

Simon, R. *Histoire critique du Nouveau Testament* (Rotterdam, 1689)

Skeat, T. C. 'The Length of the Standard Papyrus Roll and the Cost-Advantage of the Codex', *ZPE* 45 (1982), 169–75

Strack, H. L. and P. Billerbeck. *Kommentar zum Neuen Testament aus Talmud und Midrasch*, 6 vols. in 7 (Munich, 1922–61)

Strange, W. A. 'The Sons of Sceva and the Text of Acts 19:14', *JThS* 38 (1987), 97–106

'The Text of Acts 19.1', *NTS* 37 (1991)

Streeter, B. H. *The Four Gospels* (London, 1924)

'The Primitive Text of Acts' [Review of Clark's *Acts*], *JThS* 34 (1933), 232–41

'Codices 157, 1071 and the Caesaraean Text', in *Quantulacumque. Studies Presented to Kirsopp Lake*, ed. R. P. Casey, S. Lake, and A. K. Lake (London, 1937), pp. 149–50

Stuehrenberg P. F. 'The Study of Acts before the Reformation. A Bibliographic Introduction', *NT* 29 (1987), 100–36

Talbert, C. H. *Literary Patterns, Theological Themes, and the Genre of Luke–Acts* (SBL.MS 20; Missoula, 1974)

Theissen, G. *The First Followers of Jesus. A Sociological Analysis of the Earliest Christianity* (London, 1978)

Thiele, W., 'Ausgewählte Beispiele zur Charakterisierung des "westlichen" Textes der Apostelgeschichte', *ZNW* 56 (1965), 51–63

Tissot, Y. 'Les Prescriptions des presbytres (Actes, xv,41,D)', *RB* 77 (1970), 321–46

Torrey, C. C. *Documents of the Primitive Church* (New York, 1941)

Turner, C. H. 'Historical Introduction to the Textual Criticism of the New Testament', *JThS* 10 (1908–9), 13–28, 161–82, 354–74; 11 (1909–10), 1–27, 180–210

'A Textual Commentary on Mark 1', *JThS* 28 (1926–7), 145–58

Turner, E. G. *Greek Papyri, An Introduction* (Oxford, 1968)

Greek Manuscripts of the Ancient World (Oxford, 1971)

Unnik, W. C. van. 'Luke–Acts, A Storm-Center in Contemporary Scholarship', in *SLA*, pp. 15–32

'Luke's Second Book and the Rules of Hellenistic Historiography', in *Actes*, pp. 37–60

Valentine-Richards, A. V. 'The Western Text of Acts. A Study by A. Pott', *JThS* 2 (1901), 439–47

Waitz, C. 'Das Problem des sogennanten Aposteldekrets und die damit zusammenhängenden literarischen und geschichtlichen Probleme des apostolischen Zeitalters', *ZKG* 55 (1936), 227–63

Walter, N. 'Apostelgeschichte 6.1 und die Anfänge der Urgemeinde in Jerusalem', *NTS* 29 (1983), 370–93

Weiss, B. *Der Codex D in der Apostelgeschichte. Textkritische Untersuchung* (TU 17.1, Leipzig, 1897)

Wensinck, A. J. 'The Semitisms of Codex Bezae and their Relation to the Non-Western Text of the Gospel of Saint Luke', *BBezC* 12 (1937), 11–48

Wilcox, M. *The Semitisms of Acts* (Oxford, 1965)
'Luke and the Bezan Text of Acts', in *Actes*, pp. 447–55

Williams, C. S. C. *Alterations to the Text of the Synoptic Gospels and Acts* (Oxford, 1951)

Wilson, J. M. *The Acts of the Apostles. Translated from the Codex Bezae* (London, 1923)

Wilson, S. G. *Luke and the Pastoral Epistles* (London, 1979)
Luke and the Law (MSSNTS 50; Cambridge, 1983)

Witherington, B. 'The Anti-Feminist Tendencies of the "Western" Text in Acts', *JBL* 103 (1984), 82–4

Yoder, J. D. 'The Language of the Greek Variants of Codex Bezae Cantabrigiensis' (unpublished Th.D. thesis, Princeton Theological Seminary, 1958)
'The Language of the Greek Variants of Codex Bezae', *NT* 3 (1959), 241–8
'Semitisms in Codex Bezae', *JBL* 78 (1959), 317–21
Concordance to the Distinctive Greek Text of Codex Bezae (NTTS 2; Leiden, 1961)

Zahn, T. *Introduction to the New Testament*, 3 vols. (Eng. trans., Edinburgh, 1909)
Die Apostelgeschichte des Lucas, 2 vols. (Leipzig, 1919, 1921)

Zuntz, G. 'On the Western Text of the Acts of the Apostles', in *Opuscula Selecta* (Cambridge, 1972), pp. 189–215

Zwaan, J. de. 'Was the Book of Acts a Posthumous Edition?', *HThR* 17 (1924), 95–153

INDEX OF SUBJECTS

An asterisk following a page number indicates citation of a textual witness in the textual apparatus.

INDEX OF AUTHORS

INDEX OF BIBLICAL PASSAGES

An asterisk following a page number indicates a reference to textual evidence or discussion of a textual problem.